'*Operation Morthor* is as exciting as the best spy novels, with the enormous advantage of being completely true. Ravi Somaiya masterfully teases out the tangled strands of a Cold War mystery . . . The result is a gripping book by a gifted writer and a dogged investigator' Mitchell Zuckoff, author of *13 Hours*

'*Operation Morthor* is one of the most gripping non-fiction books I've read in a very long time. Somaiya does a masterful job sifting the evidence and building a case of murder. This is a fabulous page-turner. I highly recommend it' Douglas Preston, author of *The Monster of Florence*

'Ravi Somaiya's brilliant unwrapping of the mystery surrounding Hammarskjöld's death will convert the reader into an avid investigator the moment they pick up this book! *Operation Morthor* also raises key questions before governments who still act suspiciously: why? What are you hiding exactly?' Zeid Ra'ad Al Hussein, UN Human Rights Chief (2014–2018)

'What caused the 1961 plane crash that killed UN Secretary-General Hammarskjöld, who was attempting at the time to end a war in the Congo? Investigative journalist Somaiya lays out the evidence suggesting foul play in his impressive debut. An eye-opening account' *Publishers Weekly*, starred review

'Fans of novelists such as Tom Clancy and Robert Ludlum, as well as military history and true-crime enthusiasts, will find much to enjoy about this riveting read' *Library Journal*

'A gripping account of Hammarskjöld's death and the ensuing search for the truth about what happened to him' *InsideHook*

ABOUT THE AUTHOR

Ravi Somaiya was most recently a correspondent for *The New York Times*. He has written for the *Guardian*, *Rolling Stone* and *New York Magazine* among others, and has presented and produced documentaries for Vice and HBO. He has covered Islamic extremist terrorism, disinformation, mass shootings, Anonymous and Wikileaks, among other long-running stories.

OPERATION MORTHOR

The Death of Dag Hammarskjöld and
the Last Great Mystery of the Cold War

RAVI SOMAIYA

PENGUIN BOOKS

PENGUIN BOOKS

UK | USA | Canada | Ireland | Australia
India | New Zealand | South Africa

Penguin Books is part of the Penguin Random House group of companies
whose addresses can be found at global.penguinrandomhouse.com.

Penguin
Random House
UK

First published as *The Golden Thread* in the United States of America
by Twelve, an imprint of Grand Central Publishing 2020
First published as *Operation Morthor* in Great Britain by Viking 2020
Published in Penguin Books 2021
001

Printed and bound in Italy by Grafica Veneta S.p.A.

The authorized representative in the EEA is Penguin Random House Ireland,
Morrison Chambers, 32 Nassau Street, Dublin D02 YH68

A CIP catalogue record for this book is available from the British Library

ISBN: 978–0–241–97502–2

www.greenpenguin.co.uk

For Caroline

And for my parents, Raj and Hershi

Contents

Contents

REPUBLIC OF CONGO, 1961

Showing approximate flight path of Hammarskjöld's plane

© 2020 Jeffrey L. Ward

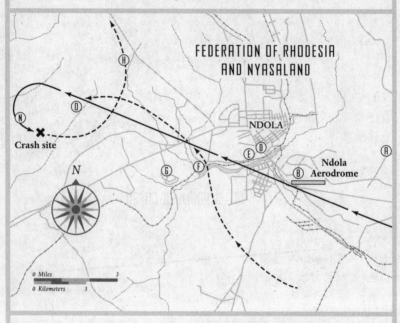

VIRVING'S RECONSTRUCTED MAP OF THE MOMENTS BEFORE THE CRASH
With eyewitnesses marked

FEDERATION OF RHODESIA AND NYASALAND

NDOLA

Crash site

N

Ndola Aerodrome

0 Miles 3
0 Kilometers 3

⟶ *Albertina* flight path

◂--- Flight path of second plane described by witnesses

EYEWITNESS LOCATIONS

Ⓐ D.A. Clarke

Ⓑ R.A. Phillips

Ⓓ D.E. Peover

Ⓔ D.J.F. Buchanan, D.D. Lowe, M.Y. van Wyk

Ⓖ T.J. Kankasa

Ⓕ D.L. Bermant

Ⓗ A. Wright

Ⓝ F. Mazibisa

Ⓘ D. Simango

© 2020 Jeffrey L. Ward

Select Characters

Cyrille Adoula—prime minister of the Congo, 1961–64.

Beukels—a Belgian pilot who says he flew as a mercenary for Katangese forces.

Larry Devlin—the Central Intelligence Agency's Leopoldville chief of station, 1960–67.

Colonel René Faulques—a French soldier who led Katangese rebel forces.

Dag Hammarskjöld*—the second secretary-general of the United Nations, 1953–61.

George Ivan Smith—a UN press representative and close friend of Hammarskjöld.

Harold Julien—an American soldier, acting head of security for the United Nations Operation in the Congo.

Joseph Kasavubu—the first democratically elected prime minister of the Congo.

Claude de Kemoularia—a French former assistant to Hammarskjöld and diplomat turned adviser and executive.

John F. Kennedy—president of the United States of America, 1961–63.

Nikita Khrushchev—leader of the Soviet Union, 1953–64.

King Leopold II—a Belgian royal who colonized, then brutalized, the Congo.

Patrice Lumumba—the first democratically elected president of the Congo.

Harold Macmillan—prime minister of the United Kingdom, 1957–63.

---

* Pronounced, roughly, *ham-ar-heuld*.

Joseph Désiré Mobutu—head of the Congolese army who eventually seized power and installed himself as a dictator.

Godefroid Munongo—interior minister of Katanga, in close contact with Katanga's Belgian advisers.

Conor Cruise O'Brien—an Irish diplomat, politician, and writer who was Hammarskjöld's representative in Katanga.

Mohamed Chande Othman—a Tanzanian jurist appointed in 2015 by the United Nations to reexamine the Hammarskjöld case.

Daphne Park (later Baroness Park of Monmouth)—the British Secret Intelligence Service's head of station in Leopoldville, 1959–61.

QJWIN—a safecracker named Jose Mankel employed by the CIA for assassination recruitment and related activities in Leopoldville.

Bengt Rösiö*—a Swedish diplomat and investigator.

Charles Southall—a US naval pilot seconded to the National Security Agency.

Jean-François Thiriart—a Belgian optometrist and a fascist ideologue and recruiter.

Harry S Truman—president of the United States of America, 1945–53.

Moïse Tshombe—a Katangese businessman appointed leader of the breakaway state.

Bo Virving—a Swedish pilot and investigator.

Roy Welensky—the last prime minister of the Federation of Rhodesia and Nyasaland.

Susan Williams—a British academic, author, and investigator.

WIROGUE—a forger and former bank robber turned CIA agent in Leopoldville. Real name either David Tzitzichivili or David de Panasket.

---

* Pronounced, roughly, *reu-scheu*.

All narrative is a kind of benevolent lie. In telling a story so it's intelligible, an author must, of necessity, leave some things out and focus on others. I have certainly done so here, and I apologize in advance to anyone who feels that their role in the story of Dag Hammarskjöld's life and death has been omitted or underplayed.

In an effort to mitigate that, I have worked to place things in context and to credit those who have worked so assiduously before me to unearth original materials. I have used dialogue only where it was precisely recalled and noted by the participants themselves. All descriptions are drawn from the recollections or accounts of those present or from contemporaneous photographs and video.

This is a story with so many twists, and so many duplicitous characters, that unraveling it drove me nearly to madness. But as with all enduring puzzles, it has at its heart a simple question: What happened to Hammarskjöld's plane in the skies over what is now Zambia in the few minutes between its last contact with the control tower and its fatal crash landing?

Between midnight and dawn, when the past is all deception,
The future futureless, before the morning watch
When time stops and time is never ending

—T. S. Eliot, "The Dry Salvages," Four Quartets

"When they killed him"

On the morning of Tuesday, September 19, 1961, Harry S Truman woke before the sun was up. He made himself breakfast, lost in thought, then bathed and dressed in a dapper gray suit, a dark-blue tie, and a gray felt hat.

He picked up his cane, pulled the door shut quietly behind him, and set out through his hometown, now home again, Independence, Missouri, on the outskirts of Kansas City.

Truman, moving slowly against the rising morning light, was seventy-seven. He had been out of the Oval Office for eight years, and had grown into the role of former president. Living quietly with his wife on a modest pension, in the peaceful Victorian home their daughter had been born in thirty-five years earlier, suited him.

He had visited the White House again several times in recent months, at the invitation of its new incumbent, John F. Kennedy. He was gratified to have been taken into his confidence.

But he visibly preferred his freedom to the constraints of high office. The eyes behind his thick glasses, amused and sharp, had come alive since his retirement. A Midwestern tendency toward bluntness had been elevated to a principle.

That morning, as he took his usual turn around the town's peaceful square, past the red-brick courthouse topped with a white clock tower, and toward Bundschu's department store, he looked unusually grave.

Truman had been sworn into office in 1945. He had helped found the United Nations that same year, as a bulwark against the kind of war that he never wanted to see again. And then he had watched as his grand hopes for peace had turned to global suspicion, antipathy, and scheming.

Few understood better how the Cold War worked. And on that morning he could not shake the idea that it had taken a particularly evil turn.

He arrived at his presidential library, a modernist complex built on a hill overlooking the Kansas City skyline. It was home to exhibits that included a replica of his old desk, complete with the little sign that said THE BUCK STOPS HERE. He climbed the broad staircase, passed through a colonnade of elegant white pillars and a set of glass doors, and made for his office. He had thinking to do, and calls to make.

Later in the day, he emerged for a formal ceremony. Soldiers of the Thirty-Fifth Infantry Division, Truman's old World War I unit, had raised $6,903.10 to donate to the library. Truman stood next to the division's major general, both men behind a podium and in front of a blue curtain, as the press photographers' magnesium bulbs flashed. He was transparently touched to collect the check, along with a flag that the division had paraded in November 1945 after the war.

He also looked, for all the world, angry. Unprompted, as he drew the ceremony to a close, he expressed his sorrow at the death of Dag Hammarskjöld, the second secretary-general of the United Nations, who had died a day or so previously while attempting to mediate a savage war in the Congo.

But he could not restrain himself there. As the soldiers and reporters began to disperse, he made a side remark.

"Mr. Hammarskjöld was on the point of getting something

done when they killed him. Notice that I said 'when they killed him.'"

The journalists pressed him to explain further.

"That's all I've got to say on the matter. Draw your own conclusions."

One reporter, likely aware of Truman's connection with Kennedy, asked whether he had any inside information. Truman walked away, ignoring the question, thinking perhaps that he had already said too much.

He had little to fear. His aside made only the bottom paragraphs of a short United Press International wire report. The local *Independence Examiner* primly elided the incident.

———

At around the same time in the Sarek National Park in the north of Sweden, an otherworldly landscape of gray-brown mountains reflected in icy blue lakes, an indigenous Swedish child, Laila, of the Sami people, was visiting the community store.

As soon as she and her parents stepped inside the building, a sturdy hut, painted red, that still smelled of sawn timber, she froze and stared at a shelf of newspapers and magazines. She saw pictures, on each front page, of the man she had met earlier in the year when she was playing outside her family kåta—a conical tent made from peat moss and long branches.

It had been a frosty morning, and he had walked past, hiking under the cold blue sub-Arctic sky, and asked her about herbs growing in the area. She talked in an excited babble, and he looked amused. She liked the man. He could see things, she felt, and he really listened when she talked. He had danced, terribly, swaying, his legs all over the place, to show her how the children danced in Africa, where he had been recently.

Before he left, he said that she and her family should visit him at his work in New York, where she could meet children from across the world. And a letter had arrived a few weeks later, inviting them all to the United Nations. But her parents had been too busy tending the family's reindeer, and they could not go immediately.

Now the headlines all said versions of the same thing: DAG FOUND DEAD IN PLANE. DAG HAMMARSKJÖLD KILLED IN THE CONGO. HAMMARSKJÖLD DEAD. And each pictured, in black-and-white halftone that turned to dots when she looked closer, the wreckage of his plane, the *Albertina*.

About five thousand miles away, in the Congo, as a guard of honor escorted Hammarskjöld's coffin across the airport for transportation back to his native Sweden, hundreds of black Congolese stood in massed ranks to pay tribute. They were, in a nation marked by near-constant noise and color utterly silent.

In the days that followed, the Congolese protested in the streets, decrying Britain and its prime minister, Harold Macmillan, and America and Kennedy, whom they felt sure were behind the death.

The new Congolese prime minister, Cyrille Adoula, had his own theory. Hammarskjöld, he said, had "fallen victim to the shameless intrigues of the great financial powers of the West" and their thirst for his country's boundless mineral riches.

"How ignoble is this assassination," he said, "not the first of its kind perpetrated by the moneyed powers. Mr. Hammarskjöld was the victim of certain financial circles for whom a human life is not equal to a gram of copper or uranium."

Outside the United Nations building, a monolithic skyscraper overlooking the East River on Manhattan's East Side, a smaller group of protesters had gathered. Their fury was undimmed by the miserable rain pelting from a mutinous gray sky. Their placards asked, WHO SHOT DOWN DAG'S PLANE? and answered themselves with a reference to the Soviet leader Nikita Khrushchev: DIAL K FOR MURDER.

Inside, thirty-eight floors above the bedraggled protesters, Hammarskjöld's staff had gathered in his elegant suite of offices, decorated with paintings and sculptures that he had chosen himself. Some discussed the mocking invitations they had received from wealthy white Europeans living in Africa to attend lavish parties they were throwing to celebrate his death.

Others reflected, in a kind of impromptu vigil, on the rarity of Hammarskjöld's awareness that humankind had a tendency to get stuck in ridiculous and destructive predicaments of its own making, and his certainty that there were always solutions to those predicaments.

They knew he would have considered the tributes to his life and work inappropriate and unseemly. But also that none really captured him. Because Hammarskjöld was, fundamentally, an honest man. And honest men are difficult to define.

In upstate New York, at the modest house Hammarskjöld had kept for hiking weekends, his colleagues found papers filled with his neat, urgent handwriting. A diary of sorts. In the early 1940s, years before he was to think in any meaningful way about the Congo, he had written: "There is only one path out of the steamy dense jungle where the battle is fought over glory and power and advantage—one escape from the snares and obstacles you yourself have set up. And that is—to accept death."

Two official inquiries, conducted shortly after the plane crash, ruled it was likely an accident. Pilot error or an act of God. Hammarskjöld was awarded the Nobel Peace Prize the same year he died—one of only two occasions on which it has been awarded posthumously.*

And that is where this story might have rested, a neat bow tied on top, his name remembered for the Manhattan plaza that would be named in his honor. Except for the work of a band of ingenious devotees who never believed the official verdict, and who kept digging for information. This book draws on their accounts, and archives in America, Britain, Sweden, and elsewhere.

It is also built on the experiences of the diplomats, soldiers, spies, and ordinary Congolese people who lived the very peculiar, very bloody, forgotten war that seized the Congo for five years between 1960 and 1965.

It pitted a black Congolese independence movement, roused to rage by centuries of genocidal colonial exploitation, against white colonialists willing to die to keep an Africa, and a way of life, they considered theirs.

It pitted the Soviet Union, eager to seize advantage and make allies in Africa, against Britain and America, willing to do whatever it took to prevent the Congo falling into the clutches of an empire they equated with the Third Reich.

And underneath it all lay the torrents of money that corporations, especially mining companies, had been able to extract from the Congo, and which they used to amass influence and connections that made them pseudo-governments in their own right.

The factions were united on only one point: that Hammarskjöld, and the United Nations, stood in their way.

---

* The other occasion was for the Swedish poet Erik Axel Karlfeldt in 1931.

PART ONE

Tar man fan i båten får man ro honom iland.
If you take the devil in the boat, you must row him ashore.

—*Swedish aphorism*

But they hated the town for the intruders who had
ruled in it and from it; and they had preferred to destroy
the town rather than take it over.

—*V. S. Naipaul,* A Bend in the River

"Godzilla"

The Congo* is shaped like a real human heart, messy and organic and the size of Western Europe. It tilts counterclockwise across the lower half of the African continent and borders nine other nations.

From above, shortly before dawn in January 1959, it appeared as an unsettlingly vast swath of darkness. As the first red glow of the sun hit, it turned into the wet, dark green of an ancient forest.

It was wreathed with mist, and studded with irresistible riches. Those who lived on its borders spoke of it as a dark, dangerous place. People who entered, the legend held, either returned wealthy and brutal or disappeared entirely.

On its eastern edge, where a row of active volcanoes spat and burbled, and the world's largest lakes gradually turned a dark blue in the morning light, the ground was marbled with gold. Oil and gas deposits were so abundant they occasionally leaked out unbidden, poisoning the locals.

On its western edge, near the modern-day border with Angola, the land was riven with veins of diamonds, both industrial and ornamental.

---

* There are two nations with the name Congo: the Republic of the Congo, and the Democratic Republic of the Congo. This book is about the latter.

In the far south, toward the point of the heart, lay Katanga, a region the size of France that is one of the most naturally rich areas on earth. Under the tan-colored dirt of its cool hills were ores of copper, nickel, tin, tungsten, and cobalt so pure, they haunted the dreams of mining geologists. Bilious yellow rocks of uranium ore littered the ground. It was the source of countless fortunes.

The Congo River, the deepest and fastest on earth, which loops for three thousand miles across the north of the country, has its sources in those hills. It feeds 1.4 million square miles of fragrant, outrageously fertile land known as the Congo Basin. Crops will grow anywhere you plant them there. And its rain forests and swamps host a wild, chaotic, crawling, flying, swinging, jumping ecosystem, featuring buffalo, elephants, chimpanzees, gorillas, and a thousand species of birds. Some Congolese scraped their yards to smooth dirt to avoid ants and snakes wending relentlessly toward their homes through the undergrowth.

The river eventually bursts through a channel on the west coast, into the South Atlantic, near Leopoldville, a port city of about three hundred thousand and the capital of a nation that has never really submitted to being governed in the Western sense of the word.

The city sits on the south bank, where the river is nearly a mile wide, and clumps of green-and-purple water hyacinth drift past on the coppery water. In the late 1950s and early 1960s, Leopoldville was often described by non-Africans as the pride of Africa. Pictures show white, modernist high-rise buildings arrayed along handsome boulevards, broken up with landscaped lawns and grand plazas. On the ground the architecture often feels like a temporary intrusion that the pale-reddish dirt and profusion of plants are working to dislodge.

Avenue Prince Baudouin ran down from the river. It was a determinedly straight line that betrayed the attempts by the Congo's Belgian colonial rulers both to impose rigor, and to name it after themselves. It went on past the giant Stade Roi Baudouin, a shallow concrete bowl like a half-buried amphitheater rising from a patch of lush green grass.

Inside, at 2 p.m. on Sunday, January 4, 1959, a soccer match between a local team, Victoria Club, in vivid green-and-black-striped shirts, and their crosstown rivals, FC Royal Leo Sport, was nearing its climax, and the voices of tens of thousands of fans echoed through the sweltering tropical afternoon.

South of the stadium, where Avenue Prince Baudouin met Avenue de la Victoire, a separate crowd of about four thousand young black Congolese men had gathered, spilling out into the broad intersection. Some of them were wearing Stetson hats, rakishly tied neckerchiefs, and cowboy-style jeans. All of them emanated a suppressed anger—a giddy, terrifying kind of potential energy.

Only the first brave souls were acting on it. As white Europeans drove past in Peugeots and Mercedes, they shouted "attack the whites" and "independence." The cars swerved, with a squeal of rubber, as rocks rained down on them.

Slightly away from the main throng, one young man had pulled his fist back to throw a punch that would loose decades of hatred and frustration. It would also begin a war that would come to kill at least a hundred thousand Congolese and one United Nations secretary-general.

It is possible to trace the motivations of that delirious blow virtually step by step back to 1482, when a Portuguese explorer named Diogo Cão, navigating his ship through the South Atlantic, noticed that the sea had turned from a cobalt blue to a rusty ocher.

He had found the mouth of the Congo River, pushing back the ocean. After he landed, he erected a monument proclaiming the Congo discovered.

It came as news to a population of two or three million native Congolese who lived in loosely linked polygamous village tribes, ruled over by local kings, busy growing bananas and yams, and raising goats, pigs, and cows.

They measured time by the cycles of the moon, and distance in marching time. They had no written language, but communicated across long distances using drum rhythms long before Morse and his code. They had a history of their own—of conquest, triumph, tragedy, of empires rising and falling—every bit as vivid as the Europeans who claimed them as property.

The white men began to take people. They loaded them onto ships. Between 1500 and 1850, one stretch of Congolese coastline 250 miles long sent four million people on slave transports. They were bound for the sugar plantations of Brazil or the Caribbean, or for the cotton plantations of the American South.

The slave trade had barely ended, in 1874, when a self-styled grand explorer, Henry Morton Stanley, arrived in the Congo with a walrus moustache, a pith helmet, and ambition in his eyes.

He had come to fame three years earlier, spinning a career as a writer and adventurer from his discovery of a lost explorer, David Livingstone, who had disappeared—from European and American view, at least—while seeking the source of the Nile.

Stanley claimed he had located Livingstone on the shores of Lake Tanganyika in 1871 and that he had the presence of mind to greet him with the line, "Dr. Livingstone, I presume?"*

By 1874, he had a new assignment: to send more tall tales from Africa for the *New York Herald* and the *London Daily Telegraph*. They were a hit, and he fed a frenzy for global exploration, and global

---

* The line, like all of the best lines, is too good to be true: Livingstone died too soon afterward to confirm or deny it, and Stanley tore out the pages of his diary that referred to the meeting.

commerce, and added fuel to a race among European nations to claim colonies.*

The Congolese called him *bula matari*—stone breaker—because he could blow up rocks with dynamite. They marveled that his entire body was covered in cloth except for his head and arms, and that his canoe rowed itself. Stanley described them in turn, privately, as "filthy, rapacious ghouls." In his stories he portrayed them as noble savages, obsequious in the face of his obvious superiority.

In Brussels, a gangling and overweening princeling with a long, gray beard that made him look like an authoritarian Santa followed each turn of Stanley's tales, and each new colony claimed, with breathless rapture.

At forty, King Leopold II had ruled over Belgium for ten years. He had grown to dislike, even resent, all the things he had—the palaces, the jewels, and the toys. He grew obsessed, instead, with colonialization and a new phenomenon, globalized business. Plummeting transport costs and a fashion for the exotic† combined to make it worth shipping tea from India or ostrich feathers from South Africa to the capitals of the West.

Leopold had calculated that if he found the right colony and allied himself with global companies keen to strip it of its natural assets, the profits were potentially endless. He tried to obtain Fiji. He lusted after the Argentine province of Entre Rios. He attempted to lease part of what is now Taiwan. But he came to

---

* By the end of the nineteenth century, Britain and France alone had claimed rights over modern-day Gambia, Ghana, Nigeria, Southern Cameroon, Sierra Leone, Kenya, Uganda, Tanzania, Senegal, Mali, Burkina Faso, Benin, Guinea, Ivory Coast, and Niger.

† The pineapple was such a status symbol that a business emerged renting them to people who could not afford to buy them, so they could at least show them off at parties.

realize that he could not merely buy a colony. He would have to take one.

He did not have an army. Nor did he have the political clout of a nation like Britain or France behind him. In order to claim territory, he had to resort to cunning. So he disguised his desire to pillage as a heartfelt wish for the furtherment of the noble savages and chiefs Stanley had depicted in his stories. He called it a fight against slavery, for the rights and lives of black Africans.

He started a society—the Association Internationale Africaine—with the stated aim of studying the blank spot in the middle of Africa by establishing outposts there. It meant he had license to explore, and to plant his flags, in the Congo. He hired Stanley, who put together a large team of subordinates.

Leopold's agents began to travel the country, negotiating with village chiefs. They persuaded them to sign contracts promising all rights to all lands, for all time, and offered bales of cloth, crates of gin, livery uniforms, coral necklaces, caps, or military coats in exchange. Many agents signed dozens of these treaties a month.

With every agreement, the white men put up a flag—a blue field, with a yellow star. It represented the darkness in which the Congolese had wandered, and the light of civilization that Leopold had bestowed on them.* In 1885, he was recognized by Germany, Britain, and the United States as the official ruler of the Congo Free State.

In London and New York, bicycles and cars had begun to fill the streets. Passengers marveled at the wonder of riding on rubber tires instead of hard wood and metal wheels. The demand for rubber spiked. And the value of the rubber vines and trees that grew wild in the Congo spiked with it.

Leopold spied an opportunity. He tasked every Congolese village with gathering rubber—three or four pounds, tapped

---

* The modern Congolese flag retains the motif.

painstakingly and cleaned, every two weeks, to be presented to Belgian officials and soldiers who now made up an army called the Force Publique. They passed it on to private companies that had signed generous export deals.

Congolese men exhausted themselves to meet ever-increasing quotas. They were seen as another commodity, a human resource to be tapped until it gave out. If they failed to produce, or were caught transgressing, the Force Publique wielded a power that a modern corporation could only dream of. Some men had their hands held against trees and beaten to a jelly with rifle butts. Others were not so lucky.

And rubber was not the only commodity in demand. Congolese elephants were harvested for their tusks. Lever Brothers, a British company, built an empire on soap made from Congolese palm oil extracted by forced labor. It later merged with a Dutch company to form Unilever.

Several of the deadliest mass murderers in history were Force Publique officers. One, René de Permentier, had the jungle around his house cleared so he could more easily target-shoot black passersby. Léon Fiévez, a district commissioner, had killed 572 people after four months in the job. He collected the severed heads of his victims for display at home.

Leopold operated with impunity. He was seen merely as an eccentric philanthropist. His excesses were forgiven because his aims were seen as laudable. In 1897, 267 Congolese traveled to Tervuren, in Belgium, as exhibits in a colonial exhibition there. They built huts by a pond in a park, and played at being themselves for families curious to see black skin and marvel at the benevolence of Belgium.

At around that time, a young Englishman, Edmund Dene Morel, visited the Congo on assignment for a shipping company. He noticed that the ships leaving were laden with rubber and ivory. The ones arriving were filled only with soldiers and guns. This was not trade, he concluded, but pillage.

His outrage began a global movement, a campaign against what amounted to a holocaust. By means of exhaustion, sickness, and murder, the regime killed between eight and ten million Congolese—about half of the population—between 1885 and 1908. One Belgian historian estimated that Leopold's personal profits amounted to more than a billion dollars in today's money.*

Fifty years later, nearly half of the Congo's fourteen million inhabitants were under eighteen. A form of apartheid known as the color bar kept them separate from, and beneath, the hundred thousand or so Belgians who ran the country.

Life in Leopoldville still came, as it had for generations, on ramshackle white barges that chugged up and down the river. These floating bazaars sold monkeys charred black to preserve them, red grubs stored in moss, smoked crocodile, furniture, and multipurpose necessities like enamel tubs—the essentials to maintain a way of life that existed between a rich tribal history and a bright future that had been promised, but never quite delivered.[†]

Millions of black Congolese had moved from their villages to Leopoldville seeking jobs and opportunities to better themselves. But by 1959, mineral prices had dropped and a recession had hit. In Leopoldville, thirty thousand people were unemployed, most of them young men.

The Belgian government had managed to suppress and divert uprising after uprising. In schools, textbooks avoided mention of American and French revolutions and of civil rights movements around the world. Trade unions had, by law, to be run by a white adviser, making them toothless. There were clubs and

---

* For a full and astounding account of this period of Congolese history, see *King Leopold's Ghost,* by Adam Hochschild.
[†] Epidemiologists think that HIV spread into the world from Leopoldville at about this time, propagated by the movement of people through the city.

associations, but they were limited only to those Congolese who adopted wholesale the lifestyles and mores of the Belgians, and who expressed fealty to them.*

At first the suppressed frustrations of the young Congolese had been grounded safely in superstition. They had long been told of Mundele Mwinda, a legendary white man who stalked the streets of the city looking for black Congolese. He paralyzed them with his lantern, then took them to Mundele Ngulu, a swineherd who fed and fattened the victims before making ham and sausages of them to feed white children.

In recent years, that had given way to other forms of release. Movie theaters had begun to open in the black neighborhoods, known as the *cité*, amid the rows of low, box-like concrete houses in pale green or pale blue.

They showed Westerns. So young Congolese men began to dress like their new hero, Buffalo Bill. They called themselves bills and were divided into gangs that each ruled an area of the city nicknamed for the American West (Santa Fe, Texas) or for other movies they enjoyed, like Godzilla.

Nearby, on that Sunday afternoon in 1959, the Congolese rumba, a mesmerizing blend of Cuban and African rhythms, spilled out of tiny bars serving mazout—beer mixed with lemonade. Clouds of marijuana smoke hung thick in the tropical air.

What had gathered the crowd of thousands that January day was far more potent than legends or movies: the nascent realization that the Belgians did not have any actual right to rule over them.

Since 1952, Kenya had fought a war to rid itself of the British; Algeria had likewise fought to expel the French. Sudan attained independence from Britain and Egypt in 1956. Tunisia broke free

---

* A wonderful and detailed recounting of modern Congolese history, as seen by the Congolese themselves, can be found in David Van Reybrouck's *Congo*.

of France three months later. In 1957 Ghana, under its charismatic leader Kwame Nkrumah, was declared free of Britain, too. Guinea, Cameroon, Togo, Mali, and Senegal followed.

The black Congolese had followed every turn. It felt like hope. Like a release. A week earlier, they had listened rapt to one of a small group of black political leaders, Patrice Lumumba, a wiry former beer distributor who seemed to have modeled his rhetorical style and his brow-line glasses on Malcolm X, as he spoke of independence for the Congo.

Another event had been scheduled at the Leopoldville YMCA for 2 p.m. that Sunday. But these gatherings struck a deep and primal fear into European officials and their leaders at home who preferred a docile Africa. At the last moment, the Belgian mayor of the city decided to ban the meeting.

Some accounts say that one of the young men turned on the manager of the YMCA when he delivered the news. It is more likely that he got into an argument with the white driver of an electric bus, one of the city's proudest achievements, who had denied him passage.

His identity is not known. Congolese history lives mostly in the memories of its people, and few have asked them about it, let alone written it down. Perhaps his grandfather had given away his lands and freedoms by signing a cross on a piece of paper he did not understand. Perhaps his grandmother had been cajoled into moving into the home of a local Belgian official, or a series of local Belgian officials, for sex, then shoved into the street pregnant to fend for herself. Or maybe he really wanted to ride the bus.

A riot is the temporary suspension of civilization. The veneer drops away much faster than anyone expects, and is replaced with a determined, collaborative destruction, both fevered and meticulous, slapstick and terrifying.

His punch landed like a battle cry.

The center of the crowd surged forward, toward the fallen bus driver. As each punch and kick landed on the unfortunate man and on the police officers who attempted to intervene, the fringes of the crowd, seeking their own damage to do, spread out. They set cars alight, or rocked them back and forth in small, spontaneous teams until they teetered satisfyingly and crashed onto their roofs with the crunch of crushed metal and powdered glass. With each act of destruction the world of rules, and of consequences for breaking them, retreated.

The crowd fanned out through the afternoon like one fevered consciousness. Each man silently dared the next to pick up a stick, or a stone, to become the savages the Belgians told them they were.

They graffitied a sign at a school: BE CLEAN, BE POLITE, BE HONORABLE became BE DIRTY, BE IMPOLITE, BE DISHONORABLE. There was a glee in destruction for its own sake. In doing the certified, universally acknowledged worst possible thing instead of pleading politely once more for incremental change. The warning shots of the police, ringing now into the vast blue sky, meant nothing. The crowd had simply ceased to accept their authority.

At that moment, the soccer match at the Stade Roi Baudouin ended. About twenty thousand supporters, their faces daubed with white, feathers in their hair, dancing, drumming, and screaming, poured out onto the avenue. Their cries soon merged with those of the rioters, as fans and fighters formed one amorphous wall of destruction.

Two men in white shirts buzzed past on a scooter and skidded to a halt, the two-cylinder engine rattling as it idled: Lumumba, scheduled to give the speech that caused the riot, and his friend and ally Joseph Kasavubu, a politician with ambitions to restore the mythical kingdom of the Congo.* (They had risen together

---

* His picture could be seen on posters around town with the slogan *roi kasa,* or "King Kasa," underneath it.

through one of the only political organizations allowed by the Belgians: the Boy Scouts.) The two gazed with disbelief at the rage of their people, released at last. Kasavubu gunned the bike, and they disappeared in a haze of exhaust smoke.

Lieutenant General Émile Janssens, unflinching as stones and bottles rained down, also watched the crowd spread out in front of him. Janssens was a veteran of the Belgian army who headed the new version of the Force Publique—the thousands-strong Belgian army that had enforced such a brutal reign of colonial terror.

By 1959, it was a national army, and most of its soldiers were black Congolese. But they were led exclusively by white Belgians who enforced a strict discipline. They remained the ultimate arbiter in the Congo.

Janssens had grown used to his power. He surveyed the fires burning out of control. The slicks of dark blood, peppered with shards and fragments of his city. He watched looters, some trailing yards of vivid floral fabric as they ran from smashed stores. The word had come down from the Belgian officials who ran the city that the riot zone now extended about seven miles.

Pictures of Janssens from his youth reveal a small, sensitive-looking soldier. Over years of careful conditioning and military campaigns in Ethiopia and in Europe during World War II, he had turned his fear into disdain for the fearful, and his sensitivity into contempt for those in pain.

The transformation was etched on his face. Weathered and ruggedly handsome, with a low brow and a suspicious gaze like the actor Robert Forster, he was by 1959 the very picture of a general commanding his troops.

He ordered his soldiers to open fire with live rounds. Other Belgians, too, colonial officials mostly, felt themselves fill with terror that they would fall victim to this post-colonial rage. They grabbed their hunting rifles and joined in, gazing down the oily barrels of their guns and firing into the dusk.

Night near the equator comes fast. At around 6 p.m., after four crazed, terrible, brutal hours, the red ball of the sun plunged below the horizon and Leopoldville fell dark, save for the flickering orange light of the flames.

Darkness achieved, on a strictly temporary basis, what no quantity of bullets could: The crowd dispersed as quickly as it had risen up. The wave had broken. But it would swell again. The riots continued for days.

A procession of European cars, their windows hanging from their frames, their bodywork crumpled like tinfoil, limped and rattled toward the Red Cross hospital. They crunched to a halt outside the stately white building ringed with verandas, to form a spontaneous monument to the bruised dignity of their occupants.

The Congolese wounded made do with whatever treatments they had on hand. Feticheurs—witch doctors who created elaborate figures and masks for healing and destruction—were still active in 1959. The scale and success of their efforts is not recorded; only that as many as three hundred Congolese were dead.

"We killed them because they were thieves, because they were pillagers," Janssens said. "If they don't keep quiet, we are ready to recommence the sport."

Years later, when the war was over, and when Belgium was nothing more than a bitter memory in Africa, they found Janssens in Brussels at the foot of a statue of King Leopold II. "Sire," he was heard to say, "*ils vous l'ont cochonné.*" They've made you dirty.*

---

* He eventually became a far-right politician.

Chapter 1

"That's independence"

The United Nations is so ubiquitous, and so often dismissed as a pointless, hand-wringing bureaucracy, that we forget what it is for.

The name itself was coined by Franklin D. Roosevelt for a declaration on New Year's Day 1942 by twenty-six nations* that they would continue to fight the Axis powers with every means at their disposal, and that none would make a separate peace.

After the war, representatives of fifty countries, shaken by the specter of the grubby, selfish, destructive part of humanity, gathered in San Francisco.

Over two months, they negotiated—with the care and determination that only people who have recently lived through horror can muster—a better way. On June 25, 1945, they voted on the final charter. A show of hands was deemed insufficient for such a moment, and so the delegates, about three thousand of them, stood up to show their assent. The next day they brought the International Court of Justice into existence and signed the United Nations charter, which opens thus:

---

* The next day, twenty-two more signed on to the declaration.

WE THE PEOPLES OF THE UNITED NATIONS
DETERMINED to save succeeding generations from the
scourge of war, which twice in our lifetime has brought
untold sorrow to mankind, and to reaffirm faith in fundamental human rights, in the dignity and worth of the
human person, in the equal rights of men and women and
of nations large and small...

When Roosevelt's successor, Truman, addressed the delegates,
he described the charter as a victory against war itself. "If we fail to
use it," he said, "we shall betray all those who have died so that we
might meet here in freedom and safety to create it. If we seek to use
it selfishly—for the advantage of any one nation or any small group
of nations—we shall be equally guilty of that betrayal."

———

By July 1960, as the Congo was dragged over a precipice, Dag
Hammarskjöld had been UN secretary-general for seven years.
He believed in his mission with a sincerity that his enemies, men
of expedience rather than principle, simply could not grasp. He
carried the charter with him at all times, in a small and worn
booklet. And he tried to apply it as precisely and fairly as he could.
It would not have occurred to him to do anything else.

He was, on the surface, every inch the deft diplomat. He was
nearly six feet tall, and looked at least a decade younger than his
fifty-five years. His face, halfway between handsome and possum-
like, gave away nothing.

His hair, sandy with graying edges atop a high forehead, was
swept back neatly. His suits, elegantly cut, were always immacu-
late over a crisp shirt and tie, or bow tie. His shoes were polished
to a shine that stopped discreetly short of showiness. He smoked,
on occasion, a pipe.

He was trained as an economist. He loved to figure out the system, the essence, of a thing before forming a plan and executing it with precision. He spoke very fast, in a distinct lilting Swedish accent, the words tumbling out as if they could not keep up with his thoughts. He walked even faster. His security detail dreaded keeping up with him.

Those who worked closely with him admired him greatly— but as one admires a view or a monument. They recalled his capacity to work virtually without sleep. His tendency to see the good in nearly anyone. His ability to talk with deftness and perception about nearly anything—medieval literature, economics, painting, poetry—in fluent Swedish, English, French, or German. He numbered John Steinbeck, Barbara Hepworth, and W. H. Auden among his friends. But very few felt they really knew him.

Sture Linnér, a Swedish mining executive, Greek scholar, and UN official whom Hammarskjöld counted among his closer friends, once recalled being invited to dinner at his Manhattan apartment. It was a classic duplex on the Upper East Side, built around a grand, curved staircase, that he had elegantly decorated with Scandinavian furniture and art including works by Matisse and the Swedish painter Bo Beskow.

He came and opened the door himself, no servants around. We had a simple meal while he played recordings of Bach in an adjacent room. Not a word was said during dinner. After we had finished, he said let's go to the library. And we continued listening. Toward 11 o'clock I said that it was time to say goodbye. He said I think so. And he kindly escorted me to the door. He hadn't said anything. When we shook hands, he looked at me and said, "I want you to know that the talk we had tonight is one of the most enriching I have had in a long time."

Hammarskjöld seems only to have been truly free with animals, and with those in severe pain. He recalled an incident in Stockholm, when he was thirty and working as an official in the Swedish treasury. He often worked through the night, and was walking home through the island city, with its clarifying gusts of Baltic wind and pale northern light, at dawn.

He saw a man nearby throw a package to a woman. The woman took the package and walked away. And then the young man walked over to the water, dotted with squares of ice and viscous with cold, and threw himself in. By the time Hammarskjöld got to him, he was floating facedown, unconscious. Hammarskjöld pulled him to shore with a nearby boat hook.

He had recently come out of the army, he told Hammarskjöld. The bundle he had thrown to the woman contained love letters she had written him. But she had found somebody else while he was away and wanted her letters back.

Hammarskjöld prevented him from running back to the water and persuaded him to get a cab home. It was one of four occasions on which he had witnessed suicides or attempted suicides. He was fascinated, his diaries reveal, with self-inflicted death, with resisting its temptations, and with the balance of the animal and the civilized that exists in all of us.

As secretary-general, years later in 1960, unbeknown to all but a small circle of friends, he kept a monkey in his grand Manhattan apartment. It had been presented to him earlier in the year, in Somaliland, an autonomous territory that was once part of Somalia, on one of the last stops of a monthlong tour of Africa. It was a vervet, a chittering baby the size of a small dog, its animated little face framed with a fluffy ring of white hair. It proved within seconds to be an irrepressible ham, playing shamelessly to whoever was near it.

Hammarskjöld couldn't resist it. Maybe it was a reaction to the grueling schedule of pleasantries on the tour; the shaking hands and standing near buildings, statues, and boats in Senegal, Kenya, Ghana—twenty-seven stops in twenty-four different nations or regions—smiling alongside freshly spruced local dignitaries; the small talk. (He hated small talk. He called it "the hell of spiritual death.")

He named the monkey Greenback, for the greenish tint in its fur, and made arrangements to have it smuggled back to America. Greenback was as comfortable in Manhattan as Truman Capote would have been joining a vervet troop in the jungles of Somalia.* But the monkey quickly found a feeling of safety on the window-sill, playing with the dangling curtain cord or staring out into the snowy New York night, watching the cars.

On the same tour of Africa, Hammarskjöld had grown pro-foundly concerned about the Congo. It was, he had discovered, catastrophically seductive to world powers. It was right in the middle of Africa, with two prime airfields. It had the world's pur-est uranium. The head of the largest Belgian mining company, Union Minière, had been given the American Medal for Merit for supplying the Manhattan Project. And it had the best supply of cobalt—vital for circuits in the American and Russian nuclear missiles that carried nuclear payloads.

The first national elections had taken place in May 1960. Each new African party made lavish promises. Their pamphlets pledged the perfect, the impossible. "When independence arrives," said one, "the whites will have to leave the country. The goods left behind will become the property of the black population. That is to say: the houses, the shops, the trucks, the merchandise, the factories and fields will be given back . . ."

Patrice Lumumba narrowly gained the most votes. He was the

---

* Vervet monkeys, also known as green monkeys, share 90 percent of their genetic makeup with human beings. They feel joy, sadness, and anger. They can adapt to nearly any environment. And they are among the only nonhuman primates that suffer from stress and high blood pressure in the same ways we do.

only candidate that appealed to all regions, and all tribes, partly because he campaigned, using brightly colored vans playing music and blasting political messages, more broadly than his rivals.

His supporters considered him passionate and honest, and with an advanced grasp of social justice and a plan for advancement for his people based in his Christian values. They held that he was the Congo's best chance for a functioning democracy on its own terms.

He would be prime minister, and his friend and ally Joseph Kasavubu would be president. The Force Publique would be renamed the Armée Nationale Congolaise (ANC) and run by a thin, ascetic soldier named Joseph Désiré Mobutu. The rest of the cabinet was formed of their allies.

Parliament sat for the first time on June 24, 1960. It was made up of hundreds of new politicians, most of them taking public roles for the first time. The new government sent tremors through the network of corporations that had been extracting the Congo's natural resources unimpeded for decades. Belgium had let them operate with near-complete autonomy. When they chose to be benevolent—as they did when building homes and providing education and health care for their thousands of workers—nobody stood in their way. When they chose to drive those same workers like slaves to exhausted deaths, they were allowed to do so. They craved continuity and the election of a leader sympathetic to capitalism.

Continuity is not a word that anyone ever applied to Lumumba. His supporters would have said, with pride, that he could not be controlled or diverted but would relentlessly do what he felt was correct in any given moment. His detractors would have said the same, but with horror.

The Belgians, the Brits, and the Americans saw him as a dangerously left-leaning firebrand. In military radio transmissions between Belgian officials who remained in the country, his code name was "Satan." General Janssens described him thus: "Moral character: none; intellectual character: entirely superficial; physical character: his nervous system made him seem more feline than human."

On June 30, 1960, Hammarskjöld watched as Leopold's successor, King Baudouin of Belgium, stood up in a white military uniform festooned with medals and, with the bitterness of a reluctant divorcée, declared the Congo free at last.

"The independence of Congo constitutes the completion of the work that arose from the genius of King Leopold II," he said, "that was undertaken by him with undaunted courage and set forth by the determination of Belgium." He asked that the Congolese show that Belgium was right to have offered independence, and said that he would offer counsel if asked.

Lumumba stood to give his own unscheduled riposte. "The fate that befell us during eighty years of colonial rule," he said, "is not something we can eradicate from our memory, our wounds are still too fresh and too painful. We have known grueling labor, demanded from us in return for wages that did not allow us to eat decently, to clothe ourselves or have housing, nor to raise our children as loved ones.

"We have known mockery and insult, blows that we underwent in the morning, in the afternoon and evening, because we were Negroes," he continued. "We have seen our raw materials stolen in the name of documents that were called legal, but which recognized only the right of the most powerful." He spoke of magnificent houses for the whites, and hovels for the blacks, and railed against the apartheid that meant separate white movie theaters, restaurants, and shops. Lumumba's supporters broke into applause. The king went as pale as his dress uniform. He never forgot the slight.

The plan was for the Congolese army, with twenty-five thousand well-drilled and beautifully turned-out soldiers, to remain a bulwark for law and order. But though it had been renamed the Armee Nationale Congolaise (ANC), and was no longer the Force Publique, its role as overseer had never been forgotten by the black Congolese.

Its uniformly white officers, about six hundred of them, had spent years brutalizing both their men and the populace they nominally protected, often with a stiff whip called a chicote made from dried hippopotamus hide that could leave a man hobbled for life.

In early July, the Congo formally joined the United Nations. And at around the same time, black Congolese soldiers, who had been promised nearly immediate changes in their quality of life after the election, finally ran out of patience.

Camp Thysville, about a hundred miles outside Leopoldville, housed the ANC's Fourth Brigade with the Second and Third Infantry Battalions. There, about two thousand men, unsure, and unmoored, mulled the idea that they might be free, and that those they had previously feared might now fear them. Their hatred extended beyond their officers, to anyone European.

Hammarskjöld received cables, on paper so thin it was translucent, containing alarming fragments of what happened next. A Belgian parliamentary report, compiled later, described the events that followed in greater detail, with names redacted. It is a list of dozens of incidents, each laying out unimaginable horrors.

One woman had been at home, on July 5, 1960, the report said, with her mother and four children. At around 4 p.m. a group of four soldiers broke in, pushed her into a bedroom and raped her in turn, then left. Three hours later, as she processed what had just happened, a group of thirteen soldiers and policemen entered the house. Twelve of those also raped her.

On July 6, a Belgian man was snatched up and taken to an army jail. He was forced to flatten coils of barbed wire with his feet. Another man, Swiss, not Belgian, was arrested two days later, the report said. He was hit in the back of the head with rifle butts while a Congolese policeman said, "That's independence." The documented examples alone continued for thirteen pages.

Belgians began to flee by any means open to them. Groups of cars, with smashed windows and suitcases strapped haphazardly to their roofs, sped across the borders. Parents handed their children loaded guns. Men dressed as women to sneak aboard transportation home. They destroyed the blueprints and operating instructions for the country's major pieces of infrastructure as they left, out of spite.

The Europeans who chose to remain, about thirty thousand of them, fled south to the province of Katanga. It bordered the white-controlled Federation of Rhodesia and Nyasaland, and its capital Elisabethville was the center of the white-controlled mining industry. It would be their stronghold.

On July 11, 1960, Katanga's council of ministers, led by a local businessman named Moïse Tshombe and backed by the federation, Belgium, and the Katangese mining industry, declared that the province had seceded and would form its own government.

It took with it most of the Congo's mineral wealth and somewhere between half and two-thirds of its revenues as a nation. Quite simply, the Congo could not survive or even function without Katanga.

———

At about 2 p.m. the next day, Hammarskjöld received a formal request from the Congolese government for military assistance. Lumumba was determined to overturn the secession by any means necessary. He simply had to reclaim Katanga and make the Congo one nation. And at first, while Katanga had only a small, ragtag army of mercenaries to defend it, the odds were in the new prime minister's favor.

Hammarskjöld began to work on the problem as he always worked, deep into the nights, all alone, by the light of a desk lamp.

He sifted the mass of data he had gathered about the country. Its history, the long-term probabilities, the practical possibilities, and the support required. He wrote notes: what the UN could do, what it should do, its objectives and operating principles. If he knew his aim, the speed and confidence to navigate the inferno would follow.

On July 14, 1960, the UN Security Council passed Resolution 143 calling on foreign troops to depart the Congo, and giving Hammarskjöld the power to provide military assistance to the crumbling Congolese government as it sought to reunite the country.

Transport planes began landing in Leopoldville, disgorging thousands of United Nations peacekeepers drawn from Morocco, Sweden, and India, among other smaller nations.

But Katanga had virtually unlimited resources and connections. It was filled with Europeans who had fled what they felt was a vicious and unjustified attack. It did not plan to let the black revolution proceed unchecked. A British journalist, Sandy Gall, captured a conversation between two white residents at this moment.

"They're not fit to run a shamba [farm] let alone a country, man."

"Yes, but that's a matter of training. In a few years' time..."

"But Jesus, man, you don't know the African. You just don't understand his mentality. These fellows were swinging from the trees when I first came here and now you want to dress them up in dinner jackets and make them run the country?"

Chapter 2

"Swindled, cheated and abused"

Jean-François Thiriart was an optometrist. A successful one. He lived in a solid, respectable Belgian home, in a solid, respectable Belgian suburb, with a solid, respectable Belgian family. He owned a chain of optical stores across Europe and, at thirty-eight, he had risen to chair the European Federation of Optometrists.

The smell at his home was the first clue that something else lay beneath the surface. Sour urine, mixed with the ferrous tang of cat food, hit visitors as soon as they walked in, to be explained moments later when one of twenty or so cats he kept strolled languidly past.

Thiriart had always felt he should not have been born in Belgium. He had bigger ideas, befitting a bigger nation—even a continent, or a planet. He grew fond of reciting a Latin maxim he had picked up from Heinrich Jordis von Lohausen, an Austrian general who had become one of the grand philosophers of white nationalism in the years after World War II: "Destiny carries the willing man," it went. "The man who is unwilling it drags."

He was trim and precise, with a pair of rectangular, silver-rimmed spectacles and a shock of dark hair. As a teenager, he had first enlisted in a left-wing student organization, the Young Socialist Guards. But then his mother had divorced his father and married a German Jew, who insisted on teaching his stepson Yiddish.

He joined the extreme-right-wing National Legion at seventeen, in 1939, and another pro-Nazi group known as the Association of the Friends of the German Reich at around the same time. He thrilled to skydive with the commandos of Austrian SS-Obersturmbannführer Otto Skorzeny.

Thiriart had been jailed for three years after the war, and had kept a low profile since. He now disdained the label *fascist*, which he felt was outdated, petty, and offensive. His vision was far grander. His theories were rigorous and should not be subjected to such simplifications. He peppered his conversation with allusions to philosophers, warriors, and poets. (Most of whom, on closer inspection, turned out to be fascist.)

Left and right were obsolete concepts, Thiriart felt. He cited Hitler, who (he had been reliably informed by people who would know) had once said that Communists made great Nazis, whereas moderates never did.

To Thiriart only race, history, and power mattered. A pan-European white nationalism. He dreamed of a sweeping white-power bloc, from Brest, in northern France, to Vladivostok, on Russia's Pacific coast, closer to Tokyo than Moscow.

In 1960, he became fixated on the Congo. The withdrawal of Belgium had angered him. The idea that Washington or Moscow might step in angered him more. He felt that to raise his own army, and to take back the Congo for Europe, would provide both an example and a base of operations for the future.

He began to rouse supporters with stump speeches, in bars and parks and grubby meeting halls, that were purest fire and fury. "We are calling the men who are ready to die for Europe . . . The Europe of the beautiful conceptions, the Europe of salons, will emerge from the Europe of guns, from the Europe of will power."

In *Belgique-Afrique*, a pamphlet published by Belgian colonialists, he was more specific.

Recruitment of soldiers, he said, should focus on "Europeans,

Belgians, Hungarians, Italians, who are sick of seeing Europe scorned and humiliated from the outside, swindled, cheated and abused from the inside."*

He had begun recruiting already, in the backstreet bars of Brussels. He and his colleagues sought the defeated, the guilty, the sick, and the sad. Those who could be brought easily to tears of outrage, who longed to attach all of life's horror and mystery to successive simple causes. They were slow to move, to decide, to commit. Their minds were not nimble or open. But once you had them, Thiriart felt, you had them. Especially for 25,000 Belgian francs a month, plus expenses. A wage that most of them could only dream of.

They came in all stripes. Fascists, who had fought for Germany. Ultra-hard-line Catholics who saw Jews as the perpetual enemies of Christ. Arch-royalists, who craved the return of Leopold and released pamphlets campaigning against democracy. Corporatists, who believed that the only way for a nation to run was in the interests of the powerful. And white supremacist colonial soldiers, veterans of wars in Kenya and South Africa.

More than anything, Thiriart spoke to those who yearned to be heard. To be respected. To have their pain accepted and approved and indulged, however repulsive its manifestations. The thing they least wanted to hear was that they were merely afraid.

They sought not comfort, or relief, but retribution.

In 1960, Katanga's capital city, Elisabethville, was a colonial idyll dotted with vivid purple jacaranda trees and trickling fountains. It was home to hundreds of thousands of people, a blend of Europeans and white Africans, who lived in homes with manicured

* Later, the Argentinian dictator General Juan Perón became an adherent of Thiriart's ideas.

lawns surrounded by low walls, and black Africans segregated into their own neighborhoods, many in houses they had built themselves.

Its center was a sunbaked sprawl of low, white and tan buildings around broad intersections and grand boulevards. They hosted a slow parade of Europeans in Volkswagens and finned Chevrolets, surrounded by black Africans on two wheels. On the outskirts the roads turned to a dark, rich dirt, and the bicycles began to outnumber the cars.

The newly anointed presidential palace of the newly founded nation of Katanga was a beautiful white house set back from such a road. That summer a car pulled up to its wrought-iron gates. A palace guard sitting in a wooden hut, wearing white pantaloons with a red sash, a green jacket with gold braiding, and a pointed gold helmet, stood up to meet it. He informed Moïse Tshombe, the president, that his visitor had arrived.

Tshombe was forty. He was a large man with a round, animated face that looked built for comedy but caught perpetually in tragedy. He was the son of a rich man—a local king, in fact. He liked fast cars, and women who liked men who liked fast cars. He had started business after business but had never managed, until leading a rogue nation, to make anything stick. It was a nice feeling. He had postcards made of himself posing, exuding a barrel-chested pride, in his ceremonial sash. He reveled, too, in the newly minted coins and stamps that legitimized his rule.

Actually running a government had, on the other hand, been one hideous calamity after another. Most recently, a giant cloud of bees had shut down the ministry of the interior, drifting from room to room with a thrumming malevolence as his ministers hid in their offices until the bees had decided to depart.

Tshombe had been selected by Belgian officials. The political campaigns he had run, and the decisions he had made as president, including secession, were strategized by those officials and the executives of Union Minière—the Belgian mining company that had arrived in the Congo with Leopold's blessing in 1906, and had effectively ruled over Katanga since.

It still extracted hundreds of thousands of tons of minerals, primarily copper, and returned the equivalent of hundreds of millions of dollars to Belgium, and its shareholders in Britain and elsewhere, each year. The *New York Times* described it as "the colossus of the Congo economy."

Its dozen or so mines and headquarters, and the roads and railroads that connected them, were like Katanga's arteries. Many of them snaked across the southern border into the Federation of Rhodesia and Nyasaland, to connect up with other white-African-controlled mines and refineries. And its communications networks were the only reliable methods of getting information to and from the province.

Union Minière felt it had found in the Congo, according to its promotional materials, malnourished and diseased savages in huts and transformed them into clean pseudo-Europeans, grateful and docile in prim white shorts and shirts. Its films showed them gamboling innocently in Union Minière compounds, little towns attached to the company's facilities. It provided housing, education, and medical care, and even sold cost-price building materials and offered cheap loans. More than twenty-two thousand black Africans worked directly for the company, and it estimated that it supported about a hundred thousand in total.

The company's executives flitted through Katanga like low-key royals. They shopped for a nice bottle of burgundy or a Christian Dior dress in town. They played tennis at Circle Albert, an exclusive sporting club, or enjoyed coq au vin or filet mignon with an appropriate wine, of course, at the Hotel Leopold II.

When one of those executives had asked Tshombe to meet his brother-in-law, visiting from Belgium, he could not refuse. So he instructed the palace guard to show the man, an envoy from

Thiriart named Pierre Joly, a sometime-journalist with a slicked ponytail, inside.

Over a bottle, perhaps, of red wine and with the scent of yellow rock roses from the garden wafting through the warm air, Joly made a proposal. It was the culmination of the recruiting and funding work he and Thiriart and other far-right campaigners had done in Brussels.

They wanted to supply a mercenary army to Katanga, led by extremist European soldiers. It would be at Tshombe's disposal—subject to consultation with Union Minière and Tshombe's network of Belgian advisers, of course.

Rumors had swirled in Katanga that the central government in Leopoldville would soon send soldiers to retake the province. Tshombe was scared. He wanted to maintain his power, and to placate his patrons. He approved the plan.

By September 1960, the first fifty mercenaries had stepped off Sabena airlines flights from Brussels to Elisabethville. The head of intelligence for the Katangese police, Armand Verdickt, ran background checks on them. Deserters. Thieves. Rapists. Addicts. One wrestled professionally as The Black Angel. These are not soldiers, Verdickt said, scanning the list. "*Ils sont les affreux.*"

Each successive group, arriving staggered over days and weeks, was ushered through customs without stopping. They boarded old flat-bed trucks, covered with sun-bleached canvas stretched over a steel frame. As they drove, rural Katanga unfolded through the canvas flaps and the cloud of billowing red dust they left in their wake.

Dirt roads, edged with a verge of short grass, gave way to a tangle of roots, branches, and vines and then a verdant green. It was punctuated occasionally with baobab trees, their trunks as squat and square as a house, their branches surreal and tiny on top. They passed husks of buildings, their exposed beams pointing skyward at strange angles, bemused and emaciated cows, bony dogs and lean chickens.

On such a journey one soldier had, according to one of the contradictory memoirs that the mercenaries would eventually write, seen a man leaning thoughtfully on a spear, considering their passing. Without knowing or caring who he was, he had pulled his pistol and snapped a shot through the open rear of the truck. He missed, and the man leapt back into the bush. The echoing report had woken the other soldiers from their daze. But none of them considered the attempt impolite.

It was a signal of the atrocities to come. And as they began to defend Katanga from enemies, real and imagined, by any means they felt necessary, the nickname Verdickt had coined spread through Katanga, and through the Congo. They would forever be *les affreux*. The deplorable ones.

Chapter 3

"The galaxy of good and evil talents"

On September 20, 1960, on a warm late-summer day in Manhattan, the fifteenth annual General Assembly of the United Nations began. Thousands of delegates were scattered around the complex of United Nations buildings that sits on the East Side of Manhattan, in New York but distinctly not of it, designed after a series of disagreements between the architects Le Corbusier and Oscar Niemeyer among others.

Kips Bay was once dominated by slaughterhouses and tenements. Now, tucked behind well-kept hedges and lawns, it hosts a rectangular glass-and-stone skyscraper so substantial that sections of cloud and sunshine play across its surface. It is home to the UN's staff, including the secretary-general. Leading away from it is a low, sweeping curved building, which hosts the General Assembly. Or rather, attempts to contain it.

Its cavernous halls—somewhere between a church and an airport—had to accommodate the egos and entourages of ten heads of state, eleven prime ministers, twenty-eight foreign ministers, and a nearly uncountable quantity of ambassadors, ministers, economic, military, and legal advisers, and first, second, and third secretaries.

The *New York Times* wrote:

Never, except at peace conferences ending great wars, has there been anything like the galaxy of good and evil talents, assembled under the glittering light of publicity, that has been shooting out sparks on the banks of the East River.

These personalities are endowed with temperaments. They lose their tempers, they embrace each other under the incongruous glare of the photographers' flashes, they pointedly ignore each other as they pass in narrow aisles, they whisper together when the speaking is going on, they cluster in the strictly guarded delegates' lounges.

President Nasser of Egypt brought every Arab chieftain he could find with him, including two kings. The Russian premier, Nikita Khrushchev, with a flair for drama disguised under a carefully constructed drabness, arrived with an entourage of nearly one hundred, including Communist bosses from Hungary, Poland, Romania, Bulgaria, and Yugoslavia.

His intention, all but avowed, was to destroy Dag Hammarskjöld, whom he saw as an agent of the West, and to replace his role with a troika of diplomats that he felt could be more easily manipulated to his ends.

At least five street brawls had broken out in the days and hours leading up to the assembly's opening. A crowd, including Ukrainian and Hungarian activists, had gathered to jeer in unison outside the Soviet delegation's headquarters on Park Avenue. The NYPD intervened when they began throwing firecrackers at the legs of police horses, and punches at each other. They were aided by one irate resident who slung a basin of water out of her window into the melee.

Anti-Albanian Greeks clashed with anti-Greek Albanians outside the UN building itself in a flurry of sticks and umbrellas and placards. More than a hundred police officers charged in with nightsticks.

Nearby, pro-Castro Cubans and anti-Castro Cubans put on a similar performance, with variations. Pacifists, meanwhile, held their own protest. Their signs read, WELCOME! LET'S CO-EXIST!, STAY FOR PEACE AND TALK IT OUT, and HANDS OFF CONGO. No fights were reported.

The drama was raised to a fine pitch by the fact that fourteen African nations, newly independent—including Cameroon, Togo, Somalia, Niger, Chad, the Ivory Coast, Gabon, and Senegal—were to be admitted to the UN as the first piece of business.

As the delegates took their seats in the chamber, sitting behind nameplates, wearing translation headsets, in concentric arcs in front of a marble-backed stage, Khrushchev had a point to make to these new members.

With the glee of a naughty boy, he began to pound on the desk in front of him with both fists, a UN TV producer, Emery Kelen, recalled later. "His small, alert eyes sparkled with malice, and no trace of anger was visible on his face. He looked amused, self-satisfied as a child who has just played a successful prank," Kelen said.

His foreign minister, Andrei Gromyko, sat next to him and joined in halfheartedly, confirming a statement that Khrushchev had once made: "If I tell my foreign minister to sit on a block of ice and stay there for a month he will do it without back talk."

He wanted to discredit the organization, and Hammarskjöld, with a ludicrous scene. Khrushchev had risen through a brutal and deeply unfair system. He had nothing to fear from an operator—there were none he felt he could not outmaneuver. A man like Hammarskjöld who could not be bought or bullied was a different proposition.

Dag Hjalmar Agne Carl Hammarskjöld was born in July 1905, the smallest of four sons of Hjalmar Hammarskjöld, a widely disliked former prime minister of Sweden, and Agnes Hammarskjöld, a woman described as so sensitive it was occasionally hard to tell if she was laughing or crying.

He grew up in a pink medieval castle on a hill in Sweden's bucolic center. The castle, a squat, dusky edifice with a low gray roof and towers on either end, was Hjalmar's official residence, granted to him in his new position as governor of Uppsala—the name of both an agrarian region in the middle of Sweden and its main town. It overlooks Sweden's most storied university and the cathedral that is the seat of the archbishop.

In an essay he wrote about his youth in the castle, Dag remembered the ghost of a former queen who would wander the corridors dressed in black with white lace trimmings. The bodies of swifts he used to find in the castle's deep windows, dead after flying into the cavernous, cold halls and finding themselves unable to get out. The ants fighting each other for territory among the white-star flowers of his favorite northern rock jasmine plants in the grounds.

The Hammarskjölds were an aristocratic family—the name is a version of the Swedish words for "hammer" and "shield"—granted a seat in the prestigious Nobel Academy (the body that awards the prizes).

Hjalmar, born in 1862, was the latest in a line of soldiers and government officials that extended back into Swedish antiquity. In pictures he appears positively Dickensian, wearing a top hat, a pince-nez, a long coat, and a gimlet-eyed stare that speaks of a stern intelligence held back from explosion by a thread of will.

He was trained as a lawyer and became the Swedish minister of justice in 1901. Later he served on the newly founded Court of Arbitration at the Hague. When Dag was born, he was negotiating the dissolution of a union between Sweden and its neighbor Norway. In 1914 in the midst of a governmental crisis, when Dag was eight, Hjalmar was asked by the Swedish king to form a government. World War I broke out shortly after he became prime minister.

It was Hjalmar that instituted a policy of wartime neutrality, which included declining a trade deal with Britain. He felt it a principled necessity. His people, suffering under rationing that they blamed on his isolationism, called him Hungerskjöld. The world saw it as the beginning of Sweden's awkward appeasement of German forces. In 1917, he resigned his position and returned to the castle in Uppsala to be governor of the province.

Dag remembered his father watching out of his window and laughing as the crows outside fought, fluttered, and negotiated. Their disputes reminded him of human ones in their petty fury and pointlessness.

Hjalmar was frequently away. And Dag's nearest brother was five years older. That meant he functionally grew up by himself. He became obsessed with cataloging the plants and insects around the castle. He modeled himself on an early hero, the botanist Carl Linnaeus, the father of modern genetics and the inventor of the taxonomical system, who had been a professor at Uppsala University.

The memories of his childhood that Dag put down in the essay were not of playing with other children, or of adventures, but a child's careful observations of people and of life. That may have been of necessity. Sweden is a profoundly conservative society, for all of its progressive ideals. The lot of an aristocratic young man was to conform to the expectations of his parents.* His life was expected to revolve around them.

His mother called him her little larva. To Dag she was everything his father was not—warmth, not light. She came from a

---

* Until relatively recently, Sweden had very high rates of incarceration for mental illness. That has been taken as evidence of a prevalence of mental illness there. It is more likely to be evidence of a desire to categorize away those who didn't quite fit in. Strindberg was institutionalized, for example. The country also performed involuntary lobotomies into the 1950s, and involuntary sterilization up until 1975.

long line of clergy, scholars, and poets, and embodied a child-like openness, a dislike of the rational, and a tendency toward startlingly quick intimacy with friends and strangers alike.

A friend, Sten Söderberg, told one of Hammarskjöld's biographers that Dag had been Agnes's "gentleman in waiting, her page, her faithful and considerate attendant." Others expressed concern that he was spending too much time with her.

When Dag was seventeen, and on a trip with his brother and his wife, his mother sent him a letter: "Writing to you is the most fun I have. Dag is the only one I really own on earth, the only one who cares about me."

He studied close to home, at Uppsala University, strolling out of the castle door, down one hill and slightly up another, to immerse himself in linguistics, literature, and history. It seems to have been the first moment he felt truly free. In a long-running correspondence with two friends, Rutger Moll and Jan Waldenström,* the three discussed literature—Flaubert, Emerson, and Conrad—and life.

They spent a summer studying together in Cambridge, England, in 1927, when Hammarskjöld was twenty-two. After this, their letters to each other turned playful. They began addressing each other as "dear" and "darling"—perhaps an ironic Briticism.

On one occasion in August 1927—the matter of feverish debate for those who seek a binary definition of Hammarskjöld's sexuality—he wrote to Rutger about Jan. "I regard him as 'mine'— in a few years or perhaps sooner. It won't be long."

There is no evidence that he ever attained Waldenström, in whatever sense he meant it. Or anyone else, for that matter. Hammarskjöld never had a romantic relationship that he spoke openly of, or that was recorded by his friends and colleagues.

He continued his studies, in law and economics, in Stockholm.

---

* Waldenström would later become a renowned doctor.

His parents eventually moved, too. He lived with them well into his twenties as he commenced an ascent of the Swedish government—in the ministry of justice, in the foreign ministry, and in the finance ministry—that staggered his peers with its speed. He would return home for dinner every day, with a bouquet of flowers for his mother, before going back to the office to work on into the night.

In 1943, at the height of World War II, he traveled to Britain as part of a trade delegation. The policy of neutrality instituted by his father was still in place, though Sweden allowed Hitler's Germany to move through its territory, and traded with it. The British officials he met treated him as a traitor.

His diaries reveal a split soul. A young man with a capacity for principled, logical, rigorous analysis, undertaken at a speed that astounded observers. But one who sought to push aside a sensitivity that read as shameful to him, and that found outlets in photography—which he said taught him to see—poetry, and long, solitary climbs up the mountains of the empty Swedish north, toward the Arctic Circle.

He discussed literature and life over dinners with Steinbeck—whom he pushed forward for the Nobel Prize for Literature that he won in 1962—the sculptor Barbara Hepworth, and the Swedish painter Bo Beskow, among others.

The trouble with Hammarskjöld, his friend Auden wrote, was that he was endowed with many brilliant gifts, but was "not, I think, a genius, not, that is to say, a person with a single overwhelming talent and passion for some particular activity—be it poetry or physics or bird-watching—which determines, usually early in life, exactly what his function on earth is to be ...

"To be gifted but not to know how best to make use of one's gifts, to be highly ambitious but at the same time to feel unworthy, is a dangerous combination which can often end in mental breakdown or suicide," Auden concluded.

Hammarskjöld's journal, found after his death, never mentions his work. It is, instead, a collection of thoughts and images, between Marcus Aurelius and a dream diary, unlike anything written by a working world leader in the modern era.

It reveals a deep religious faith—he was a Bible scholar of some achievement—that broadened through his life to become a precursor to modern pantheistic spirituality. And a series of obsessions that few of those who met him sensed.

How to be good in the face of evil:

Only he deserves power who every day justifies it.

How to evade the temptations of victimhood:

In spite of everything, your bitterness because others are enjoying what you are denied is always ready to flare up.

A solitude that he felt could never be assuaged. And a fixation with mortality:

Loneliness is not the sickness unto death. No, but can it be cured except by death? And does it not become the harder to bear the closer one comes to death?

In April 1953, his quiet daily life—a pleasant walk along the bucolic waterfront in Stockholm to work, days at a beautiful antique desk in a grand government building that felt more like a cathedral, summers off—was interrupted by a telegram informing him that the key nations had recommended him to run the United Nations.

"I was simply picked out of the hat," he said later, coyly setting aside the incandescent ambition that had driven him to greater and greater heights. It was partly true, anyway. America, Britain, and Russia had sought a mild, bureaucratic figure. They wanted a civil servant. And to all appearances, Hammarskjöld fit the bill. One Dutch diplomat described him, in 1953, as "an office-man without color and with a lot of care."

With a typical fervor for the driest possible expression of a glorious mandate, the UN describes the secretary-general as its "chief administrative officer." The role has been described, more grandly, as a secular version of the pope.

He—and it has, so far, always been a he—is in reality a mediator, a manager of international crises, and a cajoler of 193 member nations toward their better selves. He also sets the agenda for the UN—to focus the world on one difficulty instead of another.

When Hammarskjöld took the job, he was forty-seven. He formalized his loneliness with a declaration that he would devote himself only to his work. "In my situation in life," he wrote to a friend once, "I suppose this is part of the price of the stakes, that you are able to give yourself wholly and without reservation only if you don't steal, even in the smallest degree, from someone else."

In France, the newspapers, dripping with a haughty loathing, ran stories that he was secretly gay, at a time when homosexuality was still illegal in the United States.

He landed in New York on April 9, 1953. His predecessor, Trygve Lie, bitterly welcomed him "to the most impossible job on this earth." Hammarskjöld had, indeed, taken power over nothing and responsibility over everything. Every global crisis was his. Every powerful nation would seek to make him their scapegoat as they attempted to remake the world to their advantage. And yet it was enough to allow Hammarskjöld to put his idealistic theories into practice.

He began by meeting every delegate from every nation. He said little. But beneath his mask lay a radical idealism. "There is a simple basic morality that motivates most people," he told the *New York Times* shortly after taking office. "The great moment is the moment of realization that their desire for decency exists not only in their own groups but in others."

The *Times* story continued, "I happen to be the man selected. I happen to be the man who got the unanimous vote. I happen to have come in at the right time." Hammarskjöld added an aside, more quietly, almost to himself: "The time when there seems to be a chance."

When he took office, the Korean War had recently ended. Joseph Stalin had died, setting in motion a power struggle in Russia. President Dwight Eisenhower had refused clemency for Ethel and Julius Rosenberg, convicted of spying for the Soviet Union. Joseph McCarthy was preparing to embark on a hunt for Communists in America that would launch the country into one of its periodic paroxysms of division and hatred.

"We live in a time of peace which is no peace," Hammarskjöld said in a speech to students at Cambridge University, "in a time of technical achievement which threatens its own masters with destruction.

"There are fires burning everywhere on the horizon," he continued. "This may explain why many now show reactions which seem to reflect a kind of despair of Western civilization. But, where is the reason for such defeatism?"

In 1955, he scored a major success—he secured the release of fifteen American airmen being held in China. In 1956, he had been out walking on Mount Kebnekaise, the highest mountain in Sweden, when news broke. Egypt's president Gamal Abdel Nasser, who had already begun to accept Soviet aid—an act that was a virtual declaration of war against the West—had seized the vital Suez Canal.

The UN sent planes and local trackers out to search for Hammarskjöld. He was found thirty-six hours later, with a map in his hand, walking contentedly. The Western powers, in concert with Israel, had sent in troops. They expected Hammarskjöld's support. He condemned their decision and demanded neutral oversight instead. In 1957, he was unanimously reappointed for a second four-year term as secretary-general.

Hjalmar had died six months after his son had first taken office. And in his father's absence, Dag had started to reconsider his legacy. Hjalmar's service, he said in a radio lecture, "required a sacrifice of all personal interests, but likewise the courage to stand up unflinchingly for your convictions concerning what was right and good for the community, whatever were the views in fashion."

He wrote to Moll that he realized he had long been mediating a war inside himself, one between the stern principle of his father—"an admiration for the drawn sword that disregards the value of negotiated results and will only accept victories won in open battle"—and the "streaming, explosive power" that came from his mother.

"Where the one was light," he wrote, "the other is warmth. And who wouldn't want to integrate light and warmth?"

In October 1960, Khrushchev stood up once more to address the UN, this time specifically about the Congo and Hammarskjöld. "There are no saints on earth and there never have been. Let those who believe in saints keep their belief...Everyone has seen how vigorously the imperialist countries have been defending the position of Mr. Hammarskjöld. Is it not clear whose interests he interprets and executes, whose 'saint' he is?"

Sweden is a nation built firmly around the principle that no man should place himself above another. The concept derives, apocryphally, from Vikings passing a horn filled with mead. Each man had to sip neither too little nor too much. The principle has a word: *lagom*. And Sweden's aristocrats were willing extremists in the service of this moderation.

During World War II, Count Folke Bernadotte, the grandson of King Oscar II, the last king to rule over both Sweden and Norway, had quietly engineered the release of twenty-one thousand Jews from the concentration camps. He greeted them personally as they arrived on white buses, starved and afraid.*

Raoul Wallenberg, one of Sweden's richest men, had been appointed an envoy to Hungary in 1944. He had told senior Nazis that the war would soon end, and that when it did he would use every one of his considerable resources to pursue and destroy them unless they helped him save the Jews of Budapest. By the time the war ended, he had 350 people working for him, forging documents and smuggling people. He saved about one hundred thousand lives.†

Though on the surface Hammarskjöld was quiet and implacable, he burned with a similar righteous determination. For him it took the form of a near-mystical stoicism that drove him to neither obey nor defy, but to rise above through the rigorous application of a principle. He hated speechifying. He thought that rhetoric was cheap. But he felt he had no choice but to respond.

"It is not the Soviet Union or indeed any other big powers that need the United Nations for their protection. It is all the others." The hall stood and applauded him. "The representative of the Soviet Union spoke of courage. It is very easy to resign. It is not so easy to stay on. It is very easy to bow to the wish of a big power. It is another matter to resist."

---

* Bernadotte was later assassinated by a militant Israeli group, Lehi, after he had tried to broker a peace with Palestine in 1948. In 1983, one of Lehi's former leaders, Yitzhak Shamir, became prime minister of Israel.
† Wallenberg disappeared in Russia in 1945. He was never heard from again.

Chapter 4

"The inevitable result will at best be chaos"

The summer of 1960 was a season of hatreds in Leopoldville. One person could not merely disagree with another, but had to despise them or justify why they did not. It seemed every soul felt as though they had been treated unfairly—by life, by each other, by the government, by the Belgians, by the Congolese, by fate. The grievances were hard to dismiss as wanton self-pity because, in a way, each of them was right.

Lumumba had formed a fragile government, but it existed in name only. And he lived with the constant threat that one or other of his allies would turn and seize power.

Across the country, power stations lay idle. Telephone exchanges were unstaffed. Police stations empty. Transportation stilled. When the large steel door to one prison failed to close due to overcrowding, the wardens drove a Land Rover into it until it was snugly in place and a pool of blood was forming underneath.

In time, the traffic lights in Leopoldville would fall into disrepair and cease to work. The tractors and forklifts that were donated to try to rebuild would rust to junk, unused. A visitor to the city years later noticed that there were no old people, and that the city's most illustrious café had become a bazaar for the disabled and disfigured to offer ivory carvings and small paintings for sale.

The UN forces, now twenty thousand strong in their distinctive blue helmets, had set up in a series of rough encampments. Their light-blue flags flew over the airports in Leopoldville and Elisabethville, too. From outside the Congo, they appeared as little islands of international good intention. From inside, they were just another faction. In Katanga, where Tshombe's mercenary force had grown to twelve thousand, they were the enemy.

It was called the Congo Crisis.

An American consular official, Larry Devlin, who had recently arrived in Leopoldville with his wife and young daughter, wrote that there was "anarchy throughout the city and, no doubt, through the country at large. Central authority had broken down; there was no one in control who could prevent random acts of barbarity."

Devlin was thirty-seven, a handsome and laconic Californian with a thicket of black hair and the harried elegance and thrill at close shaves of a foreign correspondent. Though he had a banal consular title, he was, in fact, the CIA's incoming chief of station, Congo.

The official position of the US government in the summer of 1960 was support for the UN in its mission to reunite the Congo and to rid the country of foreign influences. But Devlin and his superiors saw this as mere detail in a much bigger game. It was synonymous, in his mind, with furthering the interests of the United States against Russia.

The Cold War, he would tell anyone who asked, was much better than the hot version—the version his father had fought twice, in World Wars I and II, and that he had fought, carrying his father's Colt .45 in the latter.

The details of his subsequent career in the CIA remain classified. But it seems to have included stints in Moscow and Hanoi.

And it had led him now to the second floor of the US embassy in Leopoldville, an elegant, flat-roofed block on the corner of Avenue des Aviateurs, near the river, with a facade divided into neat squares by patterned screens.

Devlin had been told that his time in Leopoldville would be dominated by dinners and golfing—that he'd mostly be subtly pulling political strings.

But Congolese soldiers, functionally answerable to nobody, patrolled the streets. They gathered in thickets at the docks, or on street corners, looking for white Europeans. They dressed in their fatigues and, because they had been trained for jungle not urban warfare, sported branches and leaves sticking up from their helmets as an indication of battle-readiness. Pedestrians learned to spot and avoid the shrubbery. To miscalculate was to be drawn, as Devlin was, into their games.

One day that summer, according to his own account, Devlin was picked up by a band of mutinous soldiers and taken to a run-down room near the Congolese quarter of the city. He protested, as the men lit up thick joints and filled the hot room with billowing and pungent clouds of smoke, that he was a diplomat.

A tall soldier in a filthy uniform walked toward him. He picked up a chair, turned its back toward Devlin, sat down astride it, and began removing one of his boots.

"Come over here and kiss my foot, flamand," he said, according to Devlin, using one of the pejorative terms for white Europeans that had proliferated in the Congo. Devlin had seen this particular game before. If the victim refused, he was beaten. If he accepted, he'd have his face kicked into the ground.

He refused.

The soldier turned his back, pulled a revolver, and began ostentatiously removing its bullets, out of sight. He got up from the chair, put the gun to Devlin's head, and asked him again to kiss his foot. He refused again.

Click. Relief flooded through Devlin. *Click.* He yelled *merde* now between each pull of the trigger. *Click.* "Just kiss my foot, patron, and you have nothing to fear." *Click. Click.* "Last chance, patron. Kiss this foot."

Click. The soldiers collapsed in laughter and the game was over. The gun had been empty. They called it Congolese roulette. They insisted that Devlin stay and help them finish a bottle of wine they had stolen, then drove him back.

Devlin learned fast that there were never any guarantees that the next game would not end in death. That no two days were precisely the same. That no rules applied. Congolese soldiers mounted checkpoints virtually at random.

The warring factions in the Congolese government might strike out against one another with a wild announcement that never came to anything. Total silence, or kind words, could end in sudden barbarity.

He began preparing for the overwhelming likelihood that a mob of Congolese soldiers would turn one day and attack the American embassy. He had been carrying either a hammer or a butcher's knife in his jacket. But neither his small team of half a dozen CIA operatives, nor the embassy security staff, he felt, had enough guns.

So he drove his battered Peugeot 403 through Leopoldville, searching for guns to buy. He exchanged a few thick wads of fresh dollar bills for an arsenal. He ended up with a Thompson sub-machine gun—the one with the big, round magazine, often seen in 1930s gangster films—two semi-automatic Browning pistols, and a box of fragmentation grenades.

Inside the embassy he and a small group of operatives piled all their secret documents into specially supplied "burn barrels"— lined with enough magnesium to blow the roof off if a match were thrown in.

If a mob did attack the building and get inside, the evidence of

America's policy on the Congo could be incinerated in a flash of white light. The CIA had created an Africa Division in 1959. The agency did not see the wave of independence movements as a triumph for African nations that had long chafed under colonialism. It saw them as new territory in the battle against the Soviets.

Devlin had placed a freshly recruited Congolese agent* at Leopoldville's N'djili Airport with a notepad. He told the man that any white person disembarking from a Russian plane was to be considered a citizen of the Soviet Union. Tallying studiously, the agent had counted several hundred.

Devlin suspected, too, that the Red Cross boxes that arrived on Soviet planes carried weapons and matériel for either Lumumba or one of the regional leaders they sought to influence. Many of those leaders were now traveling across the country to and from Leopoldville in pristine new Russian Ilyushin planes and Mil helicopters.

He briefed his superiors that if the Soviets managed to influence and control the Congo, they would use the country as "a base to infiltrate and extend their influence over the nine countries or colonies surrounding the Congo."

It would, he told them, breezily taking several dizzying hypotheticals as fact, mean that the Soviets had an "extraordinary power base in Africa." That, in turn, would foster increased influence among less developed nations, and with the UN. And enable them to outflank NATO with military bases on the Mediterranean. It would certainly give them control of the Congo's minerals—including cobalt—and thus imperil America's own weapons and space programs.

The CIA director, Allen Dulles, agreed wholeheartedly with

---

* In CIA parlance, those who work on active duty, like Devlin, are operatives. They sometimes recruit agents—locals or others who agree to work for them on a specific task.

the assessment. On August 18, Devlin sent a cable back to head-quarters. He believed that the Congo was experiencing a classic Communist takeover run by the Soviets themselves, and their Czech, Guinean, and Ghanaian proxies, both through local Communist parties and covertly. The decisive period, he said in the stilted language of cables, was not far off. "Whether or not Lumumba actually Commie or just playing Commie game to assist his solidifying power, anti-West forces rapidly increasing power Congo and there may be little time left in which take action to avoid another Cuba or Guinea."

He proposed assisting anti-Lumumba forces. The CIA's plan was to replace him with a leader, and a government, that better suited the US. On August 27, the reply arrived on the machine in Devlin's office. In "high quarters," it said, implying sign-off from the White House, the clear conclusion was that if Lumumba continued to hold high office, "the inevitable result will at best be chaos and at worst pave the way to Communist takeover of the Congo with disastrous consequences." Consequently, it said, "we conclude that his removal must be an urgent and prime objective."

The message gave Devlin broader authority, and encouraged him to take more aggressive action, so long as it was covert. He had, in a break from the usual policy, unlimited funds, and could use his discretion to conduct operations without permission from headquarters. The program he began would grow to become the largest and most expensive in the history of the CIA to that point ($12 million, or about $350 million at current prices).

Devlin's aim was to replace Lumumba with Joseph Kasavubu, Lumumba's long-term ally. The two men had birthed a revolution together, but had found victory to be much more difficult than the struggle. Their friendship and alliance had crumbled when exposed to power. Kasavubu now aligned himself with the US. And Devlin wanted to foment and quietly enact a political coup.

His operatives and agents left fat envelopes of cash on the

desks of government officials, after brief conversations. It was an attempt to addict them to the flow of dollars, so that if an important political decision needed to be made—say, if a new leader had to be chosen instead of Lumumba—they might be more persuadable.

Anti-Lumumba protests, rallies, and minor acts of violence often featured a white American standing nearby, quietly directing. And Devlin himself fostered relations with a gang known as the Binza group, made up of Congolese political leaders who had drifted away from Lumumba. It was headed by Mobutu, the army chief.

The Binza group visited his home, a nicely laid-out house run by his French wife, Colette, a former ambulance driver for the Free French forces whom he had met during World War II. She served them opulent dinners of lobster imported, packed on ice, from Angola, and cooked à l'Américaine, with a spicy sauce.

Devlin had realized that in the midst of chaos, only overwhelming force carried any weight. And so the head of the army, Mobutu, would have the last word if Kasavubu attempted to overthrow Lumumba. In his memoir, Devlin says he saved Mobutu's life in September 1960. He had gone to visit the soldier at home, when he saw "a Congolese in civilian clothes standing with his back toward me" aiming a gun at Mobutu. Devlin jumped on the gunman and grabbed the barrel of the gun as they wrestled, twisting it around so the man's finger broke inside the trigger guard.

In September 1960, Kasavubu declared himself the new leader of the Congo. Lumumba attempted to depose him right back, and the men warred in speeches and radio broadcasts, and furiously attempted to gather support in Parliament.

Mobutu, still grateful to Devlin, arrested Lumumba. He was held at a house surrounded by two cordons. One was made up of Mobutu's soldiers. The other had been supplied by Hammarskjöld, who was constantly updated on the situation in New York.

Hammarskjöld wanted, more than anything else, for the fighting to stop, so civilian reconstruction could begin. He did not accept the American view that Kasavubu was now the Congolese leader. But he also did not feel he had a mandate to do anything more than protect Lumumba.

"You try to save a drowning man," he told the assembled delegates at the UN, "without prior authorization and even when he resists you; you do not let him go even when he tries to strangle you."

Devlin saw it otherwise. This was a successfully orchestrated switch to a much friendlier government. As effective and brilliant as Iran in 1953. The UN, he wrote later, remained dangerously supportive of Lumumba, and he suspected that Hammarskjöld's forces were plotting to disarm the Congolese army, and even restore Lumumba to power. "We knew if that happened," he wrote, "it would mean civil strife, the end of Mobutu and . . . the return of the Soviets."

Chapter 5

"You there! I am a witch"

At around the same time in London, in the quiet wood-paneled office that forms the main part of the prime minister's suite at 10 Downing Street, Harold Macmillan sat behind an imposing leather-topped desk.

Macmillan, a friend of the queen who sported a gray walrus mustache and pin-striped three-piece suits, looked every inch the corporatist, conservative, and capable leader he had become after four years in office and nearly forty in government.

His official position was that Britain would support Hammar-skjöld, and the United Nations, in reuniting the Congo. But he was seasoned enough to know there were always wheels-within-wheels. A harried-looking Foreign Office official handed him a report, on thick beige paper. He began to read.

It was marked TOP SECRET PERSONAL and was a report from the Secret Intelligence Service, Britain's foreign intelligence agency, also known as MI6. It described growing Russian and Chinese influence in Africa, and an abdication by the Belgians who had run the Congo, plunging the nation into abject chaos.

Conspiracy theories were rife, it reported. The same piece of news would instantly be interpreted in five different ways, all of them hinting darkly at a grand plot by the British or the Americans. The Belgians were convinced, for example, that there was a plan in place for Britain to shove them out and take over all the lucrative mineral concessions.

Meanwhile, the Russians, the report said, without recognizing the contradiction, actually were engaged in a conspiracy. They aimed to establish bases, and to gain control of a nationalist movement "through which they can exploit trouble, wherever it may arise in Black Africa." All the tides were in their favor.

SIS decided to send Daphne Park. She was about to turn forty but had settled early into an agelessness that made it hard to guess whether she was thirty or sixty. She looked a little like Miss Marple, down to the glasses, rolling gait, and palpable intelligence.

She usually had cigarette ash on her blouse. "I have always looked like a cheerful, fat missionary," she used to say. "It wouldn't be any use if you went around looking sinister, would it?"

Park had grown up in Africa, about five hundred miles from Dar es Salaam, in what is now Tanzania but was then the British protectorate of Tanganyika. Her father was a colonial speculator who had panned for gold and grown tobacco and coffee there.

Her childhood had been spent in a mud-brick hut with no running water and kerosene lamps. By their light she read early spy novels by John Buchan, and adventure stories by Rudyard Kipling and Mark Twain.

She had won a scholarship first to school in England, then to Oxford during World War II, to study French. (Her classmates recall that she had taken part in a mock bombing, and had been so convincing in her screams and histrionics that she had alarmed the local officials.)

After Oxford, she had railed against the wartime orthodoxy that saw women only as nurses. She wanted front-line action. To be where things were happening. So she had pushed from the nursing corps into a support role that made use of her fluent French. She was to prepare Allied Special Forces soldiers who were being parachuted into France ahead of D-Day for their missions.

She got to know and like these men, with the full knowledge that many of them would die gruesome, uncelebrated deaths at the hands of desperate Nazis. In one case, it became something more. She had begun an affair with a soldier, an American called Douglas DeWitt Bazata, a marksman and boxer described as "a red-haired soldier of fortune." He called all of his superiors "sugar."* It was the only documented romantic relationship in her life.

After the war, the military machinery rearranged itself into a sprawling intelligence apparatus for a more shadowy fight in the decades to come. Park was posted to Vienna to compete with American, French, and Russian spies to recruit, or even kidnap, German scientists who might be useful. It was called dragon hunting, and was the first postwar assignment of her career as an intelligence officer. She formally joined SIS in 1948.

By 1960, Park had recently finished a tour in Moscow. Her superiors had posted her there because they felt that the Russians, hidebound by a pervasive misogyny, would not expect a woman to be a capable spy. Under the cover of her gender, she had identified missile installations that were designed to repel Western nuclear weapons, rendering unimaginable Soviet spending and planning obsolete. And she was rumored to have helped smuggle the novel *Dr. Zhivago*, banned in Russia, out of the country, to be published first in Italy in 1957.[†]

Its author, Boris Pasternak, won the Nobel Prize for Literature

---

* He later joined a ménage à trois with the Baron and Baroness von Mumm in their palace, Schloss Johannisberg, in Germany. Afterward, he restyled himself as an artist, grew a reasonable reputation, and was rumored to have had an affair with Princess Grace of Monaco.

† Its publisher, an Italian named Giangiacomo Feltrinelli, died in contentious circumstances afterward.

the next year, a grave and humiliating blow for the Kremlin. (And one of very few things that Park and Hammarskjöld, who was on the Nobel committee, agreed on.)

Her next posting was due to be Guinea, which her superiors feared had tilted to the far left. But SIS had a rule that women were not allowed to serve in majority-Muslim nations—it was felt that their gender not only impeded their attempts to gather information but also needlessly inflamed tensions. As majority-Muslim nations were often proving grounds for high fliers, this policy, and a ban on female spies marrying, made life difficult for women who wanted to climb the ranks.

Park either genuinely did not give it a second thought, or decided not to talk about it. Her attitude, when asked later in life, was that one got on with it, or didn't bother, and that she had chosen the former.

Before she traveled to the Congo, she first went to Brussels to be briefed by the SIS chief there. Then she took a train to Antwerp, then a two-week journey aboard a grand white steamer boat to Matadi, the main seaport in the Congo, about 150 miles from Leopoldville.

When she finally arrived, she found that Leopoldville was a city divided. The black Congolese lived in the *cité*, a deprived and makeshift sprawl. The Europeans lived in the highest part of the city—the only area that benefited from cooling breezes. Their large houses were like fortresses. The pristine lawns were floodlit at night, and patrolled by both guards and glossy black Doberman pinschers.

Park was warned by the Belgians that she must select a home there, among her kind. Instead, she took a house between the airport and the center of town, adjacent to the *cité*. She knew that she would get the information and connections she needed from black Africans, informally, not Europeans at soirees. She had calculated that her new address would make it easy for black Africans to visit without the added pressures of being seen to visit.*

And despite implorations from her superiors, she refused to keep the exquisite, tiny revolver with an inlaid grip that an SIS armorer had made her out of a misplaced sense of chivalry, instead of issuing a standard service gun. "If I have it at home," she reasoned, "everybody will know I have it at home. They'll come and steal it, and they'll hit me on the head in the bargain. It stays in the office."

SIS assigned Q branch, the section responsible for spy technology, to find an alternative means of defense. It suggested a device that it said had worked brilliantly in controlling crowds in Sudan. A kind of capsule, described as infallible, that she could break to release a smell so foul that it would knock out any intruders, even entire groups.

Filled with trepidation, she and a colleague took turns trying the capsules, two each, only to find that they released a smell so mild that she said "it might, just might, have been confused with a little smell of armpit."

Shortly after she had moved in, she gave a small party. After her guests had gone for the night, she had kept the music playing, and was walking around the house having a drink when she saw the handle of her front door turning slowly. She had sent the servants home—black Congolese domestic staff had to go home at night, a rule enforced by the Belgians who were afraid their servants would kill them in their sleep.

She was alone.

She picked up her Bakelite telephone and called the Congolese police. "Well, if you go to bed and pretend to be asleep," they said,

---

* The Belgians responded by removing her from the governor-general's invitation list for formal events, which she treated as a bonus.

she recalled later, "they probably won't touch you. We'll come around in the morning and see what's been taken."

Park replied that that was not her idea of a police force. They told her they were not stupid enough to go out at night in Leopoldville—it was dangerous—and suggested that she call the United Nations police instead, a unit staffed in the Congo by Nigerians.

She felt that the UN "was dead useless, full of murdering, miserable people." But she liked the Nigerians. So she called. They said, "Yes. Yes. Don't worry. We'll be around." But there was no sign of them. And she could still hear and sense the intruders, occasionally probing her home for weakness.

Park called a colleague at the embassy, Nigel Gaden, a public information officer. "Nigel, would you mind coming and visiting me and crashing through my garden," she said, "because I've got unwanted visitors, and I think if you come and make noise, they'll go away." He agreed.

She put the phone down, and kept watching the doors. About twenty minutes later, noises of smashing, falling, and shouting broke out in her garden. The Nigerians, arriving late, had arrested Nigel.

Park went outside, untangled the angry men, and explained all of their mistakes to them. They responded that they had now dealt with any intruders. "Don't worry," said one, with a tone of pity. "It will be quite all right. They won't come now."

The men departed, and Park turned out the lights, after a long day, and was climbing into bed when she heard the tinkle of broken glass. It sounded to her like the French windows. A towering rage overtook her. She got up, propelled by fury, threw open the window, and fixed her gaze on a black African who had been in the process of breaking in. In Lingala, the local language, which she spoke fluently along with Swahili, she screamed:

"You there! I am a witch, and if you go on troubling me, first your toes will drop off. Then your feet will drop off, and then other parts of your anatomy, which you would not wish to lose, will drop off. Would you please go away."

She shut the window, climbed into bed, and fell quickly into a deep sleep. The rumor of her powers spread quickly through the *cité*, she later heard. Nobody would go near her house.

She had found the only car less glamorous than Devlin's—a dull-blue Citroën 2CV that sounded, and accelerated, as though it were powered by enthusiasm alone. She said she would have chosen it again over any Aston Martin because it was so agile it could virtually climb trees, and looked so innocent that nobody ever thought to check in the back.

She had a license neither to drive nor to kill, she would joke later. But she realized nobody was enforcing the rules in Leopoldville anyway, so she improvised, terrifying passersby as she pulled up outside the British Chancery on Avenue Beernaert in downtown Leopoldville.*

She began a process vital to spying, the one that separates the spies who re-edit newspaper clippings for their reports, and the ones who deliver the bombshells: She got to know everyone of potential use. Her aim was to put together Leading Personality Reports—profiles of the main players in the Congo, and what they wanted. And then to use them to manipulate events to suit Britain.

Though she could be cold to the point of aloofness with her colleagues, she could switch on an easy charm and engagement if she so chose. And she was genuinely interested in people. Which meant that they generally liked and trusted her, too, and found themselves telling her things that they would never have expected

---

* It was above the Liberian embassy. The unfortunate Liberians often had their windows hit by anti-British protesters who couldn't quite manage to get the necessary height on their projectiles.

to tell her. Even the cagey members of Lumumba's inner circle found themselves drawn in.

The Congolese learned that they could drop by her house, to borrow books or for a chat—a novelty in a city where conversations between black and white residents were either formal or hostile. "I never said to them 'please tell me a secret,'" she told the journalist Gordon Corera later. "I just talked to them until they told me a secret."

She ingratiated herself with the 250 or so expatriate Brits in the city, and began to use one or two as agents—non-spies who gathered information. She began talking to the border guards, asking them about their families, and bringing them gifts. She volunteered to undertake the arduous three-day journeys to Accra, in Ghana, to collect the embassy's mail. She could talk to people all the way, and sense what was in the air.

She also traveled to see her MI6 counterparts Hugo Herbert-Jones in Nairobi, Kenya; Theodore "Bunny" Pantcheff in Lagos, Nigeria; Neil Ritchie in Salisbury, Rhodesia; and Michael Oatley in Kampala, Uganda. They'd compare notes, swap info, coordinate, generally help each other out.

Her travels often took her into situations so dangerous that the Americans would have sent an army. But Park didn't feel fear in the same way other people did. Or, at least, she had the capacity to think with great perception while in its grip.

As she drove down an isolated road one night, a mob surrounded her car at a checkpoint. They demanded she get out. She refused. So they began pulling her through the car's sunroof. She got stuck, which she found enormously funny. The mob saw the joke, began laughing, too, and let her pass.

On another occasion she saw a different mob approaching from a little distance, casually swinging machetes. So she got out of the 2CV, opened its hood, and affected a look of puzzlement. When the men arrived, confident and hostile, she unmanned them by greeting them warmly and asking them if they knew how to fix the carburetor. They tinkered, eager to help, and moved on.

She had also been badly beaten when her diversionary tactics had failed to work, and thrown into a pit that was to be her grave, before her attackers thought better of it. But she never spoke of the incident.

In fact she never spoke of failure, and thus developed a reputation for never failing. She said she had never experienced prejudice in her career, but she confided to friends later that she understood why, despite being a standout leader and consummate spy, she was never considered for director of MI6. The men, she said, however much they liked her, would have struggled to accommodate a woman in their little coterie.

None of it mattered, weeks away from London by boat geographically, and a world away functionally. Here, Daphne Park was director of whatever she wanted to be. And the situation she encountered was much more complex than the one described to Harold Macmillan in his intelligence briefing.

To the east of the Congo was a region known as the Federation of Rhodesia and Nyasaland. It consisted of the British protectorates of Northern and Southern Rhodesia, and Nyasaland.* What it was, in practice, was a fragment of the recent past—a series of African nations that were entirely ruled by white Europeans, mostly Brits, under a complex arrangement with the British government.

It was run by Sir Roy Welensky, a former boxer and railway engineer, who believed that colonialism had pulled him up from poverty, and that it was an unmitigated force for good.

Welensky and his intelligence chief, a former British intelligence officer named Basil de Quehen, kept in close contact with

---

* To complicate matters further, it was also known as the Central African Federation.

the forces of white Africa—apartheid security services in South Africa, and the white settlers and business interests in Katanga.

Park came to understand that British American Tobacco, Unilever, and Shell—huge, British corporations—had made major investments in the area. Their trade with Katangese companies formed an intricate and deeply lucrative web of interests that all wanted continued white rule. And all were closely linked to the British government.

The prime of those Katangese companies, Union Minière, was owned in large part—40 percent, at its height—by a British company, Tanganyika Concessions. Its chairman was a conservative former member of Parliament, Charles Waterhouse.

Waterhouse was associated with a nascent group of far-right conservative politicians that would later be known as the Monday Club and would number among its members the vice chief of SIS, Park's boss, George Kennedy Young.

Young's personal policy, and a view widely held by his cohort, he later wrote, was that "independent Africa would revert to bush and savagery." His views were not racist, he explained later, because they were "based on a lifelong interest in anthropology and comparative philology."

It was Park's job to balance the un-balance-able. The overt policy from London supported the reunification of the Congo, and Dag Hammarskjöld.

But her priority was described, euphemistically, as promoting "British interests"—and that meant British companies in the country. They were linked closely with the white settlers.

Who despised Hammarskjöld and the UN, and wanted Katanga to join the Federation of Rhodesia and Nyasaland.

And it was about to get even more complex.

Chapter 6

"Very straightforward action"

In the late summer of 1960, Lumumba remained under house arrest, surrounded by one cordon of Mobutu's soldiers and another cordon of UN soldiers.

The easiest solution to the problems of the Congo, a senior official with the British Foreign Office's Africa Department wrote on September 28, 1960, "is the simple one of ensuring Lumumba's removal from the scene by killing him." If he survived, another official replied, he would "continue to plague us all."

By that moment, Park and Devlin were effectively one operation in Leopoldville. They had become fast friends, of necessity if nothing else—sifting information from rumor by oneself was near-impossible. The people who made the decisions often didn't know themselves what they were going to do until the last moment.* They became the only two people in town who could reliably sort fact from fiction and weigh probabilities with any accuracy.

Their governments were in lockstep, too. At around the moment that the British memos were circulating, President Eisenhower had informed the CIA that he had "extremely strong

---

* One of Park's colleagues described it, in 2017, as very similar to America under Donald Trump.

feelings on the necessity for very straightforward action in this situation," and that he "wondered whether the plans as outlined were sufficient to accomplish this."

The CIA officials decided that Eisenhower was hinting at an assassination. They certainly agreed that Lumumba was still a threat. Indeed, they had imbued him with near-mystical powers.

Devlin suggested arming or supporting Lumumba's enemies. Headquarters had a different idea. Shortly afterward, a chemist from the Bronx with a clubfoot and a stutter arrived in Leopold-ville. Sydney Gottlieb had been named, for his mission, Joseph Braun, or more simply "Joe from Paris." Devlin first saw him across the street from the embassy, when he was sitting at a café. Gottlieb came over.

"I'm Joe from Paris," he said. "I've come to give you instructions about a highly sensitive operation." The two traveled to a safe house, where Gottlieb explained that he had concocted, and was carrying, a deadly biological toxin to be injected into something that Lumumba ingested—toothpaste would be perfect.

"Take this," Gottlieb said, handing over a small package that also contained hypodermic needles, gauzes, masks, and other equipment required for handling the deadly toxin. "With the stuff that's in there, no one will ever be able to know that Lumumba was assassinated."

It would appear, Gottlieb told Devlin, that he had died of polio. But ultimately, he said, it didn't matter if he used the poison or other means, as long as Lumumba ended up dead and nobody suspected the United States.*

---

* Devlin maintained until his death that he had calculated quickly: If he refused, he'd be replaced as station chief by someone who would do it. He writes, in his memoir, that he agreed but slow-rolled the operation, playing his bosses along. Another CIA operative in the Congo, Howard Imbrey, said later that Devlin had, in fact, sent the poison back to headquarters with a message: "Don't you know the Belgians are going to kill him, what do you want us to do?"

The main problem was that their target, Lumumba, was lodged in his house, surrounded by one cordon of Congolese soldiers and another of UN soldiers. "Target has not left building in several weeks," the Leopoldville station cabled to headquarters in November. "Concentric rings of defense make establishment of observation post impossible. Attempting to get coverage out of any movement into or out of house by Congolese. Target has dismissed most of servants so entry this means seems remote."

The CIA, increasingly desperate, began to send dark, mysterious agents—men recruited from the criminal underworld to perform specific tasks that required deniability. The first, a forty-three-year-old named Jose Marie Andre Mankel, arrived in Leopoldville on November 21. He had been working with the agency since 1958, on retainer, and had experience in Corsica, perhaps with mafia figures, and with the Bureau of Narcotics.

He was code-named QJWIN. Among his skills, listed in official memos, were safecracking and "assassin-recruitment" activities. His performance was listed as "excellent" and—though Devlin does not mention it in his memoir—he seems to have been assigned to the Lumumba problem.

But before Mankel could do anything, at about 10 p.m. on November 27, while most of Leopoldville was distracted by a torrential tropical rainstorm, Lumumba simply drove out of the house in a large, black car.

The Americans suspected that the UN had helped him break out. But Hammarskjöld had decided that the UN could not interfere in Congolese politics, and that he could only protect Lumumba under house arrest. The former prime minister was on his own.

Park and Devlin felt he'd head for Stanleyville, a city about a thousand miles away that was a safe harbor for Lumumba. Park was already there, waiting. The same day, Devlin sent a cable to headquarters to say he was "working with Congolese government to get roads blocked and troops alerted."

Another cable followed, though its sender is not known: "View change in location target, QJ/WIN anxious go Stanleyville and expressed desire execute plan by himself without using any apparat."

The reply came back: "Concur QJ/WIN go Stanleyville *** we are prepared consider direct action by QJ/WIN but would like your reading on security factors. How close would this place [the United States] to the action?"

Lumumba never made it to Stanleyville anyway. He had a head start on his pursuers. But, depending whether you read an account that sees him as the Congo's savior, or one that sees him as a dangerous firebrand, he either was compelled to stop and give speeches to his elated supporters, or could not resist the temptation. In any case, as he was about to cross the Sankuru River, a tributary of the mighty Congo, to safety, he was caught by Mobutu's soldiers.

United Nations troops who were nearby, on the bank of the river, declined, after consulting headquarters, to restore their protection. So he was taken back to Leopoldville by men who had learned to hate him.

Video footage shows him surrounded by dozens of soldiers who are casually abusing him in a manner that makes clear he is no longer human to them, despite his attempts to maintain his dignity and poise. He was forced to eat a copy of one of his speeches as Mobutu looked on with barely suppressed glee.

He was held at Thysville for several weeks. The Belgian historian Ludo De Witte has painstakingly pieced together what happened next.* He was tortured, repeatedly, by the soldiers at Thysville as they awaited instructions from a group of senior

---

* De Witte, in a letter to the *New York Review of Books* in 2001, also lays some of the blame for the fall of Lumumba's government at Hammarskjöld's door, for failing, essentially, to use force in his favor. Senior UN officials dispute that interpretation.

officials in Belgium who reported to the minister for African affairs, Count Harold d'Aspremont Lynden.

In January 1961, Lynden urged in a message that Lumumba "be transferred to Katanga with the least possible delay." Lumumba was so despised in Katanga that this was tantamount to a death sentence.

The next day, Lumumba and two of his colleagues were flown to Elisabethville. Their captors beat them so savagely during the flight that the pilot was forced to ask them to stop because the plane was at risk of crashing. The Belgian soldiers who were accompanying either joined in or turned away.

The plane landed not at Elisabethville airport, which was controlled by the UN, but at a Katangese military base. All that a contingent of Swedish UN troops nearby saw was unnamed prisoners being escorted by about 130 Katangese police officers. The group quickly disappeared through a hole that had been specially cut in the base's fence.

For weeks, Hammarskjöld knew only that Lumumba had been taken to Elisabethville in bad condition. But Russia accused him of complicity in his disappearance. It had, said a Soviet diplomat, been "carried out before the eyes of the 'United Nations Command' in the Congo. Thus neither the 'United Nations Command' nor the Secretary-General can divest themselves of responsibility for these acts organized for the benefit of the colonialists."

The governments of Indonesia and Morocco and several Arab nations responded by withdrawing their contingents from the UN forces, severely weakening the peacekeeping effort.

On February 13, 1961, Katanga announced formally that Lumumba was dead, but blamed the inhabitants of a mysterious village who it said had captured and set upon him.

What actually happened, according to De Witte's account, is that Lumumba and his two colleagues were taken to a home, where the leaders of Katanga, including Tshombe, attacked the prisoners until their bodies were smashed and bloodied beyond repair, and the suits of the Katangese leadership were covered in blood. They were driven into the jungle, still alive, tied to a tree, and executed by firing squad.

One of the Belgians involved, Gerard Soete, a former police commissioner, admitted later that he had helped chop Lumumba's body up to dissolve it in acid. First, though, he pulled two of his teeth, which he stored in a little box as keepsakes.*

John Kennedy was leaving his country home in Middleburg, Virginia, to return to the White House when he heard that Lumumba was confirmed dead. His immediate fear was that the murder would only escalate the violence. "We in the United States regret this tragedy," Adlai Stevenson, the US ambassador to the UN, said. "We hope that men everywhere will not seek revenge but reconciliation." The British reserved judgment but condemned the violence, too.

Lumumba's supporters were less circumspect. A mob of about three hundred African independence protesters immediately attacked the office of the Belgian envoy in Cairo with barrages of heavy stones. Another mob of about five hundred smashed up the Belgian embassy in Moscow.

UN troops in the Congo were put on alert for similar outbreaks of vengeance. Hammarskjöld had liked Lumumba, but had grown to worry that he was increasingly erratic. He described his

---

* Though the Belgian Parliament commissioned a report into De Witte's findings, which named many of those involved, nobody has been brought to justice for the crime. There was little appetite for an activity that would have required a total remaking of Belgian society. Even King Baudouin, who had never forgiven the humiliation of Lumumba's fiery independence day speech, knew of the plans to send him to his death.

conflicted feelings in a letter to Steinbeck shortly after Lumumba's death was confirmed.

> I incline to the conclusion that no one, in the long pull, will really profit from Lumumba's death; least of all those outside the Congo who now strain to do so but should one day confront a reckoning with truth and decency...
> Events in the Congo move quickly and, it seems, so far always badly or in bad directions.

Hammarskjöld had always received death threats. Now, as the world began to blame him for failing to protect Lumumba, at least, and complicity in his death at worst, they ramped up.

Russia hated Hammarskjöld as an agent of the West. The West hated him for opening the door to Russia in the Congo. The Congolese hated him for Lumumba's death. The Belgians and white Africans who had actually killed Lumumba hated him because he had attempted to stop their secession. He responded in a speech to the UN Security Council in New York.

The UN, Hammarskjöld said, had tried only to stop the war in the Congo escalating into an international conflict. "We countered effectively efforts from all sides to make the Congo a happy hunting ground for national interests," he said. "To be a roadblock to such efforts is to make yourself the target of attacks from all those who find their plans thwarted."

Chapter 7

"Stateless soldier of fortune"

The Memling Hotel, an eight-story white edifice that filled one corner of the intersection of Avenues Moulaert and Stanley in central Leopoldville, was a hub for the diplomats, journalists, and spies* who had poured in to the city during the conflict.

Inside, on December 14, 1960, a week or so after Lumumba had been taken, Jose Mankel, the safecracking CIA agent code-named QJWIN, sat in a sleek, white leather chair. He flicked his eyes from time to time at a man seated at the long bar in the double-height lobby.

Something made Mankel suspect that the man at the bar, beneath a strange haircut, was a spy like him. It was easy to spark up conversations at the Memling—everyone was out of place, really—and the two men started to talk.

The man told Mankel he was Austrian, and flashed an Austrian passport. But his German was stilted. Even his English was strange, though he said he had lived in America for eight years. When he addressed the staff to order rounds of drinks for whoever was present, he spoke French with a distinctly Parisian accent.

His main mode of conversation was boasting. He said he had lost 12,000 francs playing poker recently. When he described his

---

* These are fundamentally the same person.

journey to Leopoldville—from Switzerland, via Frankfurt and Brazzaville—he made sure to mention that he had tens of thousands more in a Swiss bank.

And then, when a moment presented itself in the conversation, he made Mankel an offer. He was a secret agent, he explained, though he remained cagey about the details, and was organizing three networks—one to gather information, one for sabotage, and one an execution squad. He could pay Mankel a $300-a-month retainer.

After a little more evasiveness, the man said what he'd been desperate to say all along—that he worked for the Americans. He said that he met his contact at the central post office in Leopoldville, and asked that if Mankel saw him there, he pretend not to know him.

He boasted that he could get Polaroid cameras into the country in diplomatic pouches, and he stepped away to call an embassy from the bar's phone—Mankel noted that it was extension 73—and spoke both English and French. He also made a call to Washington, DC, and to Switzerland, that Mankel overheard was about money.

He talked about the fact that he had three cars—one for work, a spare in case that broke down, and a third that he now realized he didn't need at all and wanted to sell. He had also taken out leases on three photographic shops in the city, and had an apartment, too.

Mankel wanted to know more, and the men arranged to meet again. Eventually Mankel decided to borrow one of the man's cars, because he had noted that the key ring also held the keys for a postal box.

He planned to make a wax indentation of the key, and copy it, to gain access and see who the man was. But Mankel had to leave the Congo earlier than expected and he never got the chance.*

---

* Mankel was later arrested and put on trial for smuggling in Europe. The CIA discussed whether it could "salvage QJ/WIN for our purposes." It is not recorded what happened after that.

CIA records, released years later, when operations in the Congo had become a public shame rather than a secret pride, show that the man was, in fact, another CIA agent. He had arrived in Leopoldville in December, after Lumumba was safely delivered to his enemies. He reported to Larry Devlin.

He was code-named WIROGUE and was an "essentially state-less soldier of fortune," a former citizen of the Soviet republic of Georgia named either David Tzitzichivili or David de Panasket who was also a forger and former bank robber.

In September 1960, unnamed members of the CIA's Africa Division had met with him to discuss an operational assignment. He was then provided with plastic surgery and a wig so that traveling Europeans would not recognize him, and plastic explosive for an unspecified purpose, and dispatched to Africa.

CIA headquarters messaged Leopoldville before he arrived to describe the agent. "He is indeed aware of the precepts of right and wrong, but if he is given an assignment that might be morally wrong in the eyes of the world, but necessary because his case officer ordered him to carry it out, then it is right, and he will dutifully undertake appropriate action for its execution without pangs of conscience. In a word, he can rationalize all actions."

The message also outlined an "intent to use him as a utility agent in order to (a) organize and conduct a surveillance team; (b) intercept packages; (c) blow up bridges; and (d) execute other assignments requiring positive action. His utilization is not to be restricted to Leopoldville."

In January 1961, days after Lumumba had died, drawing that mission to a close, WIROGUE asked to take flying lessons, to supplement his expertise in sabotage and demolitions. His assignment with the CIA did not formally end until September—the month that Hammarskjöld died.

Chapter 8

"No half-measures"

In August 1961, Hammarskjöld found his monkey, Greenback, hanging from the curtain cord in his Manhattan apartment. He was quite dead, his body limp and lifeless and suffocated as it swung in front of the sweltering skyline. He must have become tangled while playing. Hammarskjöld wrote of it in his journal, in a curious semi-poem that was the third-to-last thing he'd ever write.

> Nobody was watching—
> And who had ever understood
> His efforts to be happy,
> His moments of faith in us,
> His constant anxiety,
> Longing for something

The death hit him hard. It came at nearly the same moment that a friend in Sweden, Hjalmar Gullberg, a poet, had succumbed to a long-term degenerative disease. He wrote a letter to another friend to describe his feelings. "He was indeed one of the few and perhaps last representatives of a spiritual standard, a natural nobility, a warmth of heart and an iron-clad integrity, which is more necessary than ever in the present period of darkness and decay..."

It is likely Hammarskjöld thought of the Congo. Every time he dared hope that his efforts there might have lifted it from the mire of global proxy fights, it plunged in deeper.

By the time Greenback died, horror had overtaken Katanga. Tshombe's government had ceased, effectively, to function except as a mercenary force determined to defeat both the UN and the Congolese central government and retain independence. UN soldiers were under attack, and fighting daily, against those forces.

In Elisabethville prisoners had escaped and were out looting. The thousands-strong Katangese army and police force, now swelled with even more mercenaries, also targeted "rebels"— certain tribes, notably the Baluba, that were loyal to Leopoldville and did not accept the secession of Katanga. One estimate suggests that, by early 1961, the Katangese and the mercenaries had massacred as many as seventy thousand. The Baluba, in turn, wandered in packs wielding sharpened bicycle chains as defense against any white European.

And cannibalism seems to have been more than just a racist rumor. One picture from the time shows a dead man, his head pointed down a slight slope, his body stretched above him. The meat from the man's lower legs has been meticulously sliced away between the dirty boots, still on his feet, their laces neatly tied, and his knee-length shorts. The tibia and fibula are exposed in clean, sun-bleached white.

Civilians had learned to stay indoors, even if that meant sitting through the frequent power outages, and brushing their teeth with the local Simba beer when the water stopped.

———

The chaos was driven in part by forces that Hammarskjöld could not have known about. In the Élysée Palace in Paris, Jacques Foccart, Charles de Gaulle's adviser on Africa and a supreme creature of French politics, elegant and secretive, had spent the preceding months focused on Katanga.

Foccart was short, pudgy, and always wore a gray suit. His one eccentricity was keeping a parrot.* But he had been a resistance fighter during World War II. And the habits of cloaks and daggers had stayed with him. He ran his own foreign policy, with the permission of his friend the general.

In 1961, a steady stream of brutal-looking soldiers had been visiting him. These men had gained their first battle experiences in the First Indochina War in Vietnam, a conflict marked more than most by misery and torture. In the mid-1950s they had decamped to Algeria, a French colony, as it mounted guerrilla operations for independence.

They were willing to perpetrate casual horrors to prevent the country leaving France. They established a dozen or so torture chambers across the country. One of them, in a beautiful house called Villa Susini, became infamous. Two bathtubs sat in its courtyard, for drowning. One of its torturers became known as The Doctor, because he liked to use a scalpel. Women were subjected to systematic rape.

When it became clear that the French would lose, and that their government would negotiate with the Algerians, many of those soldiers had formed a terrorist organization, the Organisation Armée Secrète. They killed and injured thousands of people in both Algeria and France in a brutal terrorist campaign to continue colonial rule.

The CIA had intelligence that suggested Foccart had offered these men a pardon for their crimes in Algeria if they would go to Katanga. De Gaulle wanted the uranium, cobalt, and copper for France if the Congo collapsed. And having home soldiers in place

---

* It was also gray.

was a good start. Besides, many hated De Gaulle, and it might be better if they were far away.

It did not escape Foccart's attention, as the soldiers began arriving in Katanga, that these ascetic and brutal men also hated Hammarskjöld. They blamed him for undermining the French empire in Algeria.

When they arrived in Katanga, they did not hide their loathing for the UN. One UN official had been attending a cocktail party when he felt a hard object pushed into his back. He turned to find the scarred and twisted face of a French soldier that had been partly shot away, pressed close to his. "You are betraying the last bastion of the white man in Africa," the soldier said in a French accent. "You will get a knife in your back one of these days."

The same soldier had boasted to journalists at the Hotel Leopold II that the UN was *"pas de probleme! Vingt kilos de plastique et je m'en charge."* (No problem! Twenty pounds of plastic explosive and I'll take care of it.)

The official leader of the French mercenaries, and effectively of the forces in Katanga, had been a guerrilla warfare expert called Roger Trinquier. He had always wanted to be a schoolteacher, until two years of national service gave him a taste for fighting.

Trinquier treated bloodshed with a chillingly academic mindset, as though each death helped him refine his theories. "If the prisoner gives the information requested," he wrote of interrogations in a book of his theories titled *Modern Warfare*, "the examination is quickly terminated; if not, specialists must force his secret from him."

The book counseled the use of terrorism as a weapon of war. Most notably, it advised turning local residents against the state, and making them believe that only the terrorists, or in this case the mercenaries, would protect them. It had worked flawlessly in Katanga. Its residents, mostly white Europeans, occasionally even stopped to cheer outbreaks of fighting, and jeer their enemies, as if they were attending a sporting event.

Trinquier was expelled from Katanga in March 1961. But one of his most avid students, a brilliant soldier, Colonel René Faulques,* stayed on and became, effectively but without any formal notification, the leader of all mercenary forces in Katanga. Faulques, lean and scarred, had headed the armed branch of French intelligence and became notorious, even admired, for his role at Villa Susini as one of Trinquier's "specialists."

By August 1961, he had established a command post, in the middle of Elisabethville, from which he conducted a meticulous campaign against the UN and the forces of reunification. His headquarters was surrounded with sandbags and covered over with camouflage nets. Inside, the walls were covered with large-scale maps of Katanga. Dozens of walkie-talkie radios, on chairs, on the floor, or hanging from beams by a loop, crackled and chattered. It was the nerve center of the battle.

Faulques had at his disposal thousands of mercenaries. Some, like his French colleagues, were well trained. Dick Browne, a former British Special Forces soldier whose brother, Percy, was a conservative member of Parliament, oversaw one group. Its members spoke of looting ivory and killing any passing black Congolese they didn't like the look of.

Others were cowboys seeking a payday and stories to tell women in bars. They included Hubert Julian, also known as the Black Eagle of Harlem, a fifty-eight-year-old black American adventurer who had once been styled a colonel as the head of the Emperor Haile Selassie's air force. He was eventually ejected for supplying arms to Tshombe. And at least one, a former Wehrmacht lieutenant named Siegfried Muller, wore his German World War II Iron Cross medal proudly on his chest at all times.

---

* The name sometimes appears as Roger Faulques.

They were armed with Belgian FN rifles, and mortars, and whatever else they could lay their hands on. And all of them, under Faulques's command, moved fast, in signature jeeps with a Browning .30-caliber machine gun in the back. One had a skull and crossbones mounted to the front, made of real human bones.

The jewel in Faulques' crown was a Fouga Magister jet fighter with rapier-thin wings and a distinctive V-shaped tail. Nothing the UN had could match it. And so it had become a kind of god in Katanga, omniscient and omnipotent, screaming over the horizon like death from above.

The Congolese government had changed its leader once more. Cyrille Adoula, a moderate approved of by the US, had taken over from Lumumba. In late August, he asked the UN to intercede once and for all, to expel the mercenary forces from Katanga so that he could begin to reunify the Congo.

On August 24, 1961, Hammarskjöld issued an ordinance—a kind of statement of intent—to Tshombe saying that the UN would remove all non-Congolese mercenaries and advisers unless he made arrangements to evacuate them voluntarily.

In response, Radio Katanga, a powerful propaganda force, began broadcasting violently anti-UN rhetoric in an attempt to inflame the locals. It declared "total war against the UN dogs" and advised residents to "look as peaceful citizens in the day" but to "kill UN soldiers one by one" at night. And Katangese officials spread rumors that the UN soldiers would not themselves fight the Katangese, but would instead fly in thousands of lawless and violent Congolese army troops who could be expected to rape and torture.

At 5 a.m. on August 28, 1961, the operation, code-named Rumpunch, commenced. The UN seized Radio Katanga, the headquarters of the Katangese gendarmerie, the post office, and the telephone exchange. They arrested eighty-one foreign mercenary commanders.

But the diplomatic corps in Elisabethville, from Belgium, Britain, France, and other nations, insisted they be allowed to control the process of repatriating their citizens. Instead, the diplomats just let the mercenaries go after "advising" them to leave.

The toughest mercenaries went into hiding. Gordon Hunt, an unofficial British agent in the Congo, met two fugitive French soldiers and wrote an account that was eventually released by WikiLeaks decades later.

"There are between 100-150 of us in this area who have managed to evade the expulsion order of the United Nations," they told him. They had the blessing of the Katangese leadership, and their advisers in Belgium, the soldier said, for positive action against the UN.

They wanted to ask permission from Rhodesia to establish a series of commando training units. Their aim: "to embarrass the UN by a form of guerrilla warfare, and, if necessary, sabotage."*

After Operation Rumpunch, the volume of chatter about attacks on the UN and its senior officials increased markedly. A Belgian named André Crémer, who had served for the Katangese under the command of the French mercenaries, sought the protection of the UN after falling out with his comrades. He said that he had been assigned to murder senior UN officials. He had, before his escape, selected twenty-four soldiers—he said he favored the rougher, less educated ones who would express less difficulty with their task.

In early September, a pretty woman with a black eye named Thérèse Erfield had also come to a UN representative in Katanga to seek protection. She said she was engaged in an affair with Henri-Maurice Lasimone, the second in command of the French mercenary group.

---

* The British agent passed the proposal on to Sir Roy Welensky, the leader of the Federation of Rhodesia and Nyasaland. His response is not recorded. But it certainly fit with his priorities.

Lasimone had beaten her, Erfield said. And then she revealed that his group had planned to attack UN establishments and personnel with plastic explosive and silent weapons. They even had an assassination list.

It was hard to verify the accounts. And Hammarskjöld had realized that Katanga had a strange effect on people. After a few months the place was like a fever dream—urgent, terrifying, arbitrary, and too vivid.

He had appointed Conor Cruise O'Brien, an Irish diplomat and writer, to oversee operations in Katanga. But he had been warned that O'Brien was, though brilliant, prone to both the ego and the strong emotions that afflict writers. And Hammarskjöld began to worry that O'Brien and his other men on the ground might give in to the myriad temptations to retaliate.

His officials were, indeed, both angry and planning a response. A new operation they called Morthor—the Hindi word for "twist and break"—was designed, if necessary, "to create a psychological shock in the population, which will reduce possibilities of armed opposition."

The UN got warrants from Leopoldville for the arrest of Tshombe and his senior ministers on charges of torture and murder. And they planned to seize not only the same pieces of infrastructure as they had bloodlessly in Rumpunch, but also the Katangese secret police headquarters. Their plan, with the slogan "No half-measures," was to end the secession in one go. They felt it would take about two hours.

On September 12, 1961, Hammarskjöld himself left New York for the Congo. He departed, on a special plane, shortly before Morthor was scheduled to begin. He hoped to arrive in triumph the next day as the operation wrapped up and the process of healing could begin.

Chapter 9

"We are all dying"

Violent men present a paradox for those who seek peace. If they cannot be persuaded, then the only way to defeat them is with violence. Which means ceding the moral authority to act in the first place.

It remains unclear whether Hammarskjöld fell victim to this paradox. Under the strain of Katanga, O'Brien noticed, his grave and regal manner sometimes gave way to a startling tension, or anger, as if the mask had slipped to reveal a fevered conscience. He attributed it, at first, to the strains of dealing with such a fraught conflict.

But over time he began to suspect that Hammarskjöld could not bear what he asked of himself. "So high and unreal a concept," O'Brien wrote later, "so tense and exigent a conscience, must have made the realities of flesh and blood and history—and the making of practical political calculations which could not afford to be always so very lofty—something of a torture."

The record of what Hammarskjöld knew of Morthor and when is muddled. Later, even under pressure, he refused to blame any of his subordinates for what followed, or detail their actions. The official account says that he was aware in general terms that his deputies in Katanga were pushing forward with attempts to end secession, but was not expecting such a violent operation.

Others suggest that, frustrated by the lack of a peaceful solution in the Congo, he resorted to violence himself in the name of justice. He must have known, that argument goes, what Operation Morthor would bring. It is certainly the case that he could have stopped the operation as soon as it began, but did not.

Morthor started at 4 a.m. on September 13, 1961, in the blue dark of the predawn. A company of about a hundred Indian Gurkhas, the elite fighters of the UN forces, tense and precise, moved toward the post office, a white building in the center of Elisabethville that served as a communications hub for all of Katanga. At the same moment, another company was walking quietly but purposefully to the radio station. And two Swedish platoons—or about eighty soldiers—were doing the same outside the home of Godefroid Munongo, Katanga's interior minister and the official most closely linked to its Belgian advisers. They had Congolese flags ready to run up in a gesture of victory as soon as they had seized these key points.

Tshombe and Munongo had said they would resist any attempts to interfere with Katanga's communications or military by force. They had said that before, though, and UN troops had found no resistance on the ground. But Faulques was prepared this time. Katangese soldiers, under his command, were already dug in at each key location. He had moved his headquarters from Elisabethville to Kolwezi, a mining town that effectively belonged to Union Minière, and was outside the control of the UN.

The UN soldiers set up portable loudspeakers. Their message crackled into the morning in French and Swahili, the lingua franca of Africa. It was the same at the post office, the radio station, and Munongo's house. *You are surrounded*, they said. *We do not seek to disarm you, only to take control of these locations.*

About thirty Katangese paratroops were fortified into the post office. Their reply was a burst of fire from two machine guns on the roof. The Gurkhas, with armored cars in support, ran into an alley and entered the building. They fought room-to-room, throwing in a grenade, waiting for the shattering jolt and the dust and blood to blow through the door, and clearing each in turn with submachine guns. The *New York Times* correspondent there, David Halberstam, phoned in to the post office. Someone answered. He said, "We are all dying."

By 8 a.m., the battle for the key points was over. The Gurkhas had filed Katangese prisoners out of the post office. The building was filled with smashed furniture, abandoned weapons and equipment, and the dead and bleeding bodies of soldiers. The white Europeans of Elisabethville, some former officers in the Katangese army, stood outside jeering the UN.

Skirmishes continued through the day and into the night. Morthor had been planned as a swift bloodless foray that would help end a violent secession. A violation of peace only in principle. But it had quickly devolved to wild and bloody fighting. There were reports that one UN soldier had been killed by sniper fire from the Belgian embassy at a distance of 150 yards. The Belgians denied it.

In the middle of the chaos, reported one mercenary, Faulques would be "grey with fatigue but still completely in charge of the situation." He would "rush from radio to radio barking orders or gathering information. The radio sets, each on a different frequency, were his link with the key points and mobile fireforces scattered throughout the city."

His soldiers fought from behind low brick garden walls and hedges, running across manicured lawns as though they were battlefields. They fought from crudely armored cars, their weld lines visible, parked on the empty streets. They fired their guns at UN soldiers from inside workshops and on rooftops, across parks and golf courses. The haze of gun smoke hung in the heavy air, with a strong smell of cordite, until it looked like a thin fog. Above them, in the incongruously cheery blue sky, the Fouga jet fighter, piloted by a Belgian named Magain who insisted he flew best while drunk, strafed and bombed at will.

He bombed UN headquarters. He bombed UN soldiers coming to the aid of an Irish troop that was besieged in Jadotville, which left them isolated, outgunned, for six days.* His attacks caused one UN plane to crash-land, kicking up clouds of dust and burnt rubber, at a nearby air base.

Jittery and paranoid UN soldiers opened fire on a Red Cross ambulance, wounding a medic in uniform. A reporter for the BBC and a cameraman for NBC were hit by stray bullets, too.

When a car filled with Katangese gendarmes, an informal part of the fighting forces, approached the post office, the UN opened fire. "Two of the policemen had been killed instantly, two more were dying, and a fifth was walking dazedly away, wounded in the arm," Halberstam witnessed. "Some Europeans followed the wounded man, shouting at him: Why don't you fight? Why do you leave your men? Fight, coward!"

Life stopped in Elisabethville. The streets were deserted. Between thirty and two hundred were dead, mostly Katangese, and scores more were wounded. Tshombe and Munongo had fled to Rhodesia, under Welensky's protection. Tshombe said in a statement that the UN had promised not to move against the Katangese government but had tricked him.

Hammarskjöld landed in Leopoldville on September 13, as scheduled, hours after Morthor had begun. The Congolese ministers who greeted him on the tarmac, including the new prime minister Cyrille Adoula, were jubilant, and emphasized that the UN had acted on their wishes. "The Katanga secession is over," one told a reporter anonymously. "We have fulfilled our promise to reunify the Congo."

Hammarskjöld himself refused to comment to the gathered press. But he feared as he watched it unfold that the UN had gone too far. Welensky's Rhodesian Federation had sent troops,

* The subject of the book and movie *The Siege of Jadotville*.

armored cars, and planes to the border, and threatened total war with the UN if Hammarskjöld did not withdraw his soldiers. Belgium had compared his peacekeepers to Nazis. A *New York Times* editorial pondered where his use of force would stop. Would the UN become an international army, making war for peace?

In London, Harold Macmillan had been handed a report on Morthor and its aftermath:

> There have been a good many casualties and grave atrocities. Hammarskjöld has either blundered, or his agents have acted without his authority...Unless we and the Americans act quickly and resolutely, we shall have undone in a week all we have done—at huge expense—in a year. Congo will be handed to Russia on a plate. The Union Minière properties will be "nationalized" and run by Russian Communists, and a most dangerous situation created in Africa—as well as great financial and moral blow to the West and especially to European civilization.

It was the worst possible outcome, Macmillan thought. If the Congo collapsed because of the UN, it was eminently possible that one of the Congolese officials who had taken Soviet money and Soviet guns might seize the country. He dropped the report on the green leather desktop and asked to be connected with John F. Kennedy in the White House.

Kennedy, after returning from his daily trip to the White House swimming pool, had just met with his advisers on Africa in the Oval Office when Macmillan's call reached the Resolute desk. The older man had pulled no punches. And Kennedy decided to defer to his opinion. The two resolved to apply pressure to Hammarskjöld.

The overt message they sent was that Britain and America funded the UN, and could stop anytime they wanted. Macmillan had also decided that he would deny Hammarskjöld's request for jet fighters to protect UN officials and to help the UN counter the Fouga in Katanga. Hammarskjöld could only guess what the governments had done covertly.*

He sent a message to Washington. "It is better for the UN to lose the support of the US because it is faithful to laws and principles than to survive as an agent whose activities are geared to political purposes." But he knew that his grand words meant little now.

Hammarskjöld asked for a meeting with Tshombe. If he could isolate the Katangese leader, away from his mercenary advisers, Hammarskjöld hoped Tshombe could be persuaded to agree to a cease-fire. Tshombe agreed to the conference, to be held at a tiny airfield called Ndola, inside Rhodesian territory.

The summit that could end the war would take place in the minute and shabby office of a colonial airport manager, on Sunday, September 17, 1961. In Elisabethville, a plane—a DC-6 named the *Albertina*—was readied for Hammarskjöld's mission.

---

* The UN has no spies.

Chapter 10

"Ja må han leva"

Nobody knows for sure how the *Albertina* was first attacked. We know it happened the day before it crashed, probably at Elisabethville airfield, a small runway of lit asphalt squares in the middle of empty acres of dark Congolese savanna.

It must have been shortly before 4 a.m. on September 17, 1961, as the stray gunshots of Morthor echoed and the plane departed to pick up Hammarskjöld. And the most likely explanation is a mercenary somewhere in the moonlit scrub, armed with a slim black Belgian FN assault rifle.

Through its telescopic sight, his circle of vision must have caught the UN soldiers dotted across the complex in their matching blue hats, concentrated near the hangars that housed their planes. He would have noted with a grim thrill that there were more of them than usual and, if he shared the common reflex of his mercenary colleagues, he probably began to catalog their races.

They looked wary. On high alert. The pilot of the mercenary Fouga had hit the airfield often on his daily rounds, screaming over the horizon, his guns rattling. The glass in the terminal had visibly fallen away in crashing sheets.

A hangar door began to drift open, and a splutter and roar echoed across the grassland as four muscular engines sparked to life. The nose of a United Nations DC-6 airliner came into view through the light-filled gap, stubby and a little comical. The name ALBERTINA was painted, carefully but imperfectly, on one side. The body of the plane, a fresh white, was large and inviting. Its wings looked too delicate to lift it.

Its propellers appeared to spin backward momentarily until they found their speed. Then it lurched forward and began to skate along the runway, intermittently lit, and its rumble rose in pitch and fury.

The *Albertina* lifted into the air. Its wings began to flex as they bore its weight aloft. And the mercenary fired. Perhaps he pictured an explosion that would scatter torn chunks of DC-6. Or a hopeful rise, a panicked drop to earth, and then, after a pause, the first tendrils of flame. Instead, the bullet punched a hole in the aluminum cowling of the engine closest to the body on the right side and lodged harmlessly next to the exhaust.

The plane continued to rise into the night, oblivious, as its blinking lights faded into a blanket of bright stars, headed for Leopoldville to collect Hammarskjöld and transport him to meet Tshombe.

At 7 a.m., the *Albertina* made radio contact with Leopoldville's N'djili Airport to request an approach. It reduced its speed to 140 miles an hour, dropped through the morning mist above the city, and banked over the broad, glassy expanse of the Congo River.

It touched down before 8 a.m. on September 17. By the time the sun reached its stifling peak at noon, the Swedish UN ground crew had found the bullet lodged in engine number two, removed it, marveled that it had not done more damage, replaced the parts, and pumped fuel into the plane's tanks. They felt it was safe to leave the plane unattended for a little while, and to forget the rigors of war.

Harald Noork, a flight attendant, was scheduled to get back on the *Albertina* for its return journey once Hammarskjöld arrived.

While they waited, the crew surprised Noork with a cream cake and forty candles to celebrate his fortieth birthday.

They had sung *ja må han leva*, the Swedish birthday song.

Yes, may he live!
Yes, may he live!
Yes, may he live for a hundred years!

When Noork blew out the candles, one remained stubbornly lit.

Chapter 11

"Overhead Ndola, descending, confirm"

In Leopoldville, before 4 p.m. that same day, a convoy of white cars, low Ford Galaxies with double headlights and downturned fins, arced into view through the rippling heat haze. They carved a parabola toward the *Albertina*.

Inside one of them, Hammarskjöld watched the trucks, soldiers, planes, crates of supplies, petty disputes—the banal, infernal chaos of war—scan past through a rear window. It felt aggressively pointless. Like trying to give first aid to a rattlesnake.

He had slept for one sweaty, futile hour. The eyes under his black Wayfarer sunglasses were drawn. And his face threatened, at the merest provocation, to give way to a mass of furrows.

The heat hit him like a physical force as he opened the car door and stepped out onto the airport's apron, at the edge of the DC-6's shadow. Behind him, his security detail was already climbing the plane's metal stairs, their footsteps resonating with efficient purpose, to sweep it for stowaways and bombs.

One of them carried aboard a small, dark-gray metal box with an identity plate that read CRYPTO AG, SWITZERLAND and CX-52. It was used for encoding secret messages before transmitting them over the radio, back to Leopoldville or to New York, where equivalent machines decoded them.

Hammarskjöld's staff fell into place around him in two broad circles: the outer made up of soldiers and aides who hurried back and forth with bags, and the inner of more senior officials, most of whom were dressed exactly as he was, in light suits, white shirts, and dark ties.

He was handed a printout of a telex, on flimsy rolled paper. An update. Information on Morthor was sparse and imperfect. But he could not deny the scandal, and could not shake the knowledge that hundreds lay dead at the hands of the UN.

A signal broke his reverie. It was time to board. Hammarskjöld climbed the stairs, passed through the thick portal of a door, turned left, settled into a blue cloth seat at the rear of the plane, and buckled himself in. His features, out of public view, settled into a mask of concern, and his foot began to tap.

The shadows of the late-afternoon sun passed across his features as the plane taxied and took off. Through the window Leopoldville, and safety, dwindled first to a series of boxes and lines, then dots, and was finally swallowed by the endless green.

Hammarskjöld was surrounded by his aides, a security detail of five, and the aircrew, fifteen other souls in all. He was also alone. Without allies, and without support. It was a familiar feeling.

In recent weeks, the images he recorded in his diary had turned much darker. In one, he felt that he was drowned, suspended in water, while he searched in vain for the light and respite of the surface. But the last thing he wrote took a different tone.

The seasons have changed
And the light
And the weather
And the hour.
But it is the same land.
And I begin to know the map
And to get my bearings

If he failed to persuade Tshombe to declare a cease-fire, he had decided, he would resign his position, write and hike and let the world take care of itself. But he would not give up without a fight.

Hammarskjöld opened his briefcase and lifted out a pile of books. The New Testament and Psalms. Rainer Maria Rilke's *Duineser Elegien / Die Sonette*. Jean Giono's *Noé*. He selected the philosopher Martin Buber's *Ich und Du*, flicking past the personal inscription by its author, a version of the same book in English, and a notepad.

He wanted to switch off his mind by translating the text, a complex work of theology, into Swedish. He believed the words contained, in their examination of human miscommunication and mistrust, the key to the Cold War.

In the cockpit, a cocoon of instruments, the pilot, Per Hallonqvist, flicked his eyes toward the windows. Hallonqvist was known for his affability and the gap in his front teeth. The latter remained intact.

He knew that this DC-6 had been designed as a transport for oil executives before it was seconded to the UN. It was bloated. Built for comfort, not agility. The bottom of the food chain. His only defense, if a threat rose up out of the night, was to dive, veer sharply, and head for an airfield.

He flew in a long, straight line across the Congo, then turned over Lake Tanganyika and headed south toward Ndola to minimize the time over hostile Congolese territory. At two minutes after 10 p.m. local time, he broke his radio silence to tell air traffic controllers that he would arrive at approximately half past midnight.

An hour later, he dropped to sixteen thousand feet. Forty minutes after that, he asked Ndola for clearance to descend further. He locked the landing gear into position and set the flaps at a conventional thirty-degree angle.

"Your lights in sight," he told the tower after midnight, "overhead Ndola, descending, confirm."

Chapter 12

"A light pinkish red"

Ndola was the center of Northern Rhodesia's mining industry. It was a small town surrounded by stands of miombo forest—thin evergreen trees with leaves like ferns, over a carpet of flowering shrubs and grasses below, that provide shelter for both dormice and lions, bright-yellow weaver birds and black rhinos.

Six miles away, an open-cast copper mine blasted through the night. Refineries processed ores from the region, crushing, grinding, and dissolving twenty-four hours a day. Their workers, and colonial officials, lived near the airport.

Many black African workers were dotted through the woods. They had spent the day cutting down trees, then chopping the wood into small pieces to turn into charcoal that they planned to sell by the side of the road. They had packed the wood into large metal kilns and waited for nightfall so they could make sure that each part of the stack was brought to a controlled smolder. By midnight the kilns were pouring thick columns of smoke into the air as they tended them.

At the airfield, a strip cut into the grass and steamrollered flat, with a clump of buildings to its left and a stubby tower, strange things had been happening. That morning the tower spotted an unidentified plane circling. The air traffic controllers attempted to make contact, but the plane stayed silent.

Now a set of metal stairs waited on the runway, leading surreally up to nowhere. Kenneth Hammond, a senior technician in charge of the ground crew, stood and waited to push them into place under the *Albertina*'s door. Shortly after midnight, he heard a plane and looked up into the blackness. He saw a steady red light and watched it fly right along the runway for two minutes, then disappear.

Robert Read, a senior superintendent with the Northern Rhodesia Police, also watched the red light track through the night like a tracer bullet. He was certain that he saw a second light behind it. And a third light, either green or white, to the left of it.

Donald Peover, an architect who lived in a nearby building, was on his balcony with his wife, plane-spotting. They saw the red light, too. Peover thought it was coming in faster than usual. The engines sounded like they were running at full power, in fact. Then the plane disappeared.

Adelaide Wright had lived near the airport for seven years. She was a heavy sleeper, and a little deaf, and had never been woken by a plane. The sound of this one washed over her with such a powerful low-frequency rumble that it jarred her out of her bed and set her dogs barking. She had never heard one come in so close to the ground or so powerful.

Yvonne Joubert was reading at home when she heard the distinctive whine of a jet aircraft fly overhead, and then another aircraft that sounded like a piston-engined plane. She fell asleep in her chair shortly after the sound of the engines had died away.

William Chappell, a local resident, heard a double bang, then a single bang. They were sharper sounds than blasting for mining, and louder than a backfire, he thought. He heard two planes, too— one piston-engined and, simultaneously, one jet.

Davidson Simango, a charcoal burner, was under the trees, out of the reach of the moon and starlight, gathering wood. He, too, heard the sound of aircraft engines, at a deafening pitch. He saw two lights. It seemed like two planes, close together.

First the noise faded. But then it returned. He saw a white flash, and heard a crashing sound so loud and so close that he simply lay down where he was in the forest undergrowth, covered his head, and didn't move for some time.

An airfield oil technician, Ralph Philips, saw two flashes over the pitch-black silhouette of the jungle trees that rose into the sky. The center of the larger was a deep red, which blossomed, with a perverse beauty, to a light pinkish red. A second, less violent, explosion followed, slightly to the right of the first.

Nigel Vaughan, an assistant inspector with the Northern Rhodesia Police, was driving near the airport. To him it looked like a lightbulb, bright white, that had been switched on suddenly and then blown out. It was followed by a smaller light that fell vertically from the first explosion and took about two seconds to move from the top of his windshield to below the tree line.

Ledison Daka, a charcoal burner, was asleep in a nearby village when he was woken by a loud, sudden noise. He rubbed the sleep from his eyes in time to see a plane smashing into the trees. He gathered two of his friends, Moyo and Banda, and the three began to pick their way through the forest toward the scene. Inch-long camel and buffalo thorn branches left itchy welts in the balls of their thumbs and on their wrists as they pushed them aside. A red glow began to grow through the dark silhouettes of the thin trees. It spread until it cast long, moving shadows over their faces.

The forest should have been alive, on the ground and in the trees they set swaying. But it was still and silent. They followed the smoke. It was wispy at first. As it thickened, it began to take on an acrid smell. Through the black cloud, Daka began to notice that the tops of the trees above him had been shredded away, leaving freshly torn trunks. The ground itself was smoldering, covered with a splintery mess of vegetation.

The heat kept them from moving too close. But they saw

burned bodies. Banda wanted to run away, but felt he could not move.

Objects were mixed into the litter. Playing cards. China plates, some smashed into tiny pieces, some perfectly intact. Knives. Forks. Books. A revolver, its grip and cylinder smashed or burned away. A pillow, pristine and still slightly indented where someone had lain their head.

A twisted and charred propeller, taller than a man, loomed from the forest floor. Bent metal spars, blackened beyond recognition, lay over fallen trees to form crude lean-to caves.

Daka saw a new cherry-red light and felt an intense, focused heat. It was masses of aluminum, fused and heated to glowing liquefaction. They began to run back, away, through the thorns and the spiderwebs.

If they were listening as they ran, they might have heard in the distance, from what must have been the far edge of the long strip of destruction, a high-pitched scream.

Chapter 13

"The ace of spades"

The Ndola airport tower, a square block with tilted panoramic windows that offered a 360-degree view of the dark airfield and beyond, had gone eerily quiet. At about a quarter past midnight, the air traffic controller on duty, A. Campbell Martin, noted that the *Albertina*'s radio was dead. He called Leopoldville to find out what had happened, but nobody who spoke English was on duty.

At 2:20 a.m., Martin issued the first of three formal indications of a missing or endangered aircraft, known as Uncertainty Phase. Two more are required before a search begins. Forty minutes later the airport manager, John H. Williams, a gray-haired veteran nicknamed "Red," and Lord Cuthbert Alport, the British high commissioner to Salisbury, the capital of Rhodesia, who had been due to meet Hammarskjöld's plane once it landed, conferred to decide what to do. They agree that the secretary-general must simply have decided to fly elsewhere. Alport went to sleep on his own plane. And Williams closed down the runway and killed the lights in the tower, leaving only a duty radio operator.

In New York, UN officials began to worry that they had not heard from Hammarskjöld and mounted an operations room to seek information. Telex messages, on narrow, brittle paper, began to tick through:

I do not know yet

For sure

Stop I simply refuse to believe it until I get everything
in black and white.

Stand by please, and prepare for the worse

Stop

We know Park's colleague Neil Ritchie, SIS's man in Salisbury and Katanga, was monitoring the situation for the British government. We know, too, that the State Department was receiving classified intelligence reports, from Devlin or one of his colleagues.

But neither Park nor Devlin ever spoke in any detail of the events of that night. Both were aware of a simple tenet of covert work, one that is usually omitted from spy movies: that the most effective way to keep a secret is simply not to tell anyone. If nobody is asking questions, one never has to lie, or evade. In fact the aim of the British secret services is to be as boring as possible. It means that profound silence—a lack of chatter—is often the echo of a seismic secret event. It worked perfectly for decades. But where Park and Devlin were, what they did, and more pressingly what they knew would eventually come to be a key issue.

After 3 a.m., two Rhodesian police officers arrived at the tower. They found the radio operator asleep. They woke him to tell him that one of their colleagues, an assistant inspector named Marius van Wyk, had seen a mysterious deep-red glow spreading upward into the sky while on patrol shortly after midnight.

Van Wyk didn't know that Hammarskjöld was expected to land at around that time, so he didn't think much more of it. But when he returned to the station later that night, he was told of the missing plane and put the events together. The two officers had been dispatched to inform the tower.

The operator blearily told them they should find Williams, the airport manager, who was staying in a nearby hotel. They drove over and dragged him out of bed, but he dismissed their report, saying that there was nothing to be done until daybreak anyway. The officers sent out Land Rovers of their own, defying Williams. But the mission, with such limited resources to search a vast area, would have needed spectacular luck in order to succeed. It did not get it.

At 4:30 a.m., as the sun began to subtly brighten the horizon, the air traffic controller, Martin, returned to the tower and made radio inquiries. He felt there was nothing to the police reports, and he did not act with any great urgency.

At about 9 a.m., three and a half hours after dawn, the airport manager Williams himself returned to the airport. He did not do anything until he received a signal from Salisbury, the Rhodesian capital, at nine forty-two, that search planes should be sent up. They were airborne by about 10 a.m.—ten hours after the *Albertina* had overflown the runway.

Planes of the Royal Rhodesian Air Force circled in a search pattern, scanning the ground for wreckage. US Air Force surveillance planes that had been on the ground in Ndola, scrambled with an emergency signal from the US ambassador to Leopoldville, soon joined them. They were in full effect by about 10:30 a.m.

At around the same time, in Katanga, O'Brien spotted the mercenary Fouga Magister jet fighter screaming toward UN headquarters, guns blazing, and took cover in a hole with a reporter from *Life* magazine. It was dramatic, but merely the latest in a series of similar attacks. So O'Brien was perplexed to receive a call from Tshombe shortly afterward telling him, unprompted and out of nowhere, that the Fouga had now been grounded.

About five hours later, a Rhodesian pilot in a Percival Provost propeller plane began slowly advancing to the west of Ndola, in the vicinity of one of the flashes in the sky the night before. As he scanned the flat, green fields, broken up with the occasional patch of darker jungle or tan-colored earth, he noticed a glint and a small burnt area. He descended to five thousand feet, where he could see more clearly. Two engines and a tail fin, smoking. Simultaneously, three charcoal burners reported the wreck at a forestry office. The Royal Ndola Police arrived at the crash site in Land Rovers at 3:55 p.m., about fifteen hours after the *Albertina*'s scheduled arrival time.

At night, the wreck had a peculiar eeriness, all shadows and flame and suggestion. By day, it was stripped bare by the sunshine, more mundane and more horrific. It looked like dozens of burnt, smoking tree trunks had been scooped by a giant hand into an untidy pile dotted with fragments of metal. The tail was behind that pile, pointing the wrong way.

The inner engines were next to the pile, having screwed themselves into the rubble. The outer engines had spun and tumbled away to the edges of the wreck zone. It smelled like death. And clouds of mopani flies were thick in the air.

The *Albertina* had crashed into a termite mound, about twelve feet of earth painstakingly turned to cement by millions of insects. It had first hit the tops of the trees, at a height of about seventy feet, about eight hundred feet away from that mound, with its engines under power, its flaps set for landing, and its left side apparently lower than its right.

The trees above had been shredded by the propellers, then crushed by the fuselage, to form a melange of metal and wood fragments in a long strip cut directly through the forest. After it hit the mound, the rest of the plane had cartwheeled 180 degrees around it, a torn shell gushing about twelve hundred gallons of fuel from its ruptured tanks over the wreckage. What had been about forty tons of aluminum alloy, china plates, foldout beds, European novels, and cipher machines, disintegrated.

The fuel had begun to burn, flashing hundreds of feet back along the trail it had left. The fire had been so hot that pieces of fused aluminum glowed red even now.

All of the bodies but two were burned. They no longer looked like people. They had started to decompose quickly in the jungle, and were covered with blankets or pieces of material from the wreckage to ward off the flies. One person was still on fire and had to be extinguished first.

Officers, all white Rhodesians, would have to pry the wedding rings from their blackened fingers in the hope of identifying them by the inscriptions inside. Any black Africans had been asked to search away from the wreck. Americans, too. Reporters who had started to arrive were kept at a distance.

Hammarskjöld was lying slightly away from the carnage. Though he was clearly dead, he looked untouched save for specks of blood on his face. His blue eyes, now lifeless, were still open. He was surrounded by playing cards. One of them, the ace of spades, was on his body.

Nearby, at the edge of the trail of destruction, an officer fanned someone or something. A gravely wounded survivor. Another policeman, with a first-aid kit, rushed over to help. The man was severely burned, and sunburned on his face, back, arms, and legs. He had head injuries and what looked to be a fractured ankle.

All he said was that his pain was drastic, and that he wanted water. The officers injected two ampoules of morphine, gave him water out of a metal container they found in the wreckage (after tasting it to make sure), and loaded him into an ambulance.

A police officer, sitting alongside for the bumpy journey, carefully emptied the man's charred pockets, for examination and in order to pass on any effects: a wallet, containing a notebook; a comb in a leather case; a thick wad of cash that amounted to 2,860 Belgian Congo francs; and a passport, vehicle licenses, and UN identification in the name of Sergeant Harold Julien, thirty-six years old, formerly of the US Marine Corps and a veteran of the Korean War, now acting head of security for the United Nations Operation in the Congo.

They turned in to the Ndola Hospital, a low, white building with a Red Cross sign and a pristine lawn in front, about forty minutes after the police had first arrived on the scene. The chief surgeon was there to meet them and to rush Julien to a private ward. Forty minutes later, the doctors called in a detective. Despite what appeared to be serious injuries, Julien wanted to speak. So the detective entered his room as a phalanx of doctors and nurses retreated.

Julien kept his eyes closed but asked, "Where am I?"

"You're in Northern Rhodesia," the detective replied. "I am a British police officer. Can you tell me anything about what happened?"

Julien recognized that he was being addressed but said nothing. So the detective continued.

"We last heard of you over the runway at Ndola, and we didn't hear anything more. What happened?"

"It blew up," Julien said.

"Was this over the runway?"

"Yes."

"What happened then?"

"There was great speed. Great speed."

"What happened then?"

"Then there was the crash." Julien slurred this time.

"What happened then?"

"There was a lot of small explosions all round."

"How did you get out?"

"I pulled the emergency tab and I ran out."

"What about the others?"

"They were just trapped."

He lapsed into unconsciousness.

At around 4 a.m., Julien woke. "I am Sergeant Harold Julien, security officer to UNO," he said, using an acronym for the United Nations operation. "Please inform Leopoldville of crash. Tell my wife and kids I'm alive before the casualty list is published. My wife is Maria Julien and she's in Florida. Miami."

The nurse noted that the precise way he spoke—the vital mission information first, and his personal information second—showed his training.

The nurses contacted Maria, Cuban-born and with a young son, Richard, to take care of. She began the long journey to Ndola.

Chapter 14

"Sparks, sparks in the sky"

The first inquiry into the crash—set up by the Rhodesian Federal Department of Civil Aviation—formally began the next day, on September 19, 1961.

The crash site was first cordoned off, and then surrounded by unforgiving, clinically bright floodlights. A team of thirteen began picking their way through the debris, human and mechanical, meticulously photographing, mapping, and collecting every piece of the wreckage that had not burned. When they were done, each piece was taken to a warehouse in Ndola and painstakingly laid out in its original place.

Only about 20 percent of the plane remained identifiable. The five tons of fused metal that had been recovered was broken, by hammer and steam hammer, into smaller fragments, about eight inches square, for visual and chemical examination.

Each piece of wreckage—"piece of fuselage with navigator's desk light," "sink and toilet"—was carefully labeled exactly where it was found. One wing, a rudder, and part of the tailplane were the only parts large enough to merit being drawn on. The bodies were marked with numbered circles.

It was nearly impossible to make sense of the fragments, to differentiate what had been smashed or burned by accident from signs of potential foul play. Over the following decades, the details the Rhodesian forensics team could map—a smear of parts and corpses—would become a resource and an agony for those determined to figure out the crash, the pieces placed together endlessly to form different patterns.

There had been no room in the morgue for all the dead. So a large marquee had been erected on the well-kept grounds of the hospital for pathologists to begin their work. They borrowed extra fridges for the bodies from a local company, Sunspan Bananas.

Three specialists, using medical and dental records, and telephones and a telegraph machine to gather information, were busy identifying the charred remains, plotted carefully on the nascent map of the wreck.

Vladimir Fabry, forty, a legal and political adviser, once a resistance fighter against the Nazis in his native Czechoslovakia, had been closest to Julien, at the back right corner of the wreck.

Harald Noork, whose birthday the crew had celebrated before the *Albertina* took off, was a few yards closer to the plane.

Sergeant Stig Olof Hjelte, one of the soldiers aboard, was found under the wing.

Heinrich Wieschhoff, who had advised the secretary-general on African affairs, lay within the bulk of the wrecked plane itself, as did Bill Ranallo, who had worked his way up from Hammarskjöld's chauffeur to his head of security, general assistant, and friend.

The flight engineer, Nils Göran Wilhelmsson, and another of the soldiers, Francis Eivers, were discovered at the edges of a large piece of the burnt fuselage that contained the plane's toilet. They were a few yards from the last soldier, Private Per Edvald Persson.

The flight crew—Captain Nils Erik Åhréus, Captain Lars Litton, and the flight captain, Per Hallonqvist—were found in the wreckage of the cockpit, as one would expect.

Near them, unexpectedly, were Alice Lalande, Linnér's secretary, who was French Canadian, and a Haitian security official, Serge Barrau. There was no reason that one of them, let alone both, should have been anywhere near the cockpit. The only thing that obviously united the two among those aboard was a fluency in French.

Most of the bodies contained bullets—either 7.62mm NATO or 9mm, matching the ammunition aboard. But they did not bear the rifling marks indicating that they had passed through the barrel of a gun.

The pathologists, in consultation with ballistics experts, decided that the heat of the fire had set off ammunition and that it had exploded in every direction. It explained the holes in pieces of fuselage, too. In total, in the bodies and in the wreckage, they found 201 live rounds, 342 bullets, and 362 cartridge cases.

One of the bodies, that of the radio operator, Carl Erik Gabriel Rosén, was brought in later. It had been hidden under a piece of cabin fuselage. Rosén was also riddled with what appeared to be bullet holes. The officers making the search found a 9mm submachine gun nearby, and surmised that it might have been in his lap, perhaps in preparation for a hostile landing.

The Rhodesians, though professional and experienced, had a profound, and barely disguised, disdain for the UN and the observers it had sent to help. They resented the very suggestion that the crash might have been anything other than an accident.

On September 20, Knut Hammarskjöld, Dag's nephew, arrived as a representative both of his uncle's family and of the Swedish government. Knut, then thirty-nine and an executive at the European Free Trade Association, found an atmosphere of "organized disinterest." It crossed his mind that Hammarskjöld had been an enemy to many Rhodesians—a man said to be taking their way of life.

Lord Alport, the British high commissioner to Salisbury and a staunch Rhodesian ally, had decided he and the Rhodesians needed to grab Hammarskjöld's briefcase, which had lain next to the secretary-general in the wreckage, apparently unharmed.

He kept it for some time. His stated reason was to ensure that it was given quickly to either a member of Hammarskjöld's family or a UN official. But when one senior official, Björn Egge, a Norwegian soldier who was the head of military intelligence for the UN in the Congo, drove after Alport's car to secure it, Alport evaded him.

And Egge recalled another oddity that stayed with him for the rest of his life. In the mortuary at Ndola, a cool, dark room amid the tropical fug, he briefly viewed Hammarskjöld's body. He swore until his death that he had seen a small, round hole in his forehead. A hole that was missing from pathology images he later received. He could never adequately explain the disparity.

His experience was echoed by Knut Hammarskjöld. Before he left Africa, a Rhodesian police officer took him aside. He handed over a manila envelope and said, "You may find these interesting." The envelope contained photographs of his uncle's body. When Knut shuffled through them, curious what the police officer had meant, he was shocked to see head injuries that were not visible on the official images.

Over the next six days, Julien drifted in and out of sedation. Some of the team of twenty-five nurses that took care of him in that time described him as incoherent. Others felt he was lucid, or at least obviously rational, but restless.

He had been through the unimaginable trauma of a plane crash, followed by hours of dehydration and sunburn. His kidneys were failing him. When he spoke, it was to ask for water. But he also seemed aware of what was happening around him. When nurses quietly discussed changing shift, he asked them not to leave.

And he was panicked by the sound of aircraft overhead. "Plane, plane," he said on Thursday, September 21, three days after the crash, before he was reassured that he was safe.

He told another nurse, Angela McGrath, that he was the only one who got out. That the rest of those aboard were trapped. "We were on the runway when Mr. Hammarskjöld said to go back, then there was an explosion."

"Sparks, sparks in the sky," he said to another, on Friday, September 22. And then the name Bob, twice.

Maria arrived on the morning of Saturday, September 23, five days after the crash.

"Honey, take me home," he said, later that day. "We must get out of here quickly. You will take me home?" She said she would.

He was anxious. "Where's the book?" he asked. "The book! The book!" Maria did not know what he meant, but she reassured him that she had it, whatever it was. He relaxed.

An hour later Julien, the one person who both knew for sure what had happened to the *Albertina* and was willing to say, died.

PART TWO

In its purest form, "dead reckoning," short for
"deduced reckoning," involves picking a compass head-
ing and holding it until you reach the next waypoint,
while using elapsed time to calculate your position...

—*Aircraft Owners and Pilots Association of America*

Chapter 15

"Next of kin"

George Ivan Smith, press representative for the UN and one of Hammarskjöld's closest confidants, was supposed to have been aboard the *Albertina*. But by September 1961, he had been away from his family too often, on foreign assignments. So instead he was on vacation, approved by Hammarskjöld, on a road trip across America.

He heard the news on the car radio, on a long road through the bright desert in Arizona. Those who knew Ivan Smith* well said that there was a George before that moment, garrulous and alpha, and a George afterward, more withdrawn and subdued.

Ivan Smith looked, at first blush, the very cliché of a robust Australian. At forty-six, he had an intelligent gaze, a ruddy face under lustrous slicked hair, a thick neck, and an avuncular mustache. He naturally elicited trust and sympathy from others.

He was the son of a prison warden, George Franklin Smith, a former amateur boxing champion of Australia who had pioneered a kinder treatment of prisoners that we would now call rehabilitation. Franklin Smith was a big man, and a thoroughly Victorian father. Ivan Smith joked that until he had died, he had never

---

* Both names made up his last name, without hyphen.

noticed his father had a bald spot on the top of his head. He had never seen him from that angle.

He demanded that his son, too, become a big man. One of the attractions at the annual agricultural show near his father's jail in Goulburn, about 120 miles from Sydney, was a boxing troupe, which always featured an aging former national champion. "Is anyone here brave enough," the barker would call out, "to fight this man?" Ivan Smith knew that if nobody spoke up, he would hear his father's voice saying, "Yes, here is a challenger—my son." He realized later in life that he'd been knocked out by more retired champions than nearly anyone else alive.

As a teenager he had become addicted to alcohol, and after a stint in recovery had attended Sydney University, near the family home, and then Cambridge University, on the other side of the world. He had been intimidated by the pitiless condescension there, and had felt profoundly alone (signs in pubs and restaurants at the time still read NO AUSTRALIANS as well as NO BLACKS).

Ivan Smith craved action, and to withstand real pressures. But he was also a sensitive soul who read poetry at night, and who medicated bouts of depression with fizzing glasses of gin and tonic, occasionally balanced on the dashboard of his car as he drove.

So he became a journalist—that last refuge of the vaguely talented—for the Australian Broadcasting Corporation. He rose to head its foreign arm, Radio Australia, and covered World War II for the BBC, where he developed a friendly acquaintance with George Orwell.

Ivan Smith was appointed the UN's head of external affairs in 1947. He had a deft and witty way of neither lying, nor revealing anything he didn't want to reveal, that endeared him to both his colleagues and the press. But he came alive in the job in 1953, when Hammarskjöld became secretary-general. Here, at last, was someone who was both tough and sensitive. "I suddenly realized

I was in the presence of a very great man," he said of their first meeting. "His background I knew nothing about but the presence he carried with him was one of authority and of genius."

He spent most of his time attempting to correct mistakes in the way the UN and Hammarskjöld were portrayed. He assiduously explained, in letter after letter and meeting after meeting with reporter after reporter, the careful and nuanced steps required for international diplomacy. When they ignored him and printed the sugary story instead, he did it all over again.

Ivan Smith was one of the few who accompanied Hammarskjöld on both his diplomatic missions and his long walks. In pictures, the two men often mirror each other's body language. When they arrived in Cairo for a summit, one newspaper described Ivan Smith as Mr. Fluid, and Hammarskjöld as Mr. Flexible, because they both often used the words in press conferences. They adopted the nicknames in correspondence to each other.

When the BBC asked Ivan Smith for background on Hammarskjöld for a documentary, Ivan Smith wrote a lyrical note, explaining that Hammarskjöld saw the world in his own way. For him, music, painting, literature, diplomacy, and war were all of a piece—different expressions of the same humanity. After he sent it, Ivan Smith began to worry that it was too personal. So he showed it to the secretary-general. Hammarskjöld sat silent. Ivan Smith worried he was about to be fired. Eventually he said, "You are the first person who has understood this about me."

After Hammarskjöld's death, Ivan Smith returned immediately to work in New York. While Hammarskjöld had been alive, many at the UN had resented his relationship with the secretary-general. Now they showed their disdain in frosty gestures and quiet contempt.

Others were more generous. He found a spate of letters, from those who understood his loss, on his desk. "Somehow you have always seemed to me to be the SG's next of kin," read one. "You must feel it so very much," it concluded. "I sincerely hope you will find some consolation in the many fond memories you have of him," ended another.

But consolation can never be found in memories alone. He wrote a flurry of letters—to the prime minister of Sweden, to the BBC and the *Times* of London—to defend Hammarskjöld's legacy, arrange memorials and donations, and correct errors.

Ivan Smith collected press clippings. Among them was a torrent of tributes from world leaders, their frustrations forgotten. Macmillan described him as "a world servant who has pursued his duty with courage, single-mindedness and devotion." Kennedy ordered all flags on US government buildings and installations to be flown at half-mast.

The American president spoke, too, at the UN. "We meet in an hour of grief and challenge," his address opened. "Dag Hammarskjöld is dead. But the United Nations lives on. His tragedy is deep in our hearts, but the task for which he died is at the top of our agenda. A noble servant for peace is gone. But the quest for peace lies before us."

In the *New York Herald Tribune*, Walter Lippmann concluded that Hammarskjöld had been a peculiarly pioneering figure. He appeared docile, Lippmann wrote, but had taken extravagant risks to prevent a race war in Katanga from becoming entangled with the burgeoning Cold War. "If the world is not ready for what Hammarskjöld felt compelled to try in the Congo, it is also true, I hate to say, that this present world is not ready for the kind of man Hammarskjöld was," he wrote.

Peace negotiations with Katanga did, in fact, go ahead despite the crash, out of a fear that Hammarskjöld's death might escalate an already bloody war. A tentative cease-fire was agreed to on September 21.

When Hammarskjöld's body was brought back to Uppsala, one hundred thousand Swedes lined the streets to welcome him home for the last time. They marched to the mournful sound of drums. Some held flaming torches aloft to light the way. Reporters described a strange hush, as though the entire nation had fallen silent. He was buried next to his father and mother, in a quiet graveyard near the castle in which he had grown up.

Ivan Smith also began to piece together what was known of the crash. He had to be able to answer questions from the press in New York about what was quickly becoming an international mystery.

A Democratic lawmaker from New York had introduced a bill in the US Senate that offered a $50,000 reward for information "leading to the identification of any person or group subsequently shown to have been responsible for the death of UN Secretary-General Dag Hammarskjöld."

Newspapers around the world puzzled over the delay in beginning a search for the *Albertina*. They wondered in print why Hammarskjöld had been forced to fly without fighter plane protection and aired wild accusations of plots by the British and others. One official told reporters that "nobody within the UN believes the theory that the crash was caused by an accident."

Stories that would not have been news previously—like two UN planes being fired on in Katanga—were suddenly worth the column inches. Kennedy's press secretary, Pierre Salinger, refused to divulge what the president had been told about the crash, and he would not comment on the reports that sabotage might have been a factor.

The Rhodesians, meanwhile, were briefing reporters in Ndola that the crash did not look like an act of aggression. They also anonymously dismissed reports of Julien's hospital statements that alleged there had been an explosion. "The uninformed insistence in overseas newspapers that Hammarskjöld's death is a result of foul play is causing considerable bitterness here," a Rhodesian government spokesman said.

Ivan Smith, with eyes relatively fresh to Katanga, had begun to notice things himself as he worked through the clippings and received briefings from within the UN. He found out that Union Minière's communication systems—the most sophisticated in the country—were being used by the Katangese mercenaries. And that the mercenary fighters had been given access to the company's sophisticated workshops in order to build and repair equipment. He began to suspect that the company and the mercenaries were connected, like a political party and a terrorist group.

"I have such strong and curious feelings about it all," he said in one letter, "that after very careful thoughts I have decided to transfer from this work here and to move to work for the UN in Africa. In the first instance I am going to the Congo."

Ivan Smith was appointed head of civilian operations in Katanga. He said a temporary goodbye to his wife, Mary, at their home in upstate New York. Both had children from previous marriages that were only recently into adulthood, and they had planned this time as a belated honeymoon. Instead he departed for the most chaotic spot on earth, just a few days after Hammarskjöld had died.

Chapter 16

"Why, if it isn't that nice Mr. Smith"

A few days after he arrived in Elisabethville, Ivan Smith and some UN colleagues were assigned to accompany a visiting American senator to a reception at the American consulate. As dusk fell on an evening in late September 1961, they approached the consulate, an elegant house draped in dense pink bougainvillea, in a convoy of cars.

The senator, Thomas Dodd, a former Nuremberg prosecutor and FBI agent with patrician white hair, was a staunch supporter of Tshombe. He felt the Katangese leader was a true warrior against Communism.* As a token of his appreciation, Tshombe had instructed dancers to hide in the yard of the house to greet the special guest and his wife.

As the cars pulled up, the women emerged from the gloaming and began to sway and chant. Their vividly colored cotton dresses and headdresses dipped in and out of the shadows, and their voices formed a mesmeric swirl.

Inside the house the guests, dressed in their most formal attire,

---

* It did not hurt that Tshombe's Washington lobbyists were friends. Dodd was among the first senators ever formally censured for improper use of his position to raise money.

circulated to and fro through French doors, between a buffet and a space for dancing. Ivan Smith was preoccupied with attempts to persuade Dodd that the UN was not supporting Communism. But as they entered, he noticed something that stopped him short.

As well as the dancers, Tshombe was represented by a group of European mercenaries, some with terrifying facial scars. They were staring. A UN military adviser approached Ivan Smith. "You should be extremely careful," he said. "Those people are pointing you out too much. You should get out of here."

The UN group and the senator were scheduled to go to another party, a reception arranged for them by the local representative of Mobil Oil, at his equally opulent home nearby. They decided it was safest to leave earlier than planned. Dodd could follow on later.

As they drove away, Ivan Smith battled a growing feeling of unease. It was justified as they pulled up to the house, and his car's headlights revealed a dirty green troop-carrying truck parked outside. A group of Katangese soldiers in camouflage uniforms jumped from it and surrounded them.

One knocked on the car's front window. He asked for documents. When a UN guard handed over his identification, the soldier threw it on the ground and began stamping on it. It was clear to Ivan Smith that the whole group of soldiers were suffused with marijuana and beer, and out of control.

Getting out of the car into the cloud of directionless rage would have been fatal. The key was to wait until they got bored. Bored Katangese soldiers often lost the stomach for arbitrary violence.

So they waited, tense and watchful, inside the car. Eventually an American with red hair emerged from the party to tell the soldiers that this was an evening to honor a friend of their president. That Tshombe himself might even attend. The troops reluctantly allowed the group to step from the car and walk as quickly as dignity would allow into the house.

They came into a large, open hallway. It adjoined an even larger drawing room, with French windows and a grand piano, to form an L-shape. A dozen or so people, including the British consul, were already milling around the conjoined rooms in full evening dress.

Ivan Smith and his group were restoring themselves with a cocktail when another group of Katangese soldiers burst through the front door of the house, this time led by two white men.

Ivan Smith hoped it was just another show of force. That it would pass as quickly as the incident outside.

And then one of the soldiers raised his gun and jabbed its heavy wooden butt into the face of a senior UN official, Brian Urquhart.* He put his hand up to his broken nose, and a vivid torrent of blood began gushing through his fingers. The rest of the soldiers set upon him.

Behind Ivan Smith, another group of soldiers came through the French windows. The danger was real. But his response was drawn from childhood: to put the piano between himself and the attackers as though they were playing a spirited game of tag.

It didn't work. There were too many of them. They seized him and forced him to the ground. He covered his head with his arms as they pummeled the air from his body with their guns. When they stopped he found he could draw breath only in ragged, painful jags.

He lay still. The men standing over him were unsure of what to do next. They kept loading and unloading their guns. He hoped that they might be placated by the attack and move on. But yet another group of Katangese soldiers entered, visibly older and angrier.

They pulled Ivan Smith roughly to his feet and grabbed

---

* Also a close confidant of Hammarskjöld, he subsequently wrote the definitive biography of his time at the UN.

Urquhart, bruised and covered in sticky dark-brown blood. One of his trouser legs and his shirt had been torn off, but he still had his tie knotted neatly around his neck. When a Belgian banker* tried to intervene to stop them marching the two UN officials from the room, the soldiers grabbed him, too. They dragged the three men outside and across the yard into the road. They ushered and pushed them up onto the oily steel bed of the truck, underneath a canvas canopy.

It was empty except for two low metal benches. The soldiers told them to lie down. The other two men began, reluctantly, to lower themselves. Ivan Smith knew that his chances of survival would drop precipitously if the truck was allowed to drive into the night. He felt compelled, by what he later felt was a primal stubbornness, to refuse.

He pushed his back against the cab of the truck and began kicking out as the soldiers moved toward him. Other soldiers, behind them, began stomping and kicking the other two men, and beating them once more with swinging rifles.

The scene was suddenly illuminated by headlights. Senator Dodd's car, a huge black Dodge provided by Tshombe, flanked with motorcycle outriders in plumed helmets, had pulled up behind them.

The soldiers looked up. Ivan Smith felt a chance. He pushed their guns away, and shoved and ran and jumped out onto the dirt road toward the Dodge's grinning chrome visage. He saw the US consul, Lew Hoffacker, leap from the car and move toward him. He heard Senator Dodd's wife say, incongruously, from the backseat, "Why, if it isn't that nice Mr. Smith," before someone told her to get down.

Ivan Smith felt Hoffacker grab him and pull him toward the safety of the motorcade. He saw the door of the Dodge open and

---

* Who turned out to be the president of the Bank of Congo.

clambered in. Hoffacker went away and came back with the Belgian banker, who jumbled in with them, crouching in the back on the white leather seat.

Hoffacker left again. Ivan Smith heard a debate, a negotiation for the last man. He heard the soldiers outside the window cock their guns to load bullets into the chambers. There was a pause. Then he felt Hoffacker dive on top of them at speed and the rumbling V-8 engine gun underneath them all, before the car peeled away in a whir of tires and dust.*

As Ivan Smith lay awkwardly in the car, looking across at the terrified senator and his wife, he suspected through increasingly painful breaths that his ribs were broken. And slowly the traumas of that night began to sift themselves into conclusions.

The mercenaries knew the UN was approaching a reconciliation with Tshombe. That meant they would lose their paychecks and, more important, their fight. They had wanted hostages tonight, Ivan Smith decided, to use as leverage.

His mind flashed to Hammarskjöld. What if they had attempted to abduct his plane with him on it? To talk it down on the radio, or force it to another airfield with their own jet fighters. What if it had all turned to violent farce like tonight's raid, and Hammarskjöld's plane had been shot down, or crashed in the chaos?

It made little sense as a military strategy.† But mercenaries, he came to realize, were men who habitually fished in troubled waters. They were not academics or clerics. In fact, many of them were obviously psychotic, or at least unstable to the point that a formal diagnosis made no difference.

---

* The final man, Urquhart, was subsequently rescued, though not before he suffered further injury, when Tshombe himself intervened.

† Though, in fact, the cease-fire deal brokered with Katanga after Hammarskjöld died was a generous one that effectively allowed some European soldiers to remain.

And they were more inspired by their Katangese leaders than under their direct control. Nobody could call them off—only wind them up, set them off, and semi-legitimately deny any involvement in the destruction that followed. The realization set Ivan Smith on a lifelong quest to solve what he now considered a murder.

Bo Virving *(Courtesy of Björn Virving)*

Bullets found in the wreckage
(Courtesy of Björn Virving)

Dag Hammarskjöld's gravestone in Uppsala
(Conny Odenfrund, CC BY-SA 3.0)

A Fouga Magister jet
(Philippe Dulac, C BY-SA 3.0)

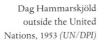

Dag Hammarskjöld
outside the United
Nations, 1953 *(UN/DPI)*

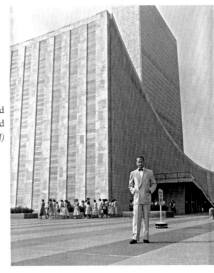

The crash site
*(Courtesy of Björn
Virving)*

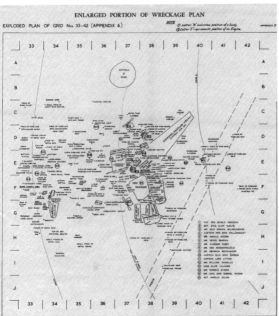

Enlarged wreckage plan *(from the Rhodesian report, 1961)*

One of the *Albertina*'s four engines *(Courtesy of Björn Virving)*

George Ivan Smith,
March 1957 (UN Photo)

King Leopold II

Lt. Gen. Sean MacEoin and Dr. Conor Cruise O'Brien, Leopoldville, June
1961 (UN Photo)

Secretary-General António Guterres and Justice Mohamed Chande Othman, June 2019 *(UN Photo)*

Daphne Park, 1943 *(Somerville College, Oxford)*

The *Albertina (Courtesy of Björn Virving)*

Moise Tshombe

Godefroid Munongo
(Munongo family website)

Patrice Lumumba

Dag Hammarskjöld at Elisabethville airport, Katanga, August 1960 *(UN Photo)*

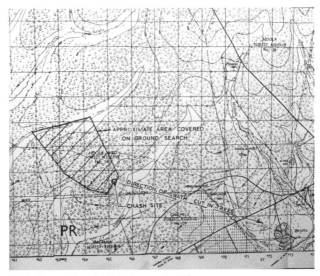

Crash site map *(from the Rhodesian report, 1961)*

A Katangan Fouga, destroyed in fighting later in 1961 *(UN Photo)*

Chapter 17

"It was not a normal flying accident"

Ivan Smith decided to visit the scene of the crime: the patch of charred forest eight miles from the Ndola airport where the *Albertina* had been found. He arrived on a hot day in late summer 1961, and picked his way through the ragged bush, humid and hostile.

When he stepped into the artificial clearing he could still see, despite the tramplings of the departed forensics team and nature's best efforts to reclaim the land, where the *Albertina* had cut into the trees in a long curve.

The site felt holy, he decided. Like an impromptu memorial. The tops of the trees, which usually blocked out the sun, were gone, and he felt the weight of the blue sky, with a bright ball of sun piercing from behind a single cloud. The damaged foliage had been cauterized into strange shapes. It reminded him of climbing a mountain with Hammarskjöld in New Zealand, and the delight his friend had felt at the unfamiliar plants there.

He went, next, to the airfield itself, and climbed the steps to the control tower to see Williams, the airport manager. They spoke, with a sweeping view of Ndola stretched out on all sides around them, for an hour. Williams was polite, but obviously reticent and very formal.

Ivan Smith asked him question after question. Each was dismissed. When he asked how it was that the tower had not seen the fire after the crash, for example, Williams said that it was the time of year for bush fires anyway. And that in any case he had grown very busy at around that time, and had not looked out beyond the airport.

Ivan Smith had seen news, in the papers in Leopoldville and Elisabethville, of a Rhodesian public inquiry that would follow the technical examination. It was being conducted by the Rhodesian chief justice, Sir John Clayden, a silver-haired and thoroughly establishment character who favored dark, double-breasted suits even in the tropical heat. Clayden had been appealing for witnesses on the radio, for a public portion of the inquiry. But he had already been privately interviewing those known to have important information.

Ivan Smith realized, as he spoke to Williams, that the airport manager must have been questioned as part of both the technical examination and the new public inquiry. He would have had those two sworn accounts in his mind to keep straight. Finally, as he sensed the interview drawing to a close, Ivan Smith grew frustrated. I am not a formal inquiry, he said. I knew the men who died. This is personal.

Williams, nervously, opened up. His tone changed. "You are right to inquire," he said. "It was not a normal flying accident." In his conversations with the crew, Williams said, they had mentioned there were things they wanted to discuss with him when they were on the ground. "It is very mysterious," Williams concluded.

To Ivan Smith it sounded like an admission.

In January 1962, several months after the crash, the Clayden inquiry began to call witnesses at the high court in Ndola, an imposing red-brick building with four white columns surrounding its entrance.

The mystery it confronted was far more confounding than any modern plane crash. There were no global positioning satellites that tracked planes moment-to-moment. Black box recorders—which store vital flight information for recovery after a crash—were not ubiquitous. The wreckage, and witness accounts, were virtually all anyone had to go on.

A cast of characters linked together by the crash drifted in and out of the stuffy wooden courtroom over several days. They included those who had seen the last moments of the *Albertina*, the officials who had discovered the plane, and the doctors and nurses who had treated the last survivor, Harold Julien, and had noted his statements about explosions and sparks in the sky.

Every day a tall, bespectacled man, with a precise air and shirt-sleeves rolled up in the tropical heat, sat on one of the benches at the back, watching attentively. Bo Virving was a seasoned Swedish pilot, who had flown every kind of plane across every kind of African terrain.

He was the protégé of Count Carl Gustaf von Rosen, a Swedish nobleman and a professional stunt pilot. Von Rosen's aunt had married the Nazi leader Hermann Göring a decade before World War II. He despised his uncle-by-marriage, who headed the German air force, and after the war broke out he quit the flying circus to wage a one-man aerial campaign against fascism. He flew first in Europe and Russia, but later moved to Africa. He sustained mustard gas burns while flying guerrilla-style, in makeshift warplanes, against Mussolini's air force.

Virving had lived alongside von Rosen in Ethiopia for a decade after the war as the two attempted to establish an airline there. He had lost count of the hours they had flown over hostile and unmapped terrain, the landings at makeshift dirt airfields, the close shaves as they evaded thunderstorms, flocks of birds and anti-aircraft guns over a wild continent racked with conflict.

He was a seasoned African bush pilot, comfortable clearing warthogs or ostriches from the runway before takeoff, and buzzing low before landing to scare away herds of elephants or giraffes. He knew how to fly without radar, without help from air traffic controllers, without weather alerts, tuned in only to his own instincts and the feel of the plane. He knew well that many of the presumptions the Rhodesians made were driven, at best, by a lack of knowledge of flying on the edge in Africa.

By 1962, Virving was a senior official for the Swedish air company, Transair, that had supplied Hammarskjöld's plane. Two days after the crash, he had received a call at his home in Malmö, in the south of Sweden: Transair and the Swedish government wanted him to observe the Rhodesian investigation in Ndola. He left his wife and three children and arrived days later to attend the tense examination of the smashed metal that had once been the *Albertina*.

He was not an overtly political man, nor one motivated by a grand sense of moral justice. But he had a quiet attachment to what was right, or more precisely what was correct, that he would never have dreamed of identifying as notable or unusual. It was simply how life had to work.

So he balked at seeing white officials give terse orders to the black Africans who were sifting the residue of the plane in the hot tent. And they were no less terse with him. Virving had known the pilots of the *Albertina* well. They were experienced, and had navigated the treacherous skies of the Congo repeatedly. He could not imagine a scenario in which they pulled off the complex maneuvers and evasions necessary to get Hammarskjöld above Ndola and then made an obvious mistake while landing and planted the plane in a forest.

And so he, with von Rosen, focused on other explanations.

He asked the Rhodesian officials, at every turn, about the possibility that a bullet, a shell, explosives, or a fire might have caused the crash. They felt the questions were offensive. It had clearly been an accident. And such loose talk, one official suggested, might even sway the malleable minds of the black African witnesses.

In court Virving watched those same black witnesses, mostly the charcoal burners who had been the last to notice the plane in the sky before the crash, give evidence. White witnesses had been scrupulously referred to as Mr. or Mrs. The charcoal burners were instead called "African," so that Davidson Simango, who had distinctly remembered two planes in the sky that night, became "African Simango."

Virving knew that most of them were appearing against their better judgment. It was lore among black Africans that no good came of trying to help their white counterparts. If you reported a car crash, you'd be accused of stealing from the wreck.

Virving was shocked that there was no interpreter to help them. They were rushed through questions by a panel of four lawyers—one from Sweden, one from Britain, one from the federation, and another from the UN—and forced to give a plain yes or no to sum up issues Virving knew to be profoundly complex.

Timothy Kankasa, a high-ranking official in a black African township, and an air force signalman with extensive aviation experience,* was one of seven black Africans who testified that he had noticed a smaller plane flying above the *Albertina*.

Geoffrey Lawrence, the lawyer for the federation, was described in one magazine as a "puckish, mousy little man with a mind as orderly as a calculating machine." He had become famous after securing the acquittal of a doctor suspected of murdering hundreds of his elderly patients in Britain.

---

* He later became a state minister in Zambia.

"What you have told us," he said to Kankasa, in the clipped and dismissive tones that British lawyers use to suggest that witnesses are laughably stupid, "is completely unacceptable. You made a mistake."

Virving's disappointment was more than casual. He had been developing a theory of his own about the crash. He had hoped the hearings might answer a key question. But it was clear to him that the intention of the inquiry was merely to tuck the issue of Hammarskjöld's death away as quickly as possible.

So one day he waited outside of the court. He watched the door for two of the witnesses in particular, Davidson Simango and Farie Mazibisa. Both were charcoal burners, and both had, from different vantage points, recalled two planes in the sky that night. They had also mentioned other details—flashes and bangs, mostly—that were incongruous or strange if taken in isolation. But Virving believed he had a way of making sense of them.

When the two men emerged, they looked nervous. A white police officer was standing near them, and their eyes kept returning to him. Virving walked over and asked to talk to them. They were reluctant to explain again, in the presence of the police officer. But they repeated their stories with remarkable consistency. In doing so they provided the confirmation Virving needed for his theories.

Chapter 18

"Black hole"

On January 23, 1962, the Rhodesian Commission of Inquiry report was released in freshly printed piles. It was bound in blue, with a thick cover of cream card stock, and it contained the final results of the most comprehensive report on the crash that would ever be completed.

It opened by explaining its methodology. The investigation— centered on the remains of the *Albertina* in the tent in Ndola— was exhaustive, whatever the biases of its instigators. It had taken statements from 130 people and gathered reams of fresh, firsthand forensic and other evidence. About 120 witnesses had also given testimony in hearings. Even the Rhodesians did not quite understand the mass of data they had gathered.

It was divided into eleven parts, and began with the basics. On September 17, 1961, a Transair Douglas DC-6B, identifier SE-BDY, known as the *Albertina*, flew from Leopoldville in the Congo to Ndola, a small town in the Federation of Rhodesia and Nyasaland. It carried the secretary-general of the United Nations, Dag Hammarskjöld, nine other UN staff, and six crew.

It took off at around 4 p.m. local time. Shortly after it was scheduled to land, six hours later at around midnight local time, it crashed in a forest of hardwood trees and bush grass. All sixteen aboard died—fifteen at the scene, and one, Sergeant Harold Julien, later in hospital after giving cryptic statements that described the crash.

The three pilots, the report said, had nearly twenty thousand hours of flying experience among them—two thousand of them in the DC-6. The weather was clear, with a slight haze and visibility between five and ten miles.

The *Albertina* itself was well maintained and in prime condition. It had suffered no ill effects from the bullet that had been lodged in its engine. Nor did it show any other signs of mechanical difficulty. It had been left unattended, but there was no way to say for sure whether anyone had planted an explosive aboard.

Because the plane had deliberately flown in stealth mode, Captain Per Hallonqvist had not filed a flight plan, and had navigated by what is known as dead reckoning. Instead of communicating with radio beacons at airfields on the route, which guide the plane but log movements, Hallonqvist, a chief navigator for the airline, had flown using landmarks like the giant Lake Tanganyika, dark blue-black below him in the night. By calculating from these known locations using his speed and bearing, he could plot his own route without ever alerting anyone.

"We express no opinion on whether security measures justified these actions," the report said, thereby raising the question in the first place.

At around midnight, the plane had overflown Ndola airport, at the correct height of six thousand feet, on the correct bearing of 280 degrees. Thirty seconds after it picked up Ndola's radio beacon—a signal to landing planes—it had turned right, as expected, at the same height, then turned back again on a bearing of one hundred degrees and dropped a thousand feet in a textbook preparation for landing.

Then it disappeared. Airport staff, aware of the need for secrecy, presumed that it had its own purposes for going silent, or that Hammarskjöld had changed his mind about meeting with Tshombe.

Dozens of witnesses saw the plane in the sky. Seven of them saw two planes. Its angle of descent was less than five degrees, its flaps set to thirty degrees—appropriate for an approach. Its engines were under power and its landing gear was down. Its controls, communications equipment, and gauges were working correctly, according to forensic analysis.

There was evidence that at least six of those aboard were wearing their seat belts when it crashed, five minutes after it was expected, nine and a half miles from Ndola. The ferocity and spread of the subsequent fire showed it had not been brought down by a lack of fuel.

Fourteen were either killed by the impact, or knocked mercifully unconscious to burn to death. Hammarskjöld was thrown clear to die nearby. Medically speaking, Harold Julien had died of renal failure, but ultimately the cause was burns across 55 percent of his body, and the effects of fifteen hours of exposure before he was found. He had a compound fracture of one of his ankles, which suggested that he must have crawled from the wreckage rather than run. Had he been found sooner, he would likely have survived.

The delay in sending help was partly a result of the chaotic political situation, the report said. It was plausible in the minds of airport staff that Hammarskjöld might have chosen to fly elsewhere. Two groups of police officers had, on their own initiative, begun searches in the night. Had they been aided by the resources, including spotter planes, that were brought to bear hours later, they would doubtless have found the wreckage, and with it the truth from a less grievously injured Julien.

But they did not, and the report went on—at great length—to absolve them of any responsibility for this decision, and to set Julien's own testimony aside. It went through each line Julien had spoken, describing an explosion and sparks in the sky, and made the argument that he could not possibly have meant what he said.

One of his doctors, Mark Lowenthal, had testified that Julien was "lucid and coherent." But the report did not mention Lowenthal's view, and took instead the word of a more senior surgeon who felt otherwise.

The blood of the pilots contained no alcohol, and analysis for carboxyhemoglobin—which indicates carbon monoxide in the blood and can show whether a person was exposed to fire before death—revealed nothing significant. That ruled out, for the Rhodesians, that they might have perished in an explosion before the crash itself, or that a fire had spontaneously broken out inside the *Albertina*.

About 20 percent of the plane was salvageable for forensic analysis. In that small section, only one hole was found that could plausibly have been a bullet hole. Spectrography indicated no traces of metals commonly associated with bullets.

The flotsam and jetsam of the wreckage had yielded other clues. Pilots used what were known as manuals—books that contained updated information on the precise approaches for different airports—before landing. There was evidence that they had used the correct chart for Ndola.

But another manual found in the wreck, intriguingly, had fallen open to the page for Ndolo, a totally different airport with a similar name. It meant the pilots could have caused the crash by setting the plane incorrectly for landing.

There were even notes on that particular page. But when the handwriting was analyzed, it did not match that of any of the pilots. And in any case the plane had been making a correct descent, using visual cues like lights on the runway that were not subject to any manual.

The puzzle boiled down to a silent period between the *Albertina*'s last communication with the tower at Ndola, at ten minutes past midnight, and the crash itself a few minutes later. The report, which called the crash an accident in its title, was keen to dismiss the idea, suggested by seven different witnesses, that this period had included another plane.

"At the outset we would say that no reason was suggested, and we cannot think of one, why anyone who might have been able to attack this aircraft from the air should ever have wanted to attack it as it carried Mr. Hammarskjöld on the mission he was then undertaking," it said. "We have investigated the position of aircraft capable of offensive action not because of suggestions that there was such action but to eliminate any known aircraft within range."

If the plane had been attacked, it said, it should have communicated that with the tower. It did not. And it suggested that no pilot would have been able to find and target the *Albertina*, given the short window of time it had to do so.

It then listed a cursory survey of fighter aircraft available in the area, and said that in the most likely case—the single Fouga available to the mercenaries—its pilot had told them repeatedly he had not been up that night, and that they trusted him.

Trust seems to have been an important quality for the Rhodesians sifting this mountain of evidence. They went to great lengths to dismiss the character and recollection of each of the seven witnesses who had seen something different.

"This witness was completely unreliable," the report's authors said of William Chappell, a local resident who had heard two planes. "He contradicted himself again and again, and gave evidence in a most unconvincing manner."

The three charcoal burners who had first seen the wreck, Moyo, Daka, and Banda, "were unsatisfactory. Apart from that finding, their evidence discloses so improbable an attack that it could carry no weight." The former air force signalman, Kankasa, must have mistaken the *Albertina*'s own tail for another plane, it said.

Yet another witness, Buleni, was dismissed as not reliable.

Mazibisa and Simango, whom Virving had questioned again outside the courthouse, had both said they had seen another plane. But Mazibisa "was not impressive," it said. The explosions he heard must have been the cartridges popping in the fire that followed the crash. Simango was "very vague" and had also likely mistaken the tail of the *Albertina* for a second plane.

It laid out a conclusion that its authors felt was far more plausible. After the *Albertina* had passed the lights of Ndola and turned back toward it, the topography of the area at night dictated that the pilots would have seen only blackness ahead.

"This is what is known in the language of the air as a 'black hole,'" it explained. "And if in the course of the turn the aircraft came far too low the slight rise in the ground between the place of the crash and the airport would obscure the lights of the runway, and of Ndola."

The authors of the report had been urged to consider other causes, they wrote. But "the conclusion to which we are forced is that the aircraft was allowed by the pilots to descend too low so that it struck the trees and was brought to the ground."

Chapter 19

"Position L"

The Swedish foreign ministry is a rectangular box of a building with large windows framed by ornate pillars. Its grand, arched entrance, surrounded by flagpoles, overlooks a cobbled Stockholm plaza and a statue of the legendary Swedish king Gustav II Adolf.

In 1962, a few months after the Rhodesian report had been released, Bo Virving waited anxiously inside, under the cold gloom of double-height ceilings. He heard steps on the stone floor, and a polite functionary led him from the lobby, through a maze of paneled corridors, up narrow wooden stairs, and into an elaborately decorated office built on the scale of a small cathedral.

He placed a sheaf of papers on the table, sat down, and began to present an argument he felt sure would move the Swedish government to bring its resources to bear in the case of Hammarskjöld's murder.

Virving had grown obsessed with finding a theory to explain the blank spot at the heart of the Rhodesian report: the silent minutes before the *Albertina* crashed. And after endless hours of work, his living room covered in maps, marker pens, and sheets of acetate, he had come upon one.

His task had been made easier by the fact that the top-secret underlying evidence the Rhodesian report had been based on—reams of typewritten paper, maps, and confidential intelligence reports—was held in two places. One copy was locked up safely in Salisbury, the capital of the Federation of Rhodesia and Nyasaland. The other was spilling out of an increasingly tired and sagging white cardboard box, which had originally contained fifteen packages of instant macaroni and cheese, in Virving's house in Sweden.

He had begun to gather it in Ndola. Sifting it all was a problem that he came to see as partly very human and partly mathematical. A puzzle that had to reconcile each known factor: the perspective of each witness, the bursts of radio communication the *Albertina* had shared with air traffic controllers, the statements of Harold Julien, and the technical capabilities of both the DC-6 and any other planes that might have been in the sky that night.

He told the Swedish officials that his work had begun outside of the courthouse in January 1962, when he had spoken with one of the key witnesses, Simango. "Undoubtedly he had seen two aircraft," Virving said. And Simango had added a new and crucial detail. "Amongst other things he said that the flash he saw was moving fast like a fire arrow pointing slightly downwards and almost immediately thereafter came the crash."

That flash had pushed Virving to concentrate on one theory out of the possibilities, he explained: that a mercenary plane had attacked or attempted to divert the *Albertina* before it landed.

Hammarskjöld's plane had departed Leopoldville at 1751 Ndola time. The Rhodesians had presumed that because it filed a fake flight plan, none of its enemies could possibly have known where it was going, and when it might arrive—crucial information for any attack. (Even a bomb planted in the hold would require timing for a midair explosion.)

But it was broadly known in Congolese political circles, not noted for their discretion, that Hammarskjöld was scheduled to meet with Tshombe. And that he would fly on the *Albertina*. It was entirely plausible, Virving said, that intelligence about the flight was sent directly from Leopoldville to Katanga by one of many Katangese sources on the ground.

Even presuming perfect secrecy on takeoff, Virving explained, did not justify the Rhodesian theory that the *Albertina* had appeared out of nowhere in Ndola like an apparition. Because at 2200 Ndola time, the *Albertina* had received a request for information from flight controllers in Salisbury, the Rhodesian capital.

"SE-BDY from Leopoldville for Ndola," it replied, giving its estimated time of arrival, or ETA, as "2235 [0035 Ndola time] aircraft DC6." Six minutes later it confirmed its position over Lake Tanganyika, and continued communicating with Salisbury and Ndola. At 2331 it updated its ETA to 0020. All of this communication was easy to overhear by radio from Katanga, Virving noted, in plenty of time for Katangese intelligence to send aircraft to intercept.

The Katangese air force was held to be deeply limited; no more than two dozen planes, only half of them suitable for attack, and two helicopters. Its pilots were reputed to be erratic, and its equipment antiquated. Tshombe had wanted to improve it but was banned from buying more planes on the international market while he was at war with the Congolese central government and the UN.

But Virving presented the ministry with a copy of a secret UN intelligence assessment of Katangese and mercenary airpower that gave a very different picture. UN intelligence officers found that Union Minière's technicians, with a company foundry at their disposal, had been modifying Katangese transportation and utility planes so they, too, boasted machine guns and racks full of aerial bombs.

One of the Katangese planes had been fitted with an advanced radio compass, which would have made precise interception much easier. There was evidence that the mercenaries had installed, or

planned to install, airfield lighting to enable them to take off and
land at night.

The Rhodesians had suggested that only one Fouga Magister
jet fighter had been operational. But Tshombe had been a canny
black-market dealer. In collaboration with the governments of
Angola, South Africa, and Rhodesia itself, he had secretly bought
more than a dozen planes. Among them was at least one other
Fouga Magister.

At around the time of the crash, one of the Katangese Fougas
was used for interceptions. Its job was to wait for a radio signal
from military intelligence, scramble to a location, climb to high
altitude, and circle to wait for a second signal in order to dive
down and attack UN aircraft.

Virving told the officials that he had pored over the thick
sheaf of original witness statements—the long dialogues between
investigators and witnesses that had been reduced to quotes and
dismissals in the official report.

He felt that witnesses could be relied upon to know what they
saw and heard in broad terms. But they could not reasonably be
expected, as the Rhodesian investigators had asked, to recall precisely the location of the lights on a moving plane, differentiate
various types of engine, or give time or direction with any great
precision. So he focused on leaving aside their interpretations and
extracting only what they themselves had seen.

And he realized that the investigators had missed a crucial
trick. He took beautiful, large-scale maps of the area around
Ndola, and several sheets of clear celluloid film. He laid one sheet
of celluloid at a time over the map. On each he plotted, using thick
pens, the location of one witness at around midnight on September 17, 1961, the direction that witness was facing, and what they
had described happening in the skies. When he lay them on top
of each other, one set of intersecting lines formed a picture of the

last known route of the *Albertina*. Another set of clustered lines showed the potential path of an attack aircraft.

Next, he plotted the speed and range of the available mercenary aircraft on new transparencies. If the mercenaries had overheard the *Albertina*'s communications with air traffic control at 2200 and 2241, Virving estimated they could have dispatched a plane from one of their airfields by 2245 on a mission to attack or divert it.

If he estimated that attack plane's speed at a very conservative 155 miles per hour, which allowed for either one of the Fougas or a propeller plane like a de Havilland Dove, he found that it would have arrived just south of Ndola an hour later, or about fifteen minutes before the *Albertina*.

That matched the moment that several witnesses, plotted carefully on Virving's maps, had heard a plane overhead. He marked a range for that plane—a line of a couple of miles to represent a holding pattern—and marked it with the letter M.

Witness testimony placed the *Albertina* at the western end of the runway, traveling at about 185 miles per hour, at virtually the same time, shortly after midnight. He marked that as position L. It was the place, and the moment, at which the *Albertina* changed from a plane coming in to land to one that was crashing. The midair scene of the crime.

One witness between M and L had described a roar there and then, tracking from south to north. Virving felt he knew that sound. When one plane attempts to intercept another, the pilot nearly always misjudges the exact distance from the target, falls short, and needs to push the throttle to catch up.

Then, Virving theorized, the attacking plane dropped two bombs, or two grenades, toward the *Albertina*. The flashes that six of the witnesses, plotted in a little circle around position L, saw in the sky timed and located precisely with two bombs detonated at altitude. But, Virving said, they did not hit, or at least did not damage the plane.

Hammarskjöld and the others aboard must have heard and felt the explosions, and seen them out of the plane's windows. It would explain, Virving said, Harold Julien's statement that Hammarskjöld had said to "go back." He might, on seeing they were in danger, either have ordered the pilots to turn the plane back, or asked the passengers to get to the back of the cabin where they'd be slightly safer in the event of a crash.

The captain, Per Hallonqvist, whose fear of attack had been realized, might have attempted a quicker landing. That would have explained why he didn't have time to alert the tower or turn off his navigation lights. It would also explain Julien's recollection of the great speed that followed.

The attacking plane must have broken left after it had dropped its bombs, on a westerly course, to see what effect its attack had. It likely turned back just as the *Albertina* was making its final turn for landing and, with another bomb, caused the pilots to lose control and crash into the forest.

In total eight witnesses provided evidence of sounds or lights that Virving believed tracked with his theory. The incident had been most clearly seen, he believed, by the two men he had interviewed outside the court—Mazibisa and Simango, the latter of which had described "a white flash" followed by "an explosion."

When he plotted the attacking plane's likely path to Ndola from mercenary airfields, he found that it followed railroad tracks on the ground. UN investigators had found Katangese air force maps that advised its pilots to navigate by doing exactly this, and had marked the routes of the tracks in pen to make it easier.

Virving had one piece of information left to reveal to the foreign ministry officials. One he felt proved his case beyond doubt. The watches of the passengers on board the plane had been disabled not by the impact of the crash, but by the heat from the fire that followed it, Virving explained. That would have taken about a minute.

If the timing of his reconstruction was correct it would mean that they should have stopped, on average, at nine minutes past midnight and twenty-five seconds. When he analyzed the data from the watches, he found that the time matched exactly.

Virving had hoped for excitement. For recognition. For a team to begin work re-examining the crash. He was met with Scandinavian reserve, and the creeping sense—tantamount to death in Swedish culture—that he had embarrassed himself. Eventually someone from the ministry suggested, tactfully, that it might be better if he left the issue of the crash of the *Albertina* alone.

Von Rosen presented a similar case to the UN. When he emerged from the meeting, he was shaken. He had been told, he said, that re-opening the crash of the *Albertina* risked a global war and that he should drop the matter.

Chapter 20

"Other and more logical explanations"

The Federation of Rhodesia and Nyasaland had hoped that its investigations into the crash of the *Albertina* would draw precisely the reaction Virving had received from the Swedish government: Pilot error. Nothing to see here.

It was an eminently plausible conclusion. Flying in Africa was a dangerous business in 1961. Planes went down all the time. When they did, their loss was often cloaked in the kind of mystery inevitable on a huge, sparsely populated landmass with inconsistent aviation infrastructure.

But the report had not examined any of the groups in and around the Congo with an interest in Hammarskjöld's movements on the night of the crash. The white supremacist Katangese mercenaries. The French Special Forces soldiers who led them. The spies from Britain, America, Russia, and elsewhere. The companies Union Minière and Tanganyika Concessions.

It was fertile territory. And in the weeks and months after the Federation's report was released, fragments of both real evidence and outlandish notions emerged from it.

In January 1962, a Danish journalist floated the "seventeenth man" theory. His story posited that a hijacker had crept aboard the

Albertina, and that the crash happened when he had tried to wrestle control of the plane from its pilots. Some Rhodesians believed that Hammarskjöld had been working covertly on behalf of the Swedish and American governments to secure mining interests in Katanga, and they had killed him to keep the secret.

Ivan Smith, meanwhile, had uncovered his own theory. He had sparked up a friendship—one that would last a lifetime—with Conor Cruise O'Brien, the UN and Hammarskjöld's former representative in Katanga. And he began to visit the Elephant and Castle bar in Ndola, the informal club for the leadership of the Katangese military. It was owned by the former mayor of Ndola and his brother, the official executioner for the area. (His party trick was sizing people up for hanging.) There he got to know the flamboyant, deadly soldiers, pilots, and miscellaneous eccentrics who had been fighting the UN by any means they could think of, as long as the paychecks kept arriving from Tshombe.

Among them was an all-purpose fixer and sometime journalist named Roger Asonong. Asonong told him that a group of far-right European soldiers, led by a white mercenary named Van Rooy, had been involved in Ivan Smith's kidnapping. It heightened his sense that the same group, or a similarly motivated one, had also targeted Hammarskjöld.

Another source had told him that, during September 1961, those same mercenaries had maintained a helicopter connection between their Elisabethville operations and Ndola. It suggested, circumstantially, that the soldiers had at least been focused on the meeting between Hammarskjöld and Tshombe. And it chimed with information Ivan Smith had received from Hammarskjöld's nephew, Knut.

He told Ivan Smith that Colonel Faulques, the brutal and ascetic French commando who had essentially run the Katangese guerrilla operation, had been based in Ndola himself that month, with three other senior operatives.

The Federation had simply never looked into such leads. Its investigators had barely gone beyond the wreckage. In fact, its government had quietly tried to stop the UN mounting its own investigation to avoid further scrutiny. But its pressure and persuasion had failed.

A specialist UN team re-examined the site of the crash and sifted the wreckage once more. It interviewed nearly a hundred witnesses. They included many of those who had seen the plane in its last moments, air traffic control crew and airport staff, the police officers who had first reached the scene, and the medical personnel who had cared for Harold Julien. A quarter of them had not given evidence before. And in April 1962, it released its report. It was a moment of hope for Ivan Smith, Virving, and others who did not believe the official account.

The UN investigators dismissed the "seventeenth man" theory. Nobody had seen or heard anything to indicate that a hijacker might have sneaked on board the plane. Besides, no extra body had been found in the wreckage.

The report did note that a saboteur would theoretically have been able to access the *Albertina*'s hydraulic compartment, heating system, or undercarriage without detection as it waited unattended on the tarmac in Leopoldville before embarking.

But there was no evidence that the plane had been damaged deliberately. It was flying perfectly before the crash. And anyone trying to plant a bomb, the UN decided, would have needed to know that the *Albertina* was flying a longer route—five hours, not four—in order to time a detonation.

The only planted explosive that might have worked would be one specially—and expensively—designed to detonate by connection with the undercarriage, flaps, lights, or anything else that was activated at landing. There had been no evidence of an explosion, the UN report reiterated. But several witnesses had seen a flash or flames.

The UN had re-created the crash, as seen from the ground, by placing each of the key witnesses in their positions that night and flying test planes along the route of the *Albertina*. That exercise was calculated to help consider the idea that another plane had shot, or forced, the *Albertina* down.

No radar was operating around Ndola that night, so the possibility of an unannounced plane in the sky could not be ruled out. And the UN investigation had found two new witnesses who had seen another aircraft.

But the UN, like the Rhodesian investigators, did not trust those witnesses. They must have been mistaken, the report said. Perhaps they had compressed in their memories events that happened over a longer time period. Some of them expressed anti-federation feeling, and so their statements might have been colored by politics, too. Virving's theory, the investigators felt, was simply too complex. The events he documented were "susceptible of other and more logical explanations."

The most likely cause, the UN report concluded, lay in the landing charts given to the pilots. These were usually marked with terrain contours and spot heights where significant, so pilots could consider the topography before landing. But on the Ndola chart, the report found, neither contours nor elevations had been marked at the point the *Albertina* had crashed.

The British Foreign Office, aligned with the Rhodesian Federation, had pressured the UN to attribute the crash to pilot error. But, instead, it returned an open verdict. That meant that, should new evidence emerge, it was willing to re-assess.

The first book on the crash, which came out that August, reached a similar conclusion.

The Mysterious Death of Dag Hammarskjöld, by a veteran diplomatic correspondent, Arthur Gavshon, pointed out that the inquiries conducted so far had utterly failed to take the broader context of the conflict in Katanga into account. The book cemented the crash, one reviewer noted, in the "realm of myth and mystery."

One of the UN's investigators, Hugo Blandori, a dashing former FBI agent who smoked a spectacular curved pipe, had put together his own narrower but far more detailed report. Eleven typewritten pages, detailing the new facts he had gathered. One section stands out. It centers on a visit to one of Harold Julien's doctors, Mark Lowenthal, at his home.

Lowenthal had given evidence that Julien had been lucid after the crash. But the doctor's account had been dismissed by the Rhodesians. Lowenthal was simply not credible, the authors of the Rhodesian report had felt. And so Lowenthal wanted to clarify, to Blandori, two points about the soldier's last days.

As soon as Julien had arrived at the hospital, Lowenthal said, he had personally administered a plasma transfusion into his right arm. Doctor and patient had been very close to each other, a moment of peace in the crash's aftermath. Julien did not have to strain either to talk or to listen. And so their conversations were quiet, and calm, and not overheard by any of the hospital staff.

The Rhodesians presumed Julien had given his abstract recollections of the crash after being administered pethidine, a powerful opioid painkiller that acts quickly but can induce delirium. This was not the case, Lowenthal told Blandori. Julien was not administered pethidine until after Lowenthal had given the plasma infusion. His recollections were colored by pain and trauma, but not powerful drugs.

Ivan Smith had used his new connections to secure a tape of Julien's interview with the Rhodesian police. He felt that Julien could not be dismissed as delirious even after the drug was administered. There was something about the clear and detailed way he gave his name, address, and telephone number that made it seem, to Ivan Smith, as though he was absolutely coherent.

Most gallingly, for Ivan Smith and the others who had known

those aboard, the report detailed the missed opportunities to find the *Albertina* before daybreak. It also found that, contrary to the Rhodesian accounts, Hammarskjöld's death was probably not mercifully instantaneous. He had grasped at the grasses and plants growing underneath him. Ivan Smith knew, at last, that his friend had died alone in the forest between midnight and 3 p.m. the next day.

There were, when all the confusion and misdirection had been pushed aside, four fundamental possibilities left. The first, pushed hard by the Rhodesians, was that the crash of the *Albertina* had simply been an accident. The second was that something on board the plane—a hijacker, or a bomb—had caused it to crash. The third was that gunfire, or other ground attack, had brought it down. And the fourth was aerial interference; the presence of another plane, perhaps hostile.

Every straight line Ivan Smith had found through the thicket of clues pointed in one direction: the Rhodesian Federation itself. There was, he realized, an essential conflict of interest. The Federation had overseen the inquiries but had also supported the mercenaries and hated Hammarskjöld. It was supported, in turn, by the British, who very much wanted the entire issue to go away.

The Rhodesians simply must have known more than they were saying. And so he began what would become a lifelong relationship with a man who had stood against the UN and Hammarskjöld. Sir Roy Welensky, the prime minister of the Federation of Rhodesia and Nyasaland.

Chapter 21

"I have never been hit so hard in my life before"

Roy Welensky weighed nearly three hundred pounds. His jaw jutted forward accusingly, his bushy eyebrows bristled, and his receding hair was fashioned into a small quiff, like a question mark floating above him.

His size belied a speed and strength he had developed in his youth, on the way to becoming the national heavyweight boxing champion for Northern and Southern Rhodesia—no small feat in nations well stocked with tough, violent men. He retained a boxer's ability to get hit and remain calm.

He had grown up poor in Harare, now the capital of Zimbabwe, the seventh child of a Lithuanian Jewish father and a white South African mother. He left school at fifteen, in 1922 (by which time he was already 250 pounds), got a job working on the railways, and joined the union. He proved such an effective negotiator that he transitioned into politics in 1938, founded the Northern Rhodesian Labour Party in 1941, and was elected prime minister in 1956.

In 1961, Welensky's stated aim was for a transitional white government to ease the way for black governance. It meant that he saw a seceded Katanga, which operated mostly under the control of white advisers, as broadly a good thing—a bulwark, or an ally. Those who sought black African governance as a civil right hated him for it.

He had supported Tshombe, to the extent that he effectively spied for the Katangese, allowed free passage for mercenaries, and helped supply war matériel including planes. In one letter to relatives he compared the UN, and its efforts to remove Tshombe's mercenaries from Katanga and reunite the Congo, to Hitler and Stalin. "Where is all this leading us?" he asked rhetorically, in one message. "I think there can be only one answer—to a third world war."

He played dirty, too. He joked in one note to his intelligence chief that the "disappearance" of two teachers who were avowed black nationalists "had the most salutary effect on the rest of the teachers." He was smart enough to leave the comment at that, in writing at least. But after a while, black Africans in and around Rhodesia began calling anyone mean or violent a "Welensky."

He maintained connections with a network of white supremacist mercenaries and intelligence operatives, many of them British, and far-right lawmakers of Britain's ruling Conservative Party. And he was not scared to express his loathing for the UN and Hammarskjöld.

In April 1961, he told the British foreign secretary, Alec Douglas-Home, that he would do anything in his power to stop Tshombe being felled by "Afro Asian pressures masquerading as UN operations," and that he was willing to face the consequences for those actions.

Welensky was careful not to write down what he had in mind. But he hinted. He spoke of his dislike of Hammarskjöld. He promised to explain to one friend "the extent to which I have gone" in support of Tshombe. And two weeks before the crash of the *Albertina*, he wrote that he'd be willing to go to "the bitter end" on the issue of the UN and Katanga.

After the UN stepped up its operations against the mercenaries in September 1961, Welensky sent his elite troops, and virtually his entire air force, to the border with Katanga. Hundreds of soldiers, and dozens of planes, had been there on the night Hammarskjöld had died.

In the days after the crash, suspicion had immediately turned toward Welensky, in cahoots with Britain. It had felt, to him, as though black Africa was about to declare war on the Federation. He hotly denied any culpability or inside knowledge.

But privately he had few illusions about Katanga. In a letter the day after the wreckage of the *Albertina* had been discovered, he told relatives that he felt that "someone may have put a little package on board at Leopoldville." He never mentioned this theory again.*

Ivan Smith suspected Welensky knew much more than he was saying about Hammarskjöld's death, if not the whole story. He was an active and well-informed prime minister who did not like to be kept in the dark. He must have been involved from the moments after the *Albertina* disappeared, through the delayed search—which had been ordered from Salisbury, his base of operations, not from Ndola—and the subsequent investigations. He was also closely linked to the mercenary forces in Katanga, to Union Minière, and to the British government. If there were bodies buried, Ivan Smith felt, literal or metaphorical, Welensky must be persuaded to dig them up.

By 1962, Ivan Smith oversaw the region around the southern tip of the Congo for the UN Technical Assistance Board—a body that provides non-financial help, often in the form of expert guidance on governance. It gave him a good reason to visit the federation and Welensky and begin a painstaking, decades-long fight for information.

---

* Or not in any way that has been recorded, at least.

After his first trip that year, he wrote Welensky a letter to thank him for his hospitality. "I gather we share a common interest in boxing," he wrote. He told Welensky of his father's prowess in the ring, and the fact that he himself had been forced to face a barrage of visiting heavyweights as a boy. And he included a story about the former English boxing champion, Jem Mace, famed in the Victorian era for his technique.

The anecdote came from James Corbett, an American heavyweight champion around the turn of the twentieth century, who had won a fight in London and then gone to see Mace, by then retired and in his ninth decade and running a small pub outside of London.

Mace had taken him down a corridor next to the bar, and unchained a door to reveal a boxing ring inside. He asked Corbett to step into the ring. Corbett, to humor the old man, did so. Mace stepped in after him. He asked Corbett to punch him. "I did," Corbett said, "and am telling the truth when I say that the next thing I remember was waking up . . . where a man of 90 could pull a punch of that kind from I have no idea, but I have never been hit so hard in my life before."

More than raw power, which is an accident of nature, boxers admire superior technique—the kind that allows a ninety-year-old man to knock out a champion. Welensky loved the story. In his reply, he first briefly thanked Ivan Smith for his visit. "Now to come to the part of your letter which is sheer joy to me, the subject of boxing," he wrote. He went on to talk as one sports fan talks to another, in a barrage of names, assessments, anecdotes, and analyses. He invited Ivan Smith to visit him again, when he could arrange for a private screening of boxing films held in the government archives.

It marked the beginning of Ivan Smith's last bout with an old heavyweight. Letters between the two show Ivan Smith cajoling Welensky, no mean fighter, toward the corner of the ring in an attempt to break a vital source.

He shared minor confidences, for which he apologized, but added that he was only doing so because he wanted to encourage a full and frank exchange. He appealed to history, or at least the duty to leave behind an accurate record, and implied his aim was only to exonerate Rhodesia and Welensky himself of responsibility for the crash.

Welensky's letters took on a warmer tone. "My Dear George," he wrote in November 1962, "I thoroughly enjoyed the lunch the other day, and if I may say you made quite the impression on my son. I don't have to tell you that you have whetted our appetites for a bit of sea fishing."

Both men explained the misconceptions that surrounded them. When Welensky stepped down in 1963, the end of the federation, Ivan Smith sent him a letter praising his dignity and asking after his wife, who had recently been unwell.

The connection paid off. In a letter to another friend, Ivan Smith revealed that he and Welensky had privately been "able to discuss the whole of the Katanga operation in a way that was very profitable from my side."

Ivan Smith said he had now learned of another active group of Katangese soldiers which also had a motivation for targeting Hammarskjöld. He described them as "French mercenaries," numbering about twenty-five, who fought for themselves. "They felt that if they could show how to lead a 'victory' over the UN . . . they would be able to appeal to other extremists in the Rhodesias, Angola and South Africa. They had in mind to assist such extreme elements to prepare a last line of continental defense behind which a 'white man supremacy' could be preserved."

Ivan Smith was not alone in turning his focus to France.

Chapter 22

"Oh my God, they've done it!"

Mid-September 1961. A few days before Hammarskjöld dies. Moïse Tshombe sits in an easy chair, still safe in Katanga, and reads an illustrated newspaper. A spotlight falls upon him. And then the telephone begins to ring. An emissary for Hammarskjöld. The two talk briefly, and arrange the meeting at Ndola.

Tshombe hangs up the phone. Then he picks it up again and calls his interior minister—the feared Godefroid Munongo, sitting by his own phone, under his own spotlight, with a French soldier, Colonel Zbyre, by his side.

"Listen, Godefroid," Tshombe says. "That Swede. You know? He's coming to see me. He's throwing in the sponge! What do you think of that?"

"Nothing. How is he traveling?"

"To Ndola airport. On the seventeenth. His own aircraft, I suppose—the DC-6."

"How many in the crew? How many passengers?"

"I don't know, what does it matter? The main thing is . . ."

Tshombe sits up suddenly. His voice grows urgent. "Godefroid! Godefroid! Are you there?"

"Yes, Moïse; you sound excited. You should avoid excitement, you know."

"Godefroid, for God's sake, no tricks. Godefroid! Godefroid! Please!"

Munongo chuckled. "Take it easy Moïse—calm yourself. After all, *you* won't be on the plane."

He replaces the telephone and does a small war dance with Colonel Zbyre, who then squats and drives his bayonet into the ground.

"Can you be sure of getting him alive?" Munongo asks Zbyre.

"He presents himself favorable ... Of course, you can never be sure. We got Ben Bella. We missed Salan. We got Moumié. We missed de Gaulle. We got Mattei. Yes, we missed de Gaulle ... but the terrain here is, as you say, conducive ... Congo is provincial and also unappetizing. But is a first-rate terrain for assassination and also kidnapping."

"How, this time?"

"Our boys in Leo know what they have to do, once they get the signal. If they can, they put specialist on board plane."

"Specialist in what?"

"Kidnapping. The hijack. We have good man there—Roger Gheyssels. It is a Fleming, of course. But is trained—knows job. We get him on plane. Hammarskjöld gets in. Flight toward Ndola. Very nice, very tranquil. Then, just preparing to land, Monsieur Gheyssels puts pistol in the back of pilot's neck and he say very politely: 'I am sorry, sir, there is a little changement in flight plan. It is not Ndola any more. It is Kolwezi—K-O-L-W-E-Z-I—Kolwezi.' And pilot, he say: 'But Kolwezi is in the hands of Tshombe mercenaries!' And maybe Gheyssels, if he has time he says: 'Those you call mercenaries, sir, are the last idealists, the last *chevalerie* of the age!' Or maybe he just push pistol harder in pilot's neck. So they do not land at Ndola. They do not meet all these nice bourgeois and English milords. They do not make a nice deal. They land at Kolwezi and meet some very nasty pipple. You for example. Me for example ..."

The two men laugh.

"Of course, it may not work like that. Maybe someone just hits Gheyssels on the head and shoves him in the compartment with the valises. Or maybe Gheyssels must shoot pilot. Or maybe there is a big *bagarre* and they all crash. But are many chances for something interesting to happen."

Later, while waiting for Hammarskjöld's plane to land, Tshombe watches a brilliant flash, followed by a sustained orange glow in the distance.

"Oh my God, they've done it!"

———

A powder-blue velvet curtain, tasseled with gold, fell. The eight hundred or so people attending the Broadway opening of Conor Cruise O'Brien's play *Murderous Angels* applauded and then stood and began to gather their coats and hats.

It was December 20, 1971, a decade after Hammarskjöld had died. The crash had entered the pantheon of endlessly debated recent-historical controversies. And as the crowd milled into the marble lobby of the Playhouse Theatre for a cigarette, or filed out onto a blustery 48th Street, they mulled what they had seen. Some enjoyed the poetic recounting of real events. A few were stony with outrage at the liberties taken with history by a man who ought to know better.

O'Brien, an Irish historian, writer, politician, and diplomat, had been Hammarskjöld's special representative to Katanga. Now into his sixth decade, he was ruddy-faced, with a mop of dark hair that managed to look bookishly outraged all on its own. The nicknames his colleagues, friends, and enemies had given him across his career—the cruiser, the bruiser, Conor Cruise O'Booze, Camera Crews O'Brien—revealed a passion for firsthand experience rare in a poetic soul, and a desire to communicate his own bravery as often as possible.

Murderous Angels was based on the accusation, hotly denied, and with little backing from historians, that Hammarskjöld had brought about the downfall of Patrice Lumumba and then refrained from preventing his death. That, O'Brien theorized, had precipitated the events that would lead to the crash of the *Albertina*.

During its short run of a month or so into 1972, the play became a matter of public intrigue. Did O'Brien know something nobody else did? What was fact, and what was fiction? Was it okay to blend the two?

"It is a good, controversial political play—it excites the mind and certainly deserves to be seen," the *New York Times* wrote in its review. But, it added, "Mr. O'Brien would have done better to have told his story of these murderous angels as honest fiction and left people to place what assumptions they liked upon it." Another reviewer accused O'Brien of playing " 'God+,' imagining sequences of events that may or may not have occurred."

In the printed edition of the play, O'Brien included a lengthy preface and notes that defended and justified his decisions. Hammarskjöld, he said, speaking from firsthand experience, genuinely feared that the Congo might become Spain, or Korea: a local dispute that would draw the rest of the world into a nuclear-armed war. He also felt that he had to sell the role of the UN to reluctant world leaders, which in practical terms meant playing up geopolitical dangers. The combination gave events in Katanga a fevered atmosphere. That, in turn, meant the events he described were more than plausible, he said.

He also revealed the source for the hijacking scene that ended the play: a book, *Notre Guerre au Katanga* (Our War in Katanga),* that had come out quietly during the 1960s in French. It was co-authored by two leaders of the group of French mercenaries— the same group that Ivan Smith had heard about from Welensky.

The first was the French guerrilla warfare theorist Roger Trin-

---

* It is not clear how O'Brien came across it. But he had been a counselor to the Irish embassy in Paris before he joined the UN, and he retained connections in the city.

quier, the former schoolteacher who had been the literal leader of Tshombe's forces until he had been expelled, and its spiritual leader and chief strategist after that. The second was Jacques Duchemin, the undersecretary of defense for the Katangese government and the man in charge of the forces aligned against Hammarskjöld.

The hijacker theory came from Duchemin. According to his account, Tshombe had been intrigued to discover that Hammarskjöld's older brother, Bo, worked for a mining company. He began to suspect that the brothers were after Katanga's mineral wealth for themselves.

The Katangese president had been shaving one day when he resolved to have Hammarskjöld's plane hijacked by a Belgian pilot named Réné Gheysels. The aim was to get Hammarskjöld to divert the *Albertina* to the mercenary airfield at Kolwezi, in Rhodesia and outside of UN control.

When he arrived, he'd be held hostage until he agreed to a resolution on Katanga's terms.

By Duchemin's account, Gheysels had successfully sneaked aboard the *Albertina* at Leopoldville and hidden until the plane was close to landing. When he emerged, there was a struggle aboard. The pilot had banked the plane to throw the hijacker off balance, and had crashed in the process.

Other UN officials who had been in Katanga felt the idea was ridiculous. Duchemin had been in Paris on the night of the crash and had heard the story secondhand. And it was riddled with inconsistencies. The glaring example was that no seventeenth body had been found in the wreckage.

But O'Brien did not trust the Rhodesian police who had discovered the wreck. And even if he did, he wrote, it was not implausible that a body could have been lost amid the flames and destruction.

He thought, too, of a moment he'd shared with Welensky. They'd been discussing the crash, and O'Brien asked about the body count—in pursuit of his theory there might have been a hijacker, and therefore an extra body. Welensky gave a big, shark-like smile and said, "Was it 14, or 15?" The number was incorrect—it had been sixteen—but the implication was clear.

He also pointed out that air kidnapping, by means of hijack, had been briefly in vogue at around the time of the crash. He cited a particularly relevant example. Ahmed Ben Bella, an Algerian leader who had become the symbol for resistance against the French, had been kidnapped by the French crew of a flight from Rabat to Tunis in 1956. Ben Bella was held in France—a significant victory for Paris, which denied Algerian forces a charismatic and tough leader—until the war in Algeria ended.*

When that story had first been revealed, he said, it had been seen as absurd, too. And because *Notre Guerre au Katanga* had come out after the Rhodesian and UN investigations had concluded, nobody had ever seriously looked into the hijack theory.

Ultimately, O'Brien concluded, it had to be taken seriously that Hammarskjöld's death, during a hijacking, had been proclaimed as an exploit of Tshombe's forces by Duchemin, the man who was in charge of those forces. But even if one chose to disregard that fact, it was undisputed that the *Albertina* had been unsecured on the runway at Leopoldville. And so, if nothing else, hijacking had to be investigated as a possibility.

There had previously been a mysterious—almost poetic—corroboration of the idea that the French white supremacist forces had been closely involved. A dispatch from the UN in Leopoldville in early 1962, just a few months after the crash, noted that the nickname for the French group of about forty soldiers Duchemin and Trinquier headed had changed recently. It was now called "the crash group." No explanation was given.

---

* He became Algeria's first president, and survived at least two French assassination attempts.

Chapter 23

"I need your help desperately on this"

By 1971, Ivan Smith was director of the UN's information center in London. He had also become, in any spare moment, the informal head of a group of Hammarskjöld's prominent associates who continued to gather evidence on the crash.

He worked from a chaotic study on the ground floor of his home, on a farm in Stroud, Gloucestershire, overlooking a rolling green valley and a village of pale limestone houses in the distance. His chief tool was an Olivetti typewriter, surrounded by fallen piles of photographs and books on a leather-topped desk.

He decided that the time was right to air what he had found. He agreed to appear in a BBC documentary exploring the idea that the crash had been a murder, not an accident.

"Enough evidence has come to my notice," Ivan Smith explained, under the gaze of a giant, boxy television camera, "to make me believe that further investigation may well show the reasons for the flying accident were not the ones that many people supposed." Those who had supplied him information, he said, were afraid to speak for themselves.

"Why are they afraid to come forward?" the presenter asked, in clipped BBC English.

"Well I suppose the personal involvement, and in some cases the evidence they offer is not thoroughly tested and in other cases there are some people whom I have spoken to who do have what seems on the surface firmer ground to stand on. They are afraid of the kind of people that might have been involved in an operation of this kind."

"They are afraid of reprisal?"

"Yes."

The burst of public attention shook loose a flurry of letters and leads. A friend wrote to tell him of a conversation with Edward Goodacre, a former British intelligence operative who had been involved in the UN investigation. Goodacre joked he had been "in on the act." Lots of inconvenient facts about the flight, especially those that mitigated against the idea of an accident, he said, had been hushed up.

Ivan Smith and Virving still felt that Welensky held the final threads of the mystery, the ones that could tie their own tantalizing clues together. And by 1976, Ivan Smith felt a fresh urgency. In America, a Senate panel known informally as the Church Committee had just released blockbuster investigations into recent abuses by the CIA, NSA, FBI, and others. They included embarrassing details on the death of Lumumba. If the CIA and SIS had been involved in one elaborate conspiracy in the Congo, was it so unlikely they knew more than they had said about Hammarskjöld? Besides, Ivan Smith had been bedridden with an illness. And Welensky had had a heart attack. Neither man had forever.

Ivan Smith sent Welensky a note of support, along with a book to read while he recuperated. But the letters took on a new tone. "I need your help desperately on this," he wrote. "My health is rotten and it would mean so much for me to get this right in my own mind before I go to my fathers." He asked him to phone, reversing the charges. He asked for access to Welensky's secret papers. Most of all, he begged Welensky to "please help me to solve this. I now have everything except the last links and it has become a point of personal importance—as a close friend of Dag's, to set the record straight."

He had settled on the aerial attack theory. He told Welensky that he knew another plane had been involved on the night of the crash. He suspected that it had evaded detection by using a paved Rhodesian road, instead of an airfield with its guaranteed witnesses and inconvenient records, to take off and land.

His working theory, he said, was that the *Albertina* had been attacked by this mercenary plane. An American official had told him, he wrote to Welensky, that there had been a "U.S. aircraft on the ground passing messages to [Hammarskjöld's] aircraft." Perhaps that American aircraft had spotted the danger and warned the *Albertina* of the threat it was under. Hammarskjöld would likely have ordered the pilots to land anywhere they could. And the crash could have come in all the confusion.

Lastly, he veiled an accusation—that Welensky had been responsible for the delay in beginning the search for the wreckage—as an innocent question. "The puzzle for me, [is] why Williams, the Airport manager, took so long to start the search. It was undertaken at your instigation from Salisbury. Did he know what had happened and was that why he delayed the official search?"

Welensky replied shortly afterward. His tone had shifted. It was cold, dismissive. At points he seemed to sneer. And at others, he lied. He confirmed that an American plane had been on the ground at Ndola, and that it had a "very powerful radio." But he denied everything else.

The two inquiries established that there had been no other plane, he wrote. (One of them had, but not very convincingly, and the other had explicitly not.) If there had been, the odds of it successfully attacking the *Albertina* were astronomical. (This evades the fact that Ivan Smith did not feel the attack had been successful.) There was only one Fouga, he wrote. (Welensky knew that Tshombe had at least two, because he'd helped supply them.) There were no suitable concrete roads near the airport. (Less a lie than a willful misinterpretation.) The search had been delayed simply by confusion. And even if it had gone ahead at night, it would have taken hours to find anything in the dense bush. (Such considerations do not usually stop searches from beginning as soon as possible.)

He offered, brutally for Ivan Smith, who specifically wanted new and unpublished information, to read over the official inquiries again. And he mentioned that recently, a Swedish journalist had come out to Rhodesia to look into the crash, but had found nothing and given up. The implication was that Ivan Smith should do the same.

Ivan Smith replied less than a week later. He tried to put Welensky at ease—to say that he bore no personal blame. It had been mercenaries, he wrote, acting on their own who had killed Hammarskjöld. Tshombe did not control them. And they did not want a cease-fire—some because they didn't want to have to find another war, others, likely French, to push the cause of white supremacy. This was more than theory, Ivan Smith wrote.

He wrote with such confidence because he now had corroboration. Bo Virving had sent, by fax and mail, his entire body of evidence. Every calculation and lead. With it, as a kind of executive summary, came the full report Virving had submitted to the Swedish foreign ministry back in 1962.

Ivan Smith's sureness lent a new tension to the correspondence with Welensky. It increased in 1980, when the Swedish writer and documentarian Gunnar Möllerstedt, an ally of Ivan Smith's, aired a multi-part biographical documentary on Hammarskjöld on Swedish television. It ended with the mercenary theory.

It further emboldened Ivan Smith. He had found out, he wrote to Welensky, that Rhodesia had helped Katanga buy planes. And details from the Kennedy papers, recently made public, showed Welensky asking Tshombe to be more discreet about using Rhodesian roads as landing strips.

"I know without any argument that you could not have been party in even the most remote degree to what happened at Ndola, nor Tshombe," he said. "I want for all our sakes to put the record straight. Please help me to do that."

Shortly afterward, Ivan Smith received a reply. He was surprised to note that it was from Welensky's daughter, also his private secretary. Sir Roy had been taken sick, she wrote, using her father's formal title. Heart trouble. "It is quite likely that Sir Roy will not be dealing with any of his correspondence within a period to be of any assistance to you," she concluded.

The next letter Welensky sent to George Ivan Smith was dictated. And it meant Welensky could no longer effectively disguise his disdain in the ambiguities of written language.

He hated the Swedish documentary. "I understand how the Swedes feel," he dictated, "they really haven't had a hero since Charles XIIth, and of course, it is very difficult to swallow that the death of the one man that they had produced in all these years that has hit the world scene, should have been killed as a result of the error of a Swedish pilot, it is damned difficult to swallow."

Unprompted, perhaps guided by the mysterious mental patterns of the spoken word, he added that "neither Tshombe or I had any reason for wanting the death of Dag Hammarskjöld."

Ivan Smith replied a few days later. The odds of the theory aired in the documentary were high, he said. But "we cannot exclude the possibility of attack by other types of aircraft—indeed a friend of mine has a complete file which I hope to see. He has met two of the pilots who were involved and is in no doubt at all about what happened."

Chapter 24

"The truth about the events"

The story Ivan Smith was referring to began on the evening of Thursday, January 12, 1967, under the soaring frescoed ceilings of the Palais Garnier, the grand opera house in Paris.

Claude de Kemoularia, a French diplomat in his mid-forties with dark, piercing features that betrayed his Georgian heritage, was attending an opulent ball there. As he wandered among the hundreds of Parisians in tuxedos and gowns, sipping champagne on three sweeping marble staircases, he bumped into a man he knew. A harried and bespectacled Paris correspondent for United Press International named Robert Ahier.

By the gentle light of ornate candelabras, they spoke of the waves of chaos and change they felt were washing over the world. Paris itself would soon be riven by riots. De Kemoularia, an adviser to Prince Rainier of Monaco, had been Hammarskjöld's personal assistant until his death. And so the conversation turned, wistfully, to where global geopolitics might have been had he lived.

"Curiously," Ahier said, over the sound of echoing voices, "I have come across a man who claims to know, or pretends to know, the truth about the events." De Kemoularia asked if it would be possible to meet this man.

Ahier said he thought he could trace him, and would try to arrange it. And one Saturday nearly two weeks later, de

Kemoularia was at his Paris office, in a handsome mansion of biscuit-colored stone that had once hosted the wedding of Napoleon Bonaparte and Josephine de Beauharnais, when his phone rang. It was Ahier's source. He named himself, in a Belgian accent, as De Troye.

De Kemoularia asked if De Troye could come by. He gave his address. An hour later, De Troye arrived, with another colleague he named as Grant. (It remains unclear who these men were exactly, but their names match two soldiers who appear in UN records from the Congo, as Major Jacques de Troyer, the commander of the Katangese gendarmerie, and a mercenary fighter, Johan Mawer Grant.)

De Kemoularia concluded immediately, from their rough appearance, that these men were likely mercenaries. They were headed to Marseille, to recruit soldiers for a fight in Angola between the Portuguese colonialists and black independence guerrillas. By coincidence, De Kemoularia was about to depart for Monaco, about two hours from Marseille on the Côte d'Azur in the south of France.

De Kemoularia reserved them a room at the opulent Hotel Metropole, a palatial maze, dotted with lush plants, minutes from the casino in Monte Carlo.* And on Tuesday, January 24, De Troye and Grant arrived at de Kemoularia's home in Monaco as arranged. The men talked all afternoon, and de Kemoularia took meticulous notes.

They kept repeating that it had been an accident. That a mercenary Fouga had brought down the *Albertina*, but that had not been the plan. They knew the pilot who had flown it. They knew who had killed the secretary-general. But he had been flying a different mission.

---

* Monaco is a tiny nation that almost entirely comprises the city of Monte Carlo.

Chapter 25

"Mr. X"

The Congo Crisis had sputtered on for years after Hammar-skjöld's death. On January 14, 1963, Katangese ministers finally declared that the nation's secession had ended. The last mercenaries took refuge in Angola the day after. In February, Tshombe had fled for Northern Rhodesia. He cited poor health. But he also flew bales of money, the equivalent of between $5 and $15 million in contemporary funds, across his borders to be deposited in banks in Geneva and Brussels.

The crisis transformed, eventually, into a rolling civil war. In 1964 the Congolese central government, under Cyrille Adoula, lost control of the country. Another province, Stanleyville, in the east, seceded, and rural insurgencies rose. Tshombe, the man who had himself wanted to split the country apart, was the unlikely rescuer. He returned to be prime minister.

Until November 1965, when Mobutu, the American ally who had headed the army, launched a coup. Tshombe fled, to plot his return. In 1967 he was tried for treason in absentia in the Congo, and sentenced to death. Shortly afterward he himself was kidnapped in midair by a hijacker, a French operative named Fran-çois Bodenan, connected with his country's intelligence services and rumored to have worked with the CIA. Tshombe was flown to Algeria, where he subsequently died.

Mobutu, who wore a leopard-skin hat and carried a traditional symbol of power in the Congo, a carved stick, was beginning to set the clichés for the modern African dictator. His was to become the only political party allowed. He crushed dissent with a combination of violence, cunning, and cash. As he repeated his rallying cry, "Authenticity," he looted the treasury. He was enabled and supported by America, which still considered him an ally in the fight against Communism.

De Kemoularia's main memory of Katanga and Tshombe was chaos. As far as he could recall, back to the early 1960s, the country and its leader had acted one way one day, and another the next. It was erratic, with no obvious strategy.

Over a series of meetings in Monte Carlo and at de Kemoularia's Paris apartment, a luxurious, modern white block overlooking the Bois de Boulogne, De Troye laid out an intricate story. It explained each change of course in Katanga and showed, plausibly, de Kemoularia felt, the unknown danger that Hammarskjöld was flying into. (The other man, Grant, usually stood guard outside.)

It was the first time he had candidly heard the story of Katanga from the perspective of the mercenaries. They called themselves "foreign volunteers" and hated the idea that they were driven only by money, De Troye said. "We're not brigands. Among us there are excellent and good people, medical doctors, professors, ex-military officers, so we were not as bad as [all] that."

The story began four days before the *Albertina* took off, on Wednesday, September 13, 1961. Hammarskjöld was on his way from New York to Leopoldville. UN troops, in an attempt to resolve the situation in Katanga before he arrived, had begun taking aggressive action in two consecutive operations against the mercenary forces—Operation Rumpunch and Operation Morthor.

Tshombe nominally led Katanga, De Troye told de Kemoularia. But in actual fact, he was a dupe. The country was run by a powerful group of about a dozen European advisers, drawn from Belgium, Britain, France, and elsewhere, and representing industry and other European interests in Africa. It was led by a man he would only name as "Mr. X," a European executive who was the functional high commander of the Katangese forces and an adviser of such influence that he was more feared than Tshombe.

He acted independently of the formal Katangese government, working mainly through Munongo—a more ruthless character than Tshombe, according to De Troye. When the UN stepped up operations, Mr. X and his cohort feared it was a dangerous sign for the continued presence of Europeans, both in Katanga and across Africa. The UN was acting, effectively, as an independent force for the reunion of the Congo—somewhat against the will of both the United States and the Soviet Union, and of European business interests. It could not be allowed to stand, for the precedent it might set.

That September, he said, white-led Katangese troops overran a giant and strategically vital air base, Kamina, that was more like a small city, and attacked the UN across Katanga. They shot up UN planes, including an air ambulance.

And they arranged a trap. Europeans in Jadotville, a mining center that was considered Katanga's second city, were tasked with making the UN believe they felt endangered and required protection. A contingent of 150 Irish soldiers arrived that week during Operation Morthor. But they found themselves vastly outnumbered—some figures suggest twenty to one—by Katangese troops, led by white European mercenaries. One of the Fougas screamed over with bombs.

The Irish soldiers, led by a tactically astute commandant, Pat Quinlan, realized quickly they were in trouble and dug in, manning antiquated Gustav machine guns. They fought bravely but were eventually forced to surrender.

It was seen in Ireland, until recently, as a national shame. An act of cowardice. And it called into question the presence of Irish troops among the UN contingent. Which is precisely what the European control group had intended, De Troye said.

The mercenary commanders crowed at their victory. They felt it showed the UN who was in charge, and that they could now negotiate as equals—as opponents worthy of more favorable terms in any cease-fire. So they were elated when Hammarskjöld elected to fly into the heart of their territory—itself a concession, they felt—to talk with Tshombe.

But Tshombe chose that moment to drift away from their influence. He decided to meet with Hammarskjöld without his European advisers present. Hammarskjöld had been excited because he felt an independent negotiation might yield a better outcome for the UN. The group led by Mr. X had made the same analysis, De Troye told de Kemoularia.

The mercenaries had means of tracking UN movements, and they were notified, on Sunday the seventeenth, when the *Albertina* had taken off to bring Hammarskjöld from Leopoldville to Ndola. And it was only then that they decided to act.

The mercenary forces were based at Kolwezi, a mercenary stronghold, but planned to divert Hammarskjöld's plane to Kamina, which was 150 miles from Ndola by air. It had a runway more than adequate for a DC-6, and plenty of buildings for a quiet meeting. They wanted to talk to Hammarskjöld themselves, first, and find a more elegant solution—one in which their power and influence would not wane so quickly as it would with the end of Katanga and the reunification of the Congo.

They scrambled two Fouga Magister jets, each equipped with radar to help locate the *Albertina* and with sophisticated radios that ensured clear midair communication with the plane and with headquarters. The plan was to intercept, then fly in formation around the DC-6 and guide it to Kamina. The European group flew, in another plane, from Kolwezi to Kamina to await their guest. They were kept informed of the *Albertina*'s movements as they waited.

In the modern era, with ubiquitous monitoring of aircraft, it would have been an utterly pointless endeavor. But in the 1960s, the skies were a wilder place.* And though the idea was unorthodox, De Troye and Grant told de Kemoularia, in his Monte Carlo apartment, there was no desire to harm Hammarskjöld. The motivation was not evil.

But one of the pilots who had flown the mission could speak to that, De Troye said. His name was Beukels, a Belgian. De Kemoularia had his doubts about De Troye—he felt he might be trying to secure money for his story, perhaps from Ahier at UPI. So he very much wanted to meet Beukels for himself, to make his own judgment.

On February 8, 1967, De Troye and Grant promised to bring Beukels to de Kemoularia's apartment in Paris. De Troye and Grant showed up without him. They had not been able to arrange it after all, they said. A week later, De Troye called de Kemoularia and told him Grant had gone to Brussels to pick Beukels up. They'd be back in a day or two.

First, De Troye came alone again. He wanted a conversation to prepare the ground for Beukels's arrival, de Kemoularia felt. He said that Hammarskjöld's death had had a severe psychological effect on Beukels. He had dropped in weight from 190 pounds to 110, and was working for a construction company in between attempts to drink himself to death. In fact, that was why he wasn't here now, De Troye said. He'd been drinking and had forgotten the appointment.

De Kemoularia was beginning to feel he was being strung

---

* In fact, the world was about to enter an era of audacious aviation capers. A few years later, the number of hijackings in America alone would spike to one a week, and stay there well into the 1970s.

along, and had to bite his tongue and channel all of the patience he could muster to avoid showing his fury. After De Troye left, at about 5 p.m., de Kemoularia called Ahier.

The reporter agreed that the story required meticulous checking. Not least because he had recently heard from another mercenary that the *Albertina* had been brought down by the white supremacist forces, but in this account it was done with anti-aircraft fire.

Ahier believed, first, that mercenaries were unreliable because they often found themselves in financial trouble, and had a natural tendency to spin schemes that might help them secure money. He felt, second, that all the stories had truth in them, but none had all of it.

The following Monday, De Troye finally brought Beukels. They posted a guard downstairs again—it struck de Kemoularia that he was there as a lookout. The mercenaries feared he might call the authorities and have them arrested for their part in the events they were describing.

Beukels looked as De Troye had described him: worn thin by life and by the torments of his own mind. He had the ambient acetone smell that comes from years of drinking. But to de Kemoularia, as the men sat overlooking the bucolic park, Beukels seemed sincere. Like he wanted to get something off his conscience.

Chapter 26

"If you refuse we have orders to use force"

De Troye and Beukels told de Kemoularia that on the day of the crash, Sunday, September 17, 1961, two Fouga Magister CM.170 jets had sat ready on the runway at the mercenary air base, Kolwezi.

The Fougas were low and narrow with rapier-thin wings and tail fins. Each was armed with 75mm guns. Every fifth bullet was a phosphorous tracer that would carve a bright line in the sky. (It was important that they be visible.) And each had 990 liters of fuel in its main tanks, with a reserve of 110 in its wing tanks. The pilots had calculated that though the Fouga's technical range was twelve hundred kilometers, they could stretch it to fifteen or sixteen hundred kilometers in good conditions on a clear night.

Two pilots and two radio operators had been called earlier that evening and told to stand ready at Kolwezi for a mission. They would be informed of the precise details thirteen minutes prior to takeoff.

At ten thirty-five, they were told that their mission would be to locate a DC-6 flying from Leopoldville to Ndola, and divert it to Kamina. They did not know, Beukels said, who was aboard or why the plane had to be diverted. He presumed, he told de

Kemoularia, that it was carrying African officials or war matériel. Five minutes later they received detailed air traffic control information on the plane's speed, altitude, and line of flight.

At about ten fifty-two, they received their thirteen-minute warning. One pilot and one radio operator climbed into each Fouga, then levered down and locked a snug glass canopy that framed a 180-degree view of the black above. Beukels had been told, he said, to search along the Rhodesian border and in a northern zone around Ndola. The other Fouga would search farther north, on a more direct intercept path. It was expected that this Fouga, Fouga Two, would be more likely to find the plane first. Beukels was a backup.

When they located the plane, they were instructed to radio a request that the DC-6 divert, with wording in French, that said roughly: *Call to DC-6, this is a landing notification. Please divert to base Kamina. We will escort you. Important Europeans want to meet one of those aboard. If you refuse we have orders to use force. Please confirm your acceptance.**

They were to give the plane one minute to respond if it was headed toward the runway at Ndola, and three minutes if it was flying in another direction. If the plane failed to heed the request, they were authorized to fire a burst of the visible tracer bullets as a warning. Once the *Albertina* submitted, the plan was to fly in formation around it and ensure it landed at Kamina, where the control group, headed by Mr. X, would be waiting.

The two Fougas flew together, Beukels at about two thousand meters, and Fouga Two at five thousand meters. After about a hundred kilometers—approximately halfway—they both climbed to nine thousand meters before splitting off to their intercept zones.

---

* In French, as recalled by de Kemoularia and transcribed by Ivan Smith: *"Appelle à DC-6. Avisation aterrisage. Prière vous détourne sur base Kamina. Vous escortons. Importantes personalités Européenes desirent rencontrer personalité a bord. Si refus, avons ordres de vous contraire par force. Si OK répondez."*

Updates on the *Albertina*'s position crackled through on a rarely used frequency accessible only to advanced radios like the ones aboard. The operation they were flying, from Kolwezi to Ndola and back, was at the outside edge of the Fougas' range, and precise information was key to save flight time, and thus fuel.

Fouga Two never found the DC-6, and returned to base. But Beukels said he did not know this. The two interceptors maintained radio silence between them—they were afraid, Beukels said without specifying further, of being overheard by "America."

Beukels said he descended to seven thousand meters on the edge of his designated intercept zone. He received an update at 2358: The DC-6 was about eighty kilometers north of Ndola at two thousand to twenty-five hundred meters, about ten minutes from arrival. He said that the Ndola tower had collaborated with him at this point. It asked the *Albertina* to make another turn in order to delay it for interception. Beukels tuned his radio to hear communications between the DC-6 and the tower for further guidance.

His radio operator, a man he said was named Mertelot, advised him to climb to nine thousand meters, to better get into position, which took him nineteen seconds.

And then he realized that he was right above his target. He dove again to two thousand meters, about two hundred meters above the *Albertina*. He turned on two powerful external floodlights, used for search and rescue in the dense African bush, as a kind of signal, and radioed the DC-6 with the message he had been supplied.

"Wait, I will check," someone aboard the *Albertina* replied. Beukels dropped to the right of the DC-6, again on the advice of his radio operator, and flew parallel with it. They then heard the *Albertina* speaking to the tower at Ndola. Beukels, now flying a short distance behind the *Albertina*, felt that the pilot had hesitated and that perhaps he was preparing to pull a trick and land anyway. He turned to his left, slightly higher than the DC-6, and dropped behind it. He felt he had no choice but to fire warning shots, and he wanted them to cross the path of the *Albertina* so that the pilot would see them.

He pulled the trigger and felt the gun expel a bright fusillade. He expected to see it arc harmlessly through the night. But to his horror the *Albertina* began to weave, and it appeared to Beukels that the pilot was struggling to correct and hold it in line. He must have hit part of its tail assembly.

"Do you think I really hit it?" he asked his radio operator. "Yes," he replied. Beukels said he was so horrified that he lost his bearings and knew nothing except that he was still in the interception zone somewhere. It was his radio operator who saw that the DC-6 was burning on the ground, and informed Kolwezi, before Beukels took the plane to nine thousand meters and headed back himself.

He landed at a mercenary base at 1:05 a.m. local time. As soon as he stepped out of the aircraft and saw the faces of his superiors, he said, he knew something terrible had happened. He was brought before a panel of senior officers, and members of the control group, and interrogated. He found out then, for the first time, what he had done. He was held for ten days. He feared he would be killed, without trial or hope of appeal. But he was freed.

The tower recordings, which were noted as missing by both the UN and the Rhodesian inquiries, had been destroyed deliberately, Beukels said. The group decided to send Major Delin, another mercenary pilot, to the Rhodesian inquiry to deny any involvement—as a kind of bluff. And so the crime had disappeared.

After Hammarskjöld's death, Beukels and De Troye said, they had been shunned. They could not find work. Beukels's radio operator, Mertelot, disappeared. Lieutenant Colonel Lamoumine, the official commander of Katangese forces whom Ivan Smith had gotten to know in Ndola, was named among the interrogation panel and might also have corroborated the story. But he, too, had fled. "Left the world," they put it, to join a monastery in Europe somewhere.

Even without corroboration, de Kemoularia somehow felt that the broken man in front of him was sincere. He got the impression that Beukels had come because he wanted to defend his character, to tell someone close to Hammarskjöld that he had not intended to kill him.

Until now, the mystery of the crash of the *Albertina* had been a sprawl of rumor. Hints, whispers, and dark implications. There was evidence, from the Rhodesian and UN reports, of an accident. There were second-hand accounts, surfaced by O'Brien, that the plane had been hijacked at the behest of a group of French mercenaries. Ahier had heard tales of a ground attack.

De Kemoularia had found the first concrete evidence—a confession, no less—that Virving and Ivan Smith had been correct to focus their attentions on the skies.

Chapter 27

"Cornered on a patch of gold"

Ivan Smith first heard the story in de Kemoularia's apartment, on September 17, 1981—the twentieth anniversary of the crash. They each signed a solemn document stating their commitment to the truth, and to exposing it together.

Ivan Smith taped their meeting, with every detail of the story De Troye, Beukels, and Grant had told. And when he played it back, at home in Stroud, he was electrified. It had taken twenty years, the span of a third of his life. But at sixty-six he felt he finally had in his possession—in folders, piles, neatly folded maps, stacks of letters, and the connections in his mind—everything he needed for his final work.

He sat at his typewriter and began the process of synthesizing Beukels's account with the material he'd gleaned from Welensky, from Virving, from his travels in Africa, and from public sources of information like the Swedish documentary and the French book *Notre Guerre au Katanga*.

On December 8, 1981, he sent a seventy-one-page account, dense with excited notes, to de Kemoularia. "I am more encouraged than ever by the validity of the story," he wrote, and said he planned to focus on "getting it right in detail." He also wanted to find Beukels again, with a view to getting his full account verified and published somewhere—with all proceeds to go to the Dag Hammarskjöld Foundation.*

Virving, he said, had noted that the DC-6 was controlled, in part, by wires leading to the tailplane. Even a botched attack could easily have severed one of those wires without destroying the plane. Virving also had a picture, Ivan Smith wrote, of a mysterious hole in the DC-6's astrodome—a small, transparent bubble behind the cockpit for taking navigation sightings. It could plausibly have been caused by a bullet that had also hit the tail assembly.

Among Ivan Smith's interviews was a conversation with a Swedish trade union official, Sven Mattson. In 1961, Mattson had been helping the charcoal burners to build their own unions. After the crash, he said, many of them told him they'd seen things that contradicted the official accounts. But despite his urging, they were afraid to come forward in case they were punished.

He unearthed a previously unnoticed report from two of those charcoal burners, who had been on the ground in Ndola that night. They said they had seen two white men, in a jeep, come to the site of the crash, long before any search-and-rescue efforts were mobilized. They had looked at the wreckage, then got in their car and left again, the charcoal burners had said. "Who were they, and why did they not go immediately to the police?" Ivan Smith wrote. "Why did the search not begin until 9.00am in the morning?"

Ivan Smith had also, he wrote, confirmed for himself that the mercenaries were using Union Minière communications equipment and workshops.

When he examined the siege at Jadotville that Beukels and De Troye mentioned, he found it had gone exactly as they claimed, and had precisely the demoralizing effect they spoke of.

Ivan Smith had confirmed previous accounts that suggested there had been more than one jet fighter in operation. He spoke

---

* It was founded in 1962 and remains vibrant even today.

to a pilot who had delivered a Fouga, purchased by Tshombe from France, to Katanga. He had landed on the way at Malta, then under British control. "The British did nothing to stop those planes going through to Katanga," Ivan Smith wrote.

He suggested that, given that the story had started with Robert Ahier at UPI, Ahier might be willing to take it on. But he wasn't. And nobody else was either, apparently. It is not recorded why, or how, or where the two men tried to have their story placed. But it is a matter of record that they did not succeed.

In the twenty years since Hammarskjöld had died, the world had shifted, and shifted again. The idealistic rebellions of the 1960s had curdled into the chaos and dysfunction of the 1970s. The UN had faded, both as an emblem of a postwar hope and as a force in the world. Put bluntly, nobody seemed to care.

So Ivan Smith waited. And then, in September 1992, an Italian United Nations plane carrying aid to Sarajevo during the Balkan conflict was shot down, reportedly by a hostile missile. Four people died. Ivan Smith told Conor Cruise O'Brien he felt this was the moment: an instance on which they could build, when the world's attention had flitted back toward the injustice of an embattled nation targeting the UN.

The two men wrote a letter together, to the *Guardian* newspaper in Britain. It was printed on September 11, 1992. It was short, but powerful. "Yet again United Nations personnel are being killed in peace-keeping and humanitarian missions," it opened.

Now the Italian crew on a mercy mission to Bosnia have been shot down we feel it is time that we should say that we are convinced that UN Secretary-General Dag Hammarskjöld was killed in the same way in 1961 when his aircraft crashed over Ndola, Northern Rhodesia. He was trying to settle the Congo crisis, in many ways as complex as that in the skeleton Yugoslavia.

Perhaps it was their ages—Ivan Smith was seventy-seven and O'Brien, seventy-four. Perhaps it was that more than thirty years had passed since the crash. But the letter stated their conviction more clearly and concisely than ever before: Mercenaries had been hired, indirectly, by European industrial interests to prevent the UN from reunifying the Congo.

A unified Congo stood to ease Cold War tensions. But would also have imperiled the profits of companies like Union Minière and Tanganyika Concessions. "We saw and felt the bare fangs of commercial interests cornered on a patch of gold," they wrote.

Those commercial interests sent two planes to divert the *Albertina*, but they hit a wire to the tailplane when they fired a warning shot, causing the crash. "Two official enquiries were complete and found no evidence to the contrary. Why should they if only a wire was hit?"

Reluctantly, they wrote, they wanted to open the case again "in the interests of peace and peoples who work for it. Bosnia is subject to raw race and religious prejudice causing brigands to commit the same type of insane acts from which we suffered in the Congo."

They had every right to expect nothing. But this time the story took off. The *Guardian* ran a separate piece on their letter, expanding on each of their theories. It was followed up around the world. Union Minière felt compelled to issue a denial.

Two weeks after the initial letter, O'Brien wrote another piece for the *Guardian*, this time calling for further investigation on key points. The mercenaries, he outlined, had means, motive, and opportunity for committing the murder. The argument that they were insane—which had been used to discredit their claims of involvement—cut both ways, O'Brien felt. Who conspires to the ridiculous more often than the insane?

Why did the Rhodesians take fifteen hours to find a plane wreck so close to the airport? he mused. And why had the governments of Britain, America, France, and Belgium been so uncooperative in addressing the open questions about the crash?

O'Brien concluded that the nations were overtly supportive of the UN but had also been helping commercial interests that may have acted against it. And so the nations probably "did not conspire against Hammarskjöld, but I believe they conspired to cover up that conspiracy."

Chapter 28

"We are going to teach them"

Godefroid Munongo woke at 4:30 a.m. on May 28, 1992, in his home on the outskirts of the Congolese capital of Kinshasa. He read from the Bible as he lay in bed next to his wife. Then he walked out on to the balcony attached to his bedroom and began to pace in the cool morning air.

He had much to think about. Munongo was scheduled to address the Congolese people that afternoon. He had written a speech that he felt, according to family legend, would shake his country to its foundations, and finally set its history straight.* Shortly before 6 a.m., just as the men who guarded his walled compound changed shifts, he bathed, put on a dark Belgian suit, ate a breakfast of bananas and coffee, and prepared to leave the house.

Thirty years earlier, when Kinshasa was still called Leopold-ville, Munongo had been Tshombe's interior minister, and one of the most powerful and feared men in the Congo. He was stocky and bald, with a chillingly implacable affect, his eyes piercing through small transparent sunglasses.

He was accused of being intimately involved in killing Lumumba. And in 1962, a man named Cléophas Kanyinda had

---

* This account was provided by Munongo's son, and only the portions of it that are public could be independently verified.

told the UN he suspected Munongo had involvement in, or knowledge of, Hammarskjöld's death, too.

Kanyinda had been a clerk with the Katangese government until he abandoned Tshombe and sought refuge with the UN. He told UN officials that, before the wreckage of the *Albertina* had been found, he had witnessed Munongo pull up in a car to talk to a Belgian official. Munongo, he recalled, looked satisfied through the rolled-down window. "Mr. H has been knocked down," Munongo said. "We are going to teach them."

It chimed with other accounts. Beukels had pointed out Munongo as the contact between Mr. X, the leader of the mysterious European conglomerate, and the Katangese. And Conor Cruise O'Brien had separately felt that Munongo was among the most dangerous of the Katangese leadership.

After Katanga rejoined the rest of the Congo in 1963, Munongo had served in the central government again. In 1966 he fell in one of President Mobutu's purges and was arrested and jailed. Mobutu seized his home in Elisabethville, now renamed Lubumbashi, and housed soldiers there. Munongo was released in 1968, when he left Congolese politics and began to work in the private sector, traveling between Europe and his home in Kinshasa.

Through the decades, despite periodic pressure, Munongo had never addressed the allegations against him. He saw his silence as regal. His last remaining title was Msiri—the king of the Bayeke people, a group of his forebears who had first migrated from Tanganyika to settle Katanga at the beginning of the nineteenth century. It was not a responsibility he wore lightly. His people, he felt, had discovered Katanga and tamed and tended the region until it had become the most fruitful and prosperous for hundreds of miles around.

It was a Msiri, Godefroid's grandfather, who had resisted the Belgians when they first came, in 1891, to plunder Katanga. They shot him in front of his people. The story had become a family parable. The embodiment of the proper willingness to do whatever was necessary to maintain the kingdom. Munongo felt that he had carried on his grandfather's proud traditions during his own rule in Katanga. He did not have to justify that to anyone.

But in 1990, under international pressure to moderate his dictatorship after twenty-five brutal years, Mobutu had instituted a national conference—a kind of truth and reconciliation commission that was supposed to be a step toward democracy in the Congo. It pushed the old allegations against Munongo toward the front pages again. As the conference sprawled over months and years, Munongo grew increasingly aggrieved at what he felt was an unfair focus on him.

By 1992, Munongo, now sixty-two and increasingly concerned with his legacy, told Mobutu privately that he had decided to confront the accusations directly. Mobutu, by Munongo's account, pleaded with him not to. He said that they should discuss the matter in secret. That he wanted to talk to the nation on these topics first himself. Munongo responded that each of them would have to do what they had to do. Munongo had announced he would speak to the conference on that day, May 28, 1992, at 5 p.m.

He left the house for the conference after breakfast, so he could watch the proceedings before his speech. He was driven the forty-five minutes or so to the huge, white Congolese parliament building* in a Mazda 929 limousine, alongside Christian, the oldest of his nine children.

They pushed past the crowds outside, ignored the television cameras, and made their way to their seats on a long bench in the chamber. Munongo was excited, he told his family, to get a weight off his chest. To tell his story even if it implicated others, and clear his name and that of his people. He had asked his wife to prepare a celebratory meal of chicken, sweet potatoes, and vegetables for later.

At around noon, as Munongo was sitting by himself, a small

---

* Now named the Palais du Peuple.

group of angry men approached him. They were carrying folded newspapers whose headlines accused him of killing Lumumba. They kept throwing them, hard, onto the table in front of Munongo. It seemed bizarre to those sitting nearby.

Shortly after that Munongo started to wheeze and gasp. He could not get enough air. Christian rushed him into a car, and on to Kinshasa's Ngaliema Hospital. By the time he arrived he was barely hanging on. The doctors resuscitated Munongo, and briefly he opened his eyes. Christian said "Papa" twice. He squeezed his son's hand, hard in response.

The power had gone out at Munongo's house, so none of his family had seen the televised coverage of the emergency. They waited, in the semi-dusk, unknowing.

As soon as Christian returned, inconsolable with grief, his mother and sister collapsed. They barely needed telling that Munongo had died while holding Christian's hand. First, they informed his younger children, studying in Los Angeles and in Belgium, by phone. Then the guards in the compound. Then they left as a group to go and tell the neighbors.

When they returned, they noticed that the gate to the house was open. Usually the guards made sure that it was locked at all times. But they'd been distracted by the death, too. Upstairs, Munongo's office had been ransacked. Papers lay all over his ebony desk and the floor. The trash can had been emptied out, and its contents apparently taken.

The Munongo family is convinced that Congolese political interests, with something to lose from the truth emerging, poisoned him. They suspect the newspapers thrown in front of him were treated with one of the deadly airborne powders, made from a concoction of poisonous plants that grow wild, then in vogue in Kinshasa.*

---

* This occasionally still happens. In 2019, a mysterious poison called karuho was implicated in Congolese murders.

Munongo had suffered from heart trouble. It might merely have been a terrible coincidence. But because the Msiri's body must be left intact, according to tradition, no autopsy was done. He habitually kept few papers. And no copy of Munongo's scheduled speech was ever found. Whatever he was planning to say about the dark events of the Katangese secession died with him.

Chapter 29

"The page is gone"

By 1992, around the time Munongo died and Ivan Smith and O'Brien's letter appeared in the *Guardian*, conspiracy theorists had discovered the Hammarskjöld story.

A former Swedish archbishop said God had told him that He had instructed a charcoal burner to kill Hammarskjöld. Another theory suggested Hammarskjöld had committed an elaborate suicide by murdering the entire flight crew. A Norwegian lady insisted he had died because he wanted to bomb Katanga himself.

The Swedish government, beset by both legitimate news and a flood of lurid tabloid headlines, appointed a veteran diplomat, Bengt Rösiö, to investigate the new claims. Ivan Smith wrote to him to ask him not to close leads that "one day others may open."

Rösiö, a witty and bemused-looking man with thick glasses and unruly hair, gray at his temples, was then sixty-five. He had recently retired after forty-one years across seventeen nations in the foreign service. Among his postings, decades earlier, had been a stint as Swedish vice consul in Leopoldville in 1961. It gave him an intimate understanding of the chaos and comedy of the Congo Crisis.

Leopoldville had felt like landing on a different planet, Rösiö recalled. He visited Matadi, the main seaport, with President Kasavubu. On the way back, Kasavubu's entire gleaming motorcade got lost and went in endless winding circles because nobody had told the lead driver where to go. Stray dogs kept him up as they howled through the nights. And an invitation to a formal dinner instructed guests that the dress code was merely to "dress."

Rösiö's colleagues from other nations dropped like flies. A British diplomat contracted a tropical disease and was flown home. A Danish one was attacked by armed robbers in his bedroom. Belgian and Swiss officials had nervous breakdowns. A Russian was sent home when his alcoholism escalated past the point of disguise, a German was eaten by a crocodile, and an American military attaché was murdered in bed with his Congolese mistress.

UN officials, he discovered, were the fish who found themselves most out of water. Only one, as far as he could make out, had any grasp of the local language or culture. He had just gotten used to being perpetually off balance when a UN jeep careened up his driveway and a Swedish air force colonel jumped down with a message: Hammarskjöld was missing, probably dead.

Rösiö traveled immediately to Ndola, where he was shocked by the raw, flaming hatred he heard against the UN from white Africans. It struck him that it was not beyond the bounds of emotional logic, at least, that one of their number might have sought to harm Hammarskjöld.

Rösiö certainly didn't rule out the idea when he came to examine the evidence in 1992. But to his bafflement the Swedish foreign ministry, despite assigning him the task, provided little help and a tiny budget. He conducted hundreds of interviews anyway, mostly at his own expense, over the course of a year or so. And he gained access to Virving's boxes of evidence, too.

Rösiö was, as an investigator, a different proposition from some who had come before him. He was funny. And being funny enabled him, for better or worse, to skip a lot of dead ends that the credulous dutifully trudged.

The official inquiries and the Swedish government, he felt,

had been inept. All had been primarily concerned with hiding the core fact all established institutions protect: that nobody knew anything. Leopoldville in 1961 had baffled everyone, most of all the UN, which was utterly flailing. He learned, too, that news editors would publish any exciting-sounding junk that met the rigorous standard of both crossing their desks and not being easily corrected. This included speculations about the CIA and KGB that had virtually no evidence to support them.

The end result, he felt, as he surveyed the landscape of speculation, theory, and evidence, was that everyone fell back on their prejudices. The Rhodesians, and white Africans in general, blamed the UN, whose pilots, they had implied, were tired, ignorant, useless, and possibly drunk. Black Africans blamed the white Africans, with an increasingly conspiratorial bent.

He interviewed former Belgian mining executives who felt that it was not at all implausible that Union Minière might have been strongly connected to the mercenaries. But he remained skeptical of Ivan Smith and O'Brien's theories.

It was exceedingly unlikely, Rösiö wrote in his eventual report, released in 1993, "that even mercenaries and/or their backers could have believed that kidnapping the U.N. Secretary-General and keeping him hostage would lead to increased respect for their common sense and good judgement."

A Swedish journalist, he discovered, had been asked to pay 500,000 francs to meet Beukels in 1981, and had declined. Which cast the pilot's motives into doubt. Rösiö had not been able to find him to corroborate his story, but he noted that Beukels had never gone to the authorities, who might have been able to establish the truth of his tale.

Rösiö felt that the earlier theory, put forth by O'Brien in his play, that French mercenaries had placed a soldier named Réné Gheysels aboard the *Albertina* to hijack it, had a fatal flaw: "If his colleagues had found 'Gheysels' to be expendable, is it conceivable

that he would have concurred? A mercenary is, almost by definition, not kamikaze material."

But on the other hand, it was equally implausible that the pilots
of the *Albertina* had simply used the wrong chart—for Ndolo, a
town near Leopoldville, rather than Ndola—and planted the plane
into the ground in simple error. "To mistake Ndola for Ndolo is as
likely as explaining a crash at Geneva by believing that the pilot...
had mistaken the Alps for the Mediterranean," Rösiö wrote.

That such far-fetched theories could have gained credence, he
wrote, "could be taken as an indication that somebody has wanted
reporters to run up blind alleys."

That left only questions:

> Did the pilot feel so relieved after a long and strenuous
> flight that he made too daring a turn, like a downhill skier
> who falls when displaying a final triumphant swerve in
> front of the spectators? Might he have been frightened by
> the sudden appearance of an unexpected plane and made
> a sudden dive, much like a bus driver who skids into a
> ravine as a result of turning the wheel too sharply in order
> to avoid hitting a child who has run into the path of his
> vehicle? Was any other aircraft "up and about" at that time,
> near Ndola?

He didn't know. And he felt that nobody else did, either. Which
left him with a similar conclusion to the Rhodesian report—that
quirks of the landscape and the circumstances had combined to
leave the pilots blind, causing them to fly into the ground. He gave
the conclusion its modern name, controlled flight into terrain.

By 1992, he noted, aircraft had special ground proximity sen-
sors to warn pilots of such an error. An urgent computerized voice
would shout, "Terrain, terrain, pull up, pull up." But the DC-6 had
no such system.

It was, he wrote, "the most probable—or, if you so wish, the least improbable—reason for the crash. Even so, it is then difficult to understand why none of the four in the cockpit of the DC-6B looked at any of the three altimeters during the final descent, an established routine which they ought to have found even more imperative than usual given that they were on such an important mission."

There were still, he wrote, things that troubled him about the crash. The *Albertina's* radio was noted as dead by Ndola air traffic control five minutes after its scheduled landing time. There were eighteen planes and countless personnel at the airport. Yet nobody did anything for hours. The *Albertina* and its occupants were left to burn.

The airport manager, Williams, had been informed of sightings of flames at 5:38 a.m., Rösiö said, but had still not gotten to his desk to begin investigating until 9 a.m. The Rhodesian wing commander Maurice Barber—who had later overseen the initial investigation into the crash that exonerated Rhodesian officials—had also been informed before the sun rose. But he had roused himself to look into it even later than Williams. The explanation by other airport staff, who said that they would have initiated a search had the *Albertina's* radio not gone dead, was "a statement tantamount to wondering why a dead man does not call a doctor," Rösiö said.

He blamed Lord Alport, the British official who had been waiting at the airport for Hammarskjöld, for his eagerness to explain away the disappearance of a plane carrying the secretary-general of the United Nations as nothing.

In fact, he wrote, nobody knew what had happened because the *Albertina* did not have a black box recorder, and the records from the tower at Ndola had gone missing. That had been taken as evidence that the authorities knew of the assassination and wanted to help cover it up. But there was another, more plausible explanation, Rösiö said: that they were scared of civil unrest if the details of Hammarskjöld's death emerged, and wanted to keep a lid on it. "This would at least explain," he wrote, "why honourable and competent men at Ndola airport did not come to the succour of fellow aviators in a burning wreck nine miles from where they stood."

He pointed out, in the understated language of a diplomat, that the governments with information that might clarify matters were hardly clamoring to provide it. And that into that vacuum had rushed the "inevitable allegations behind every conspiracy theory": that evidence had been falsified and suppressed, and that those involved had gone mad, committed suicide, "or, in one case, become a monk."

His conclusions, he wrote, were ultimately:

(i) that it is not known how an experienced crew of four could lose 1,000 feet in altitude without noticing it; (ii) that there is nothing to indicate that the DC-6B crashed because of outside interference; and (iii) that professional ground staff from civil aviation, as well as members of the police, security, and air force, let 15 hours go by from the moment the radio of the 'Albertina' went dead until the scorched wreckage was found exactly where it could have been calculated to be four minutes after commencing its final descent to Ndola airport.

He cited the poet Robert Penn Warren* as his final thought.

The answer is in the back of the book
but the page is gone
And grandma told you to tell the truth
but she is dead.

---

* From the poem *The Ballad of Billie Potts*, first cited by O'Brien in his book about Katanga.

Chapter 30

"A state secret"

Rösiö did not feel comfortable with his public conclusions. Many strange things had happened in the course of his investigation. The Swedish foreign ministry—his employer for nearly his entire career, which had asked him to pursue the investigation—refused to release all of its own documents on the crash. In fact, when his report was released, the ministry quickly classified even more material related to that night in Ndola. He never found out why.

When Rösiö met Claude de Kemoularia to discuss Beukels, de Kemoularia had told him he had previously presented his findings to a Swedish diplomat, Axel Edelstam. But when Rösiö asked Edelstam—a colleague, after all—Edelstam denied it.

Rösiö found that de Kemoularia had kept Edelstam's business card. And that travel records showed that Edelstam had indeed been in Paris on the day de Kemoularia described. Edelstam refused to explain further.

He had contacted the British Foreign Office, too, to seek out Williams, the airport manager at Ndola in 1961. Because he had realized that a small fact, dismissed in every official inquiry with a glib line or two, was in fact the heart of the mystery.

Williams had insisted in 1961 that tape recording equipment at the Ndola tower, required by strict regulation to be present and operating, had been malfunctioning on the night of September 17.

The tower logs—notes taken by air traffic controllers that provide a fallback account—were missing, too.

These records are sacrosanct for even the most boring flights. For the flight of a figure such as Hammarskjöld, in circumstances like those in 1961 in Katanga, it was difficult to imagine that they would have been casually lost or destroyed.

The only record of the last moments of the flight was a reconstruction of events in the tower that Williams had made himself, from unknown source material, two days after the crash.

No explanation had been given. And apparently—to Rösiö's shock—none had ever been sought by investigators for this vital missing evidence. Williams was the only man who could provide solid answers.

When Rösiö asked the British government he was told, by an undersecretary for transnational affairs in the Foreign Office, that Williams's address was a state secret. Undeterred, Rösiö hired a private detective, who provided the address, and he wrote to Williams to say he'd be coming to see him. But a few hours before Rösiö left Sweden, Williams called him to say that he'd been contacted by British officials and was unable to meet after all. (Rösiö went anyway, but was given nearly word-for-word the account Williams had given previously to the inquiries.)

And there was one incendiary rumor that Rösiö had left out of the public version of his findings, but that he had supplied to the Swedish foreign ministry. It came, secondhand, from the Norwegian ex-wife of an American naval officer named Charles Southall, who had been stationed in Nicosia, Cyprus, on the night of Hammarskjöld's death.

The foreign ministry asked the US Department of State to locate Southall as a matter of urgency. In late 1992, the response came back: America could not find him, and did not feel there was much to it.

Chapter 31

"Never believe anything until it is officially denied"

The Department of State's Bureau of Intelligence and Research, known as INR, is America's smallest and arguably best-respected intelligence agency. Its 350 or so analysts* are spread across the Department of State's complex of dark-beige buildings on C Street in Washington, DC.

In 1992, those of its staff who interacted with the public had blank, anonymous offices on the third and fourth floors. Others worked on the eighth floor, in a leaky attic that had been constructed for the Manhattan Project. And those engaged in sensitive matters worked on the sixth floor, in what is known as a Sensitive Compartmented Information Facility, or SCIF—a secure zone designed for examination of very secret intelligence without fear of interception or eavesdropping.

INR analysts are divided into sections to address particular areas of the world—Europe, Africa, East Asia and the Pacific, and so on. Instead of being moved to a new role every few years, as is the custom in the CIA for example, analysts specialize over a

---

* The CIA has fifteen hundred and the Defense Intelligence Agency has three thousand, for comparison.

longer period. They learn the languages and build relationships with a network of their counterparts in other agencies.

It allows them to circumnavigate bureaucracy and politics with a neatly placed phone call to a friend or colleague. That means, in turn, that they can draw together information from across the vast intelligence apparatus, including the intercepts of the National Security Agency and human intelligence from CIA operatives on the ground across the world. Their aim is to weave those strands into cohesive and punchy reports that will clarify foreign policy decisions for the department's executives.

Nobody makes movies about them. But before being broken out as a part of the State Department, INR was the elite unit of the very first American intelligence operation, the Office of Strategic Services. It remains the case that once analysts make INR, they often stay put because they feel there is nowhere to go but down.

INR was pessimistic in its assessments of the Vietnam War. And when other agencies caved to the pressure to supply intelligence that supported the use of force against Iraq in the early 2000s, INR refused. It was praised, later, for its impartiality.

INR analysts are allowed to be both selective and autonomous. Their reports, a tight page or two of ruthless relevance, are analysis rather than mere information, and they want to contribute something of significance. And so it is telling that in late 1992, when the Swedish government requested help to examine Rösiö's report and the secret material it had gathered alongside it, INR took on the task.

The request landed on the desk of Bowman Miller, the director of analysis for Europe and a former US Air Force officer and special investigator. Miller worked it himself, instead of handing it off to one of his staff, along with a Nordic analyst, Karen Enstrom, who was fluent in Swedish.*

---

* As well as Dutch and Russian.

Most INR reports are put together quickly, a little like news analysis, to cover fast-breaking situations around the world. Analysts pride themselves on being able to find an answer within five minutes, for a diplomat who is about to meet a counterpart or an executive who must brief the president, even if that answer is, "Here is what will arrive tomorrow."

From what we can piece together, this case proceeded more like detective work. It was conducted from an office on the seventh corridor of the fourth floor and ran on for at least a year. That duration is an indication, within the department, that new evidence had emerged which necessitated keeping the case open.

In December 1992, at around the time the American government was telling its Swedish counterpart that it could not locate Charles Southall, Enstrom had in fact sent him a letter. "The Government of Sweden," she wrote,* "has found new information which indicates that Hammarskjöld's plane may have been shot down. We understand that you may have additional information about the plane crash in question." She, and INR, needed his help.

Southall replied on March 23. He had been waiting for such a letter for thirty years, he said. "I am an intelligence officer in the U.S. Naval Reserve with the rank of Commander," he wrote. "I served overseas for roughly a decade," he said, before a stint with the Defense Intelligence Agency. "My activities remain buried several layers deeper than anything that will be reflected in my service record." He said he'd welcome the opportunity to provide more information—or even to investigate further himself, in person. But he heard nothing back until May 14.

The letter he received said that INR had searched State and CIA files "as well as other sources" but found nothing to support the theory that the plane had been shot or forced down. But it wanted more evidence. "We have been told by the Swedish government,"

---

* According to letters seen by the writer and researcher Dr. Susan Williams.

the letter said, "that you may have listened to a taped conversation between an air tower and a Fouga plane that allegedly shot down Hammarskjöld's plane. Is that assertion true?" It asked for details. Who was involved? How did he get access to the tape? Was it connected to de Kemoularia's story about Beukels?

Southall replied a few days later. He wrote opaquely, presumably in case anyone stumbled on his letters. But he was dubious about the claim that INR had found no evidence of foul play. He cited an old adage: "Never believe anything until it is officially denied." The recording in question, he said, "should be in files not many miles from your office, along with some interesting documentation about its origin. This recording may not be the only one. I do not recall whether it is in English or French, as I speak both, but it is chilling to listen to."

His theory was that the *Albertina* "happened on the scene when an excited pilot (called by some the 'Lone Ranger') was looking for an intruder." He offered to meet to explain further. But the exchange petered out.

INR reports are routinely declassified. They're often just old news, decades later. But Enstrom and Miller's report on Hammarskjöld's death has never been released. Rösiö was never told what his counterparts had found.

It would emerge later that, as Southall suspected, it was probably not true that INR's search of State and CIA files yielded no evidence the *Albertina* had been shot down.

And another document, released years later, shows a strange coincidence, at the very least. At about the time INR must have been concluding its report, on November 1, 1993, the FBI spontaneously decided to destroy all the materials it had concerning Hammarskjöld.* It has never explained why.

---

* According to a FOIA request filed by Susan Williams, who kindly provided it to me.

Chapter 32

"I've hit it. There are flames"

In 1993 Rösiö, given a lead by the Swedish tabloid *Expressen*, found Southall without American help. Southall was working in Casablanca, Morocco. Rösiö sent him a letter asking to visit. "Neither the US nor British authorities have been very helpful," Rösiö wrote, betraying a little weariness. "And though I try and avoid believing in conspiracies, I note a marked reluctance in digging up the Ndola file."

Southall had graduated both the American University of Beirut and the University of California, Berkeley, with degrees in political science, in the late 1950s. He looked all-American, blue-eyed and blond-haired. But he had studied the Arab world under the tutelage of George Lenczowski, who helped invent the modern Western study of the region, and he spoke both Arabic and French like a native.

He joined the navy, and had become a pilot in Okinawa, Japan. But in the early 1960s he was transferred to a listening facility operated by the navy for the NSA near Nicosia, the capital of Cyprus. He was a "processing and reporting" officer, tasked with scrutinizing intercepted messages.

He was later transferred to the Defense Intelligence Agency, where he retained a focus on North Africa and the Middle East. He left in 1969 and became a private intelligence operative. He investigated counterfeiting, piracy, fraud, and embezzlement, among other transgressions, for companies across the world.

In March 1994, Rösiö landed in Casablanca, a blast of dry heat and color after the muted and vast bucolia of Sweden. He and Southall met four times across the course of three days, in Southall's office and his home—room 1019 of the Casablanca Sheraton, an imposing concrete cube just off a major highway. While Rösiö took notes for his report, and fought feelings of bewilderment at what he was hearing, Southall related his story from the night of September 17, 1961.

Cyprus, a small island in the Mediterranean, south of Turkey, east of Greece and west of Syria, is about half the size of Connecticut and is noted for its crystal-blue waters and ruggedly idyllic beaches, for its use in recent years as a center for money laundering, and as the reputed birthplace of the goddess Aphrodite.

It's also studded with British and American radio masts and dishes. By dint of its location just seventy miles off the coast of Syria, it offers unparalleled access to signals intelligence—the interception of electronic communications and other signals, such as those from weapons systems—from across the Middle East. It is strategically vital for both the NSA and its British equivalent, Government Communications Headquarters, or GCHQ.

In 1961 the NSA's listening post in Cyprus was a substantial, square cement block without windows, surrounded by dry scrub and a fence. Its entrance was carefully guarded. Southall worked in a vast room that hosted a hundred or so desks, occupied exclusively by men who were listening to intercepted phone calls and other messages flying across the air, encrypted or not.*

Southall told Rösiö that he usually worked the day shift, from 6:30 a.m. to 1 p.m. But on that evening, Southall said, he received a call at home from an officer. "Get yourself out here tonight," the

---

* According to an account Southall gave Dr. Susan Williams.

officer said, according to Southall's account. "Something interesting is going to happen." Southall got in his car and drove to the listening post.

Shortly after midnight, Southall recalled, a recording was played back for him and a group of four or five others that had gathered. It was from Ndola, about 3,500 miles away. Which means it was likely relayed—intercepted closer to Ndola, and sent to a powerful transmitter nearby to be beamed onward to the listening station. He recalled a single male voice, which he described as cool and professional, speaking over the sound of an aircraft engine in either English or French. It was a pilot, reporting to a field command post, not a control tower, though he only ever heard the pilot's voice. It did not seem, he told Rösiö, that the pilot knew who was aboard the DC-6. Which led Southall to suspect he had just been patrolling, rather than targeting Hammarskjöld specifically.

"I see a transport plane coming low. All the lights are on. I'm going down to make a run on it. Yes, it's the Transair DC-6. It's the plane."

Southall recalled the sound of gunfire. Then the voice, more animated this time, said:

"I've hit it. There are flames. It's going down. It's crashing."

He was told by an officer that it was from a Belgian pilot nicknamed "the Lone Ranger," flying a Katangese Fouga.

At virtually the same moment Rösiö was talking to Southall, in March 1994, a story appeared in one of Sweden's most prestigious newspapers, *Dagens Nyheter*. A reporter there was speaking to a Swedish flying instructor, Tore Meijer, for a mundane story.

Meijer mentioned that he had been working in Ethiopia in 1961. On the night of September 17, by coincidence at precisely the moment Hammarskjöld's plane was coming in to land, he was testing the radio by turning the dials slowly, with a fizz of static, across the frequencies. He landed on a conversation in English, and heard the name Ndola.

A voice said, "He's coming in for landing, he's turning…he's planning…another airplane is behind, what is it? He's breaking off the plan…he continues."* Then the connection was cut.

---

* In the original Swedish, from DN: *Så säger rösten att "han kommer in för landning, han svänger…han planerar"—där piloten går in mot själva landningsbanan. Så hör jag att samma röst säger att "ett annat flygplan ligger bakom, vad är det." Rösten säger, "Han avbryter planen…han fortsätter." Så avbryts sändningen.*

Chapter 33

"Kaleidoscope"

Over the years that followed, Rösiö came to see the mystery less as a jigsaw puzzle missing pieces than a kaleidoscope, filled with hundreds of clues, which could form nearly any picture if rotated.

He came to feel, like the UPI correspondent Ahier who had helped de Kemoularia find Beukels, that each of the stories he had investigated contained some element of truth. But each also had significant problems.

Rösiö was not sure about either Southall's or Meijer's stories. They added complexity, he felt, rather than reducing it. Southall had not inspired confidence during their meetings. And he felt that the conversation Meijer had heard, if it was as described, must have been an exchange between two air traffic controllers. The radio frequencies controllers use—VHF—do not carry across thousands of miles, and so could not have been overheard from Ethiopia.

The witnesses to the crash either saw two planes and flashes consistent with an attack or warning shot, or they didn't understand what a DC-6 flying at night was supposed to look like under normal conditions.

Harold Julien's last testimony, given to the doctors and nurses in Ndola, was either a dying-but-lucid man's attempt to seek justice or nonsensical burbling.

Charles Southall and Tore Meijer either heard incendiary fragments of a pivotal moment, or they were misremembering garbled messages from decades prior.

Ivan Smith was either a brilliant investigator, familiar with both the UN and Africa, or a passionate and poetic soul who had been sadly fixated on the death of a friend and mentor.

Beukels was either a psychologically wrecked accidental murderer making a confession or a drunk who'd say anything for a little money and action.

Rösiö had found no record of a Beukels in Katanga—only a Beukens, who flew cargo planes, a very different skill than piloting a jet interceptor. And he had found no evidence that there had been enough Fougas, or pilots that could fly them at night, to allow for two to escort, or attempt to escort, the *Albertina*.

De Kemoularia had never reported the stories he heard to the police, Rösiö noted. And though de Kemoularia later became French ambassador to the UN, he never told anyone there that he knew who had killed that organization's most famous leader.

As for O'Brien's theory, Rösiö simply could not get over the fact that it required a suicidal mercenary with a disappearing corpse. The French mercenaries might have claimed credit for such a plot in their book *Notre Guerre au Katanga*, but lots of people confessed to major assassinations for reasons best known to themselves.

Rösiö hated easy narratives, and the idea of a heroic United Nations decapitated by an evil force of mercenaries arrayed against them was, from his own experiences in Leopoldville, too neat entirely. But so much never made sense to him in raw, practical terms.

Hallonqvist, the *Albertina*'s pilot, was supposed to report to the Ndola tower shortly before he landed—when he had descended to six thousand feet. But according to the official record, he never did. It did not seem plausible to Rösiö that the reason was simple negligence. He was a very experienced pilot doing a very routine thing.

That omission convinced him further that someone at Ndola

had deliberately deleted records of radio traffic and amended the log for the night. Rösiö certainly could not easily accept that the tape recordings and tower logs that would have clarified the matter were simply gone.

Rösiö couldn't shake the idea that nobody had ever investigated the "enemy" side of that evening—that no authoritative account existed of the motivations and movements of the Katangese, and that the initial inquiries did not seek material from Belgium, France, Britain, America, or anywhere outside of the Congo.

Over the coming years, even as he released a stream of skeptical writings about the crash, including a short book titled Ndola, he privately allowed for his own doubts about his conclusions. He was sure that whatever happened that night was not the result of meticulous planning. But he came to believe that it was, more likely than controlled flight into terrain, the unexpectedly disastrous effect of a clumsy attempt to hijack or divert Hammarskjöld.

Whoever had made that ridiculous attempt, and had forced Hallonqvist to fly so low and so dangerously, would hardly have boasted about it. The story might have drifted into the hands of others who had heard it and were more willing to play it up. Or maybe there was an attack, and it caused the pilots to misread their altimeters in their panic.

Altimeters, Rösiö learned, have three hands, like an elaborate clock. One refers to hundreds of feet, one to thousands, and one to tens of thousands. A pilot has to make a quick and routine calculation on glancing at it. If a plane had distracted all the pilots at the wrong moment, they might have simply misread the altimeter. If that was the case—and it was pure speculation—both things were true. It was an accident and a murder.

In the middle of October 1995, George Ivan Smith went to the hospital with stomach pains. It was colon cancer, though he never told anyone so. It barely slowed him. From his hospital bed, he wrote about Africa. He wrote letters to newspapers—on the UN, on the British royal family, on anything that caught his still-voracious eye. He delighted in poetry, particularly Seamus Heaney lines about curious children wondering at telegraph poles, imagining that words traveled the wires "In the shiny pouches of raindrops / Each one seeded full with the light of the sky . . ."

He loved the vivid pictures of space from the Hubble telescope. Perhaps he marveled, as one investigator to another, that though Hubble had not solved the mysteries of the universe it had clarified them for others.

Ivan Smith still believed that the *Albertina* had been approached by a mercenary plane as it came in to land on September 17, 1961. It had either attacked the DC-6, or caused enough of a distraction that Hammarskjöld's plane had crashed in the chaos.

He died on November 21, 1995, without ever finding definitive proof. He was eighty. O'Brien wrote an obituary that celebrated him as a witty and idealistic man, a true believer in the United Nations, which for all its flaws he felt was a force for general decency. Though he never talked about it so grandly, "you could feel him believing it," O'Brien wrote. He concluded that Ivan Smith was "one of the most fully admirable people I ever knew."

Chapter 34

"Operation to be known as Celeste"

In 1998, Archbishop Desmond Tutu headed the South African Truth and Reconciliation Commission. It was a sweeping effort to deal with thirty-four years of brutal apartheid in a court that sought both an honest accounting of the repression and reconciliation between the races rather than retribution for those crimes.

Its three-year mandate had expired the month before, and Tutu was set to depart, before a report was delivered to Nelson Mandela later that year. But something inconvenient had happened at the last moment.

On August 19 Tutu, in a cozy patterned cardigan and a blue tie, blinked against flashing cameras as he took his seat behind a table in a municipal building. Above him hung a banner that read TRUTH. THE ROAD TO RECONCILIATION.

Reading from notes, he gravely intoned that the commission had discovered, in the course of its investigations into apartheid crimes, "documents purporting to be from a South African institution called the South African Institute [for] Maritime Research discussing the sabotage of the aircraft in which the United Nations Secretary-General Dag Hammarskjöld died on the night of Sept. 17, 18, 1961."

The commission had been unable to verify them, he said. But "given our commitment to transparency we feel that apart from having handed the documents to the Minister of Justice for further investigation we should release the key documents we have found."

The documents consisted of eight letters headed with a grand crest, an elaborate Gothic font over an image of the Greek goddess Nike.* It listed the institute's address as the fifth floor of a run-down building on De Villiers Street near the Park Train Station in South Africa's largest city, Johannesburg.

The letters had surfaced in the course of one of the many investigations into apartheid crimes the commission was pursuing. They had been in its possession for months, but a researcher had only recently found them.

The names in the letters were redacted. But the letters formed part of an exchange among four men. Three had given themselves military ranks: Commodore, Commander, and Captain. A fourth went by the code name Congo Red.

The letters laid out, with a mix of the plausible, the obviously absurd, and the plain baffling, a plot that involved both the CIA and British intelligence in the death of Hammarskjöld.

The first letter, with the words SECRET CONFIDENTIAL EN CLAIR underneath the letterhead, was dated July 12, 1960, two weeks after the Congo declared independence and four days before Katanga seceded. It was from the Commodore to the Captain, typewritten and seemingly arbitrarily capitalized.

"Head office is rather concerned with developments in the Congo, particularly in the Haute Katanga, where it appears that the local strong man Monsieur Moïse Tshombe, supported by

---

* Nike inspired both the sportswear company and the spirit of ecstasy figurine on the front of Rolls-Royce cars.

Union Minière, is planning a secession along with a number of emigrés," the Commodore wrote.

The institute had it on good authority that the United Nations would "want to get its greedy paws on the province." He had been instructed "to ask You to send as many agents as You think would be needed to bolster CONGO RED'S unit in case of future problems which may arise as we are sure they will."

Katangese authorities, the Commodore said, "have agreed to place at your disposal a number of private aircraft, including two military 'Fouga' jets." It was signed with a strange and very elaborate swirl of a signature.

The second letter, three days later, headed with the word ORDERS, and also from the Commodore to the Captain, added a sense of urgency. "It is essential that your combat units be put into training as soon as possible as we expect that they will be needed shortly," the Commodore wrote. He would supply guns, .762 Belgian rifles, he said, and any other necessary matériel.

The third letter, undated, but evidently later, is also marked ORDERS, and is also from the Commodore to the Captain. "Your contact with CIA is 'Dwight,'" he wrote, adding that Dwight would be staying at the Hotel Leopold II in Elisabethville. "Ensure identity is correct before giving info. Password is 'How is Celeste these days?' Reply is 'She's recovering nicely apart from the cough.'"

The fourth letter, also undated, also from the Commodore to the Captain, said that "in a meeting between MI5, Special Operations Executive" and the institute, it had emerged that the United Nations "is becoming troublesome and it is felt that Hammarskjöld should be removed."

Allen Dulles, then the CIA director, it said, "agrees and has promised full cooperation from his people. He tells us that Dag will be in Leopoldville on or about 12/9/61. The aircraft ferrying him will be a D.C.6. in the livery of 'TRANSAIR,' a Swedish Company."

"Please see that Leo airport as well as Elisabethville is covered by your people as I want his removal to be handled more efficiently than was Patrice," it continued, implying involvement in the murder of Patrice Lumumba, too.

"If time permits, send me a brief plan of action, otherwise proceed with all speed in absolute accuracy," the Commodore added. If Major-General Sean MacEoin, the commander of the UN forces in the Congo, and Conor Cruise O'Brien could also be killed simultaneously, he said, "it would be useful but not if it could compromise the main operation." The letter ended with a note: "OPERATION TO BE KNOWN AS CELESTE."

The Commodore headed the next, following his own instructions, OPERATION CELESTE. It would proceed as planned, he wrote. "Tell Your people that the op. Will not be allowed to be less than a total success. Union Minière has offered to provide logistics or other support. We have told them to have 6lbs. of tnt at all possible locations with detonaters [sic], electrical contacts and wiring batteries etc. (a full list of requirements has been given to R.) Your decision to use contact, rather than barometric devices is a wise one, we don't want mistakes or equipment failures at this late stage." It wished the Captain luck.

The next was a reply, delivered by hand, and written in a neat sloping pen. "In order to arrange for all three of the targets to be affected," it said, "an enormous amount of planning will be required." And so, it continued, "in order to ensure the success of 'Celeste' and taking into account the fact that time is of the essence, I would suggest that we concentrate on D. and leave the other two for some future date, possibly as early as next week or the week after." Hammarskjöld, it continued, "will have to be sorted out on the 17th or 18th." It signed off: "With a little luck, all will be well. Your servant, Commander."

Another reply dated September 14, 1961, is a list of numbered points. It is written in all capitals, in what seems to be pencil. The first read: "DC6 aircraft bearing Transair livery is parked at Leo to be used for transport of subject." The most salient, point two, was unambiguous: "Our technician has orders to plant 6lb TNT in the wheelbay with contact detonator to activate as wheels are retracted on taking off."

The last, on September 18, is a report on the operation that is signed by the person code-named Congo Red. It is also a handwritten list of numbered points, but the version released is barely legible. It certainly opens with the fact that the device "failed on take-off." Point three opens with the words "Device activated" and ends with the words "prior to landing." Point four seems to confirm that O'Brien and MacEoin were not aboard. And point five seems to read: "Mission accomplished: satisfactory."

The letters were big news in South Africa. Journalists speculated that if SAIMR existed, it was a front for South African soldiers or spies. The *Cape Argus*, the newspaper in Cape Town that had broken the story of the letters, had explored "a possible link to the Institute of Maritime Technology in Simon's Town, which has ties with arms maker Denel." But that institute had only been formed twenty-two years before—long after the dates on the letters.

The newspaper's own cuttings library did reveal that Armscor, the body founded by the apartheid government to secure black-market weapons while other nations imposed trade bans on it, had briefed something called the "Institute for Maritime Research" in 1994.

Both Conor Cruise O'Brien and Brian Urquhart expressed strong skepticism (though O'Brien did take the chance to say that he still felt French mercenaries had been involved). The CIA denied it had had any involvement. Its claim was lent credence by the fact that it had previously opened its archives to admit that it had plotted to kill Lumumba, even if its final role in his death remained unclear. The British Foreign Office which technically oversees, and sometimes speaks for, MI6, said that British intelligence agents "do not go around bumping people off. At this time during the Cold War, Soviet misinformation was quite rampant so [the letters] may have been put out by them."

It was, indeed, hard to believe that any group with the ability to kill a world leader, then hide that fact for more than three decades, would also lay its entire plot out on headed notepaper. But then again, cold war plots often combined the ostensibly absurd with a grain or two of truth.

Tutu admitted that the letters could well be disinformation. But, he added, his view colored by the fact he'd devoted his life to mitigating the very worst human instincts in his homeland, "it isn't something that is so bizarre. Things of that sort have happened in the past. That is why you can't dismiss it as totally, totally incredible."

The press offered less nuance. WEST PLOTTED TO KILL UN CHIEF was the headline in the *Times* of London.

The initial investigations, by the Rhodesian government and the UN, in the days after the crash marked the first phase of the detective work. The second had been carried out for decades by Ivan Smith, Virving, and others. And it drew to a close with the South African letters. By the fall of 1998, talk of the mystery had faded from the headlines.

With hindsight, at least, it feels as though there was a diminished appetite, amid broad Western prosperity, to exhume the horrors of the past. Hammarskjöld appeared in "this day in history" features every September 17 or 18 and in the obituaries of diplomats he had known. In 1999, the Belgian historian Ludo De Witte published the definitive account of the murder of Patrice

Lumumba, widely held to have solved much of the mystery.* Though it was translated into English in 2001, it inspired precisely nobody to look into Hammarskjöld's death.

Hammarskjöld came up again when the UN and Kofi Annan won the Nobel Peace Prize that same year. "His life and his death," Annan said, "his words and his actions, have done more to shape public expectations of the office, and indeed of the Organization than those of any other man or woman in its history."

Around that time the historian Matthew Hughes examined Ivan Smith's papers, which had been acquired by the Bodleian Library at Oxford University in 1993, but which had languished in obscurity. He finally revealed, with eye-catching details in the *London Review of Books* and elsewhere, Ivan Smith's research into the death. Nobody in particular followed up on his findings.

On the centennial of Hammarskjöld's birth, in 2005, the scandal was not the riddle of the crash, but criticism of Auden's role in the translation of his writings. O'Brien, the most vociferous remaining public defender of the idea that Hammarskjöld's death was not an accident, died in 2008, aged ninety-one.

Larry Devlin died the same year. He had retired from the CIA in 1974, and had worked for the diamond merchant Maurice Tempelsman, the companion of Jacqueline Kennedy Onassis, apparently liaising with ministers of mines in Africa. He knew them all.

He remained a company man until the end. On the few occasions on which he spoke of Hammarskjöld's death, he emphasized that he knew nothing. But all the information he had from his American colleagues in the Congo suggested it had been an accident.

Only later would it be revealed that the CIA in Leopoldville had its own very different theories about the crash, and the sinister forces reputed to be behind it. And that it likely knew as much

---

* See chapter 8.

as it did because Devlin was running more, and stranger, operations than he had publicly admitted.

And so the task of unraveling what happened shortly after midnight a few miles from Ndola airport on the night of September 17, 1961, fell to a new generation. Those investigators would unearth a line of inquiry that came to be known as the golden thread.

PART THREE

And the ragged rock in the restless waters,
  Waves wash over it, fogs conceal it;
On a halcyon day it is merely a monument,
In navigable weather it is always a seamark
To lay a course by, but in the sombre season
Or the sudden fury, is what it always was.

—T. S. Eliot, "The Dry Salvages," Four Quartets

Chapter 35

"For repair of your tumble drier. Phone Nick on 970890"

In the mid-2000s, Susan Williams, an author and a researcher at the University of London who specializes in the study of decolonization, set out to write a book. It was provisionally titled *White War on Africa*, and it was to be about white supremacists who had resisted majority rule by black Africans across the continent in the middle of the last century.

Often, as she searched archives related to the topic, she came across material about Hammarskjöld's death. At first she didn't take suspicions that he had been killed seriously. But then another document or report or letter would appear. And when she came across the pictures of Hammarskjöld, his colleagues, and the crew of the *Albertina* dead she felt she could no longer ignore the crash.

Williams, slight and blond with palpable determination in her clipped voice, decided to focus on the *Albertina*. She would turn over each and every clue.

She saw the conflict in Katanga as a war driven by big business and its interests. Hammarskjöld, who supported black Africans against both business interests and the white supremacists with whom they were linked, had made an enemy of thousands of white campaigners, some of them in positions of power. She admired his sense of principle. But she also began to get a sense of the forces massed against him.

The sheer quantity of intelligence operatives, agents, and offices in the Congo—a relic of the World War II battle for the nation's uranium—made operating there dangerous, if only because there could be no secrets.

She examined Rösiö's material, kept in Sweden's grand national library, the Kungliga Biblioteket in Stockholm. She examined Ivan Smith and Welensky's archives, stored across several honeyed-stone buildings at Oxford University. She scoured the earth for forgotten pieces of paper, records of the crash, its preamble and aftermath that had languished for nearly fifty years. She conducted hundreds of interviews in America, Sweden, France, Britain, Belgium, South Africa, and Zambia.

She mostly found doors closed that should have stayed open. Small ones: Rösiö was wrong to have dismissed Tore Meijer's account of a radio conversation that detailed the crash, because it was indeed plausible that the radio signals* would have reached him.

And large ones: When she met Southall, at a private members' club in London, he proved to be an honest and reliable witness. On one occasion she doubted him. The times that he cited for the events of the night just didn't fit. But she found later that Cyprus had had a different time zone in 1961, and his account matched perfectly.

She knew that the resolution the UN had passed in 1961 to investigate the crash allowed for a reopening of the investigation if significant new evidence emerged. That became her aim. A full, new investigation.

And in August 2009, she located a researcher for the South African Truth and Reconciliation Commission named Christelle

---

* They were high-frequency (HF) not very high-frequency (VHF) signals, and could have traveled the required distance to Ethiopia.

Terreblanche. Her job was to complete a section on human rights violations by the right wing for the commission's final report.

In 1998, Terreblanche had been given a batch of documents on one of the major crimes of the apartheid era—the murder of Chris Hani, the leader of the South African Communist Party. Hani rivaled Nelson Mandela for popularity within the black political movement. His murder had left black South Africans bereft and enraged. Days of rioting followed. It felt as though the very idea that South Africa could move from apartheid to equality in peace was in danger.

Hani had been shot and killed in the driveway of his home in April 1993. The police had arrested Januzu Jakub Waluz, a Polish immigrant with close links to a militant white nationalist group. He and Clive Derby-Lewis, a politician with the pro-apartheid Conservative Party who had supplied Waluz with a gun and a list of prominent targets, were found guilty in October of the same year.

The Hani files had come from South Africa's National Intelligence Agency, she told Williams, and she had the security clearance to examine them. Among the papers she found the Operation Celeste letters. She recalled about twelve—fewer than were released by the TRC.

She wanted to investigate further. But there were so many loose ends as the commission tied up its work that her superiors did not particularly want to look into another, however intriguing.

Later a woman submitted a separate grievance to the commission. It said that her daughter had worked for the South African Institute for Maritime Research in the late 1980s. She conducted what was described as AIDS research in Mozambique. But she came to believe that the group was, in fact, smuggling in contaminated vaccines. (Others have theorized that SAIMR planned to spread the disease as a kind of tool for the mass murder of black Africans.)

The woman said her daughter had planned to visit her and

tell her more in person. But she was shot during a carjacking in Johannesburg and never made it.

Terreblanche had heard other accounts, too, including allegations of gun smuggling, that corroborated at least the existence of the group, if not its role in the death of Hammarskjöld. But the original letters that referred to Hammarskjöld, she told Williams—including four that were not initially released by the commission—had disappeared.

When Williams* made inquiries, the South African Ministry of Justice said they had simply lost the box they were in. And Dullah Omar, the minister entrusted to look into them, had died in 2004.

On balance, Williams decided at first, the documents didn't make any sense anyway. Why would mercenaries spell out their plans so clearly? But as she continued to research, she found circumstantial evidence both that SAIMR existed, at least in the eighties and nineties, and of animosity toward Hammarskjöld in South Africa.

His support for black African independence had, of course, aggrieved many in the nation that stood for draconian white rule above all else. Another prominent opponent of apartheid, the Mozambique president Samora Machel, had also died in a mysterious plane crash, in 1986, while flying to a controversial political meeting. Investigators had concluded, despite significant evidence of foul play, that it must have been pilot error. One of those investigators, the South African jurist Cecil Margo, QC, had also been involved in the investigation into the crash of the *Albertina* a quarter of a century earlier.

And SAIMR itself kept coming up in tantalizing and horrifying glimpses. The man who had killed Hani, Januzu Waluz, had been interrogated in 1997, Williams found. He confirmed

---

* Via the South African History Archive, which submitted the request.

that in 1989 he had replied to an advertisement SAIMR had placed in a newspaper, *The Citizen*. It sought someone for a dangerous assignment, six months in duration, for the lavish pay of $5,000 per month. He sent a résumé to a man who called himself the Commodore, at a post office box. It connected Hani's killer with SAIMR, and thus made it plausible that the Hani file might contain strange correspondence connected with the organization.

She found a copy of a 1990 article on SAIMR by a respected South African investigative reporter, De Wet Potgieter, in the *Johannesburg Sunday Times*. The story accused SAIMR of involvement in a series of bizarre plots across Africa during the 1980s and 1990s. They included Operation Crusader, which was an attempt to unseat the president of Uganda, Yoweri Museveni, and replace him with the deposed dictator Idi Amin. And Operation Anvil, another plan for a coup, this time in the Seychelles. The group, Potgieter wrote, also smuggled gemstones.

When Williams interviewed Potgieter, he told her that he had received information from a man named Keith Maxwell, who said he had joined SAIMR after Hammarskjöld's death and had risen to become its Commodore himself. Maxwell told eyebrow-raising tales of SAIMR's activities, and supplied him with a copy of a sprawling, grandiose memoir that detailed many more. Much of it sounded too fantastical, and too lyrical, to be true. Potgieter thought it could be disinformation—an attempt to throw him off whatever the group had actually been doing.

But after Potgieter put out one story about SAIMR, he received a letter from a man who called himself Nick. Nick wrote that he had had to flee to Botswana for his own safety, but he knew that SAIMR had planned and executed a coup in Somalia the previous year. Nick would supply battle plans, if Potgieter placed an ad reading "For repair of your tumble drier. Phone Nick on 970890" on July 31.

The letter had come via the newspaper. By the time it got to

Potgieter, it was too late to place the ad. He never heard from Nick again. But Potgieter kept following the group. He gathered clippings, fragments of reporting and interviews. They included evidence of efforts to spread contaminated AIDS vaccines, and of involvement in other coups, mostly bungled. Gradually, as far as Potgieter could make out, the bulk of SAIMR's work became mercenary recruitment before it faded away.

Williams, too, heard from a former SAIMR operative who insisted on remaining anonymous. He said that the organization was certainly in existence in 1961, and that it was rumored to have existed for more than a hundred years.

The only copies of the Operation Celeste letters that existed, Williams found, were scratchy and in some cases illegible. They looked like copies of copies. The details visible were accurate. The phone number matched the format in use at the time. And the drawing of the ship on the letterhead—of the British merchant clipper *Cutty Sark*—could plausibly have been in circulation in 1961.

Williams was determined to get hold of the originals, in order to have them forensically examined. But the government insisted they could not be found.

Chapter 36

"We did it"

On April 11, 2013, a letter appeared in the *London Review of Books*. It was from David Lea, or Baron Lea of Crondall, a former trade union leader who had been elevated to Britain's House of Lords.* It was headlined WE DID IT.

Lea said that he had read, in a previous issue, a story that concluded nobody knew whether Britain had any role in the death of Patrice Lumumba. "Actually, in this particular case," he wrote, "I can report that we do." Lea said that in March 2010 he had met Daphne Park for a cup of tea.

After leaving Leopoldville in 1961, Park had been posted to Lusaka, Zambia; Hanoi, Vietnam; and Ulan Bator, Mongolia. She retired from MI6 and had become principal of Somerville College, Oxford, in 1980. She had also, after receiving official permission to reveal her former employer, become a staunch defender of Britain's intelligence apparatus in interviews with the press.

In 1990 she had been ennobled as Baroness Park of Monmouth. Since which time she had been a fixture, famous for her probing

---

* Britain has two chambers in its Parliament. The lower, the House of Commons, is made up of elected politicians. The upper, the House of Lords, used to be hereditary but is now mostly made up of appointees, selected and given titles by the government of the day.

questions, in the House of Lords. By 2010, she was most often seen whirring down its paneled corridors in an electric wheelchair.

Lea wrote in his letter to the *LRB* that he knew Park had been head of MI6 in Leopoldville from 1959 to 1961. He took the opportunity, as the two sipped their tea, to raise the controversy surrounding Lumumba's abduction and murder. He suggested that MI6 might even have had something to do with it. She replied simply, he said, "We did. I organised it." Lumumba, she told him, would have handed the whole of the Congo to Russia, uranium, diamonds, and all.

A month later, the academic Glen Newey responded with his own letter, also printed in the pages of the *LRB*, to point out that MI6's involvement in Hammarskjöld's death was also an open question. But Park had died, aged eighty-eight, just a few weeks after her conversation with Lea. The only answers she might have been able to supply to questions about Lumumba and Hammarskjöld lay in the reports she must have filed from Leopoldville in 1961.

Park's friends and colleagues said that she had been on heavy medication to treat cancer, and that in any case Lea's account sounded fanciful. But there remain a series of open questions.

The British government has insisted it has no materials relevant to the death of Hammarskjöld. But an archivist apparently made an error that revealed otherwise. Lord Alport, the British high commissioner to the Federation of Rhodesia and Nyasaland, eventually returned to England and bequeathed his papers to the University of Essex.

Williams searched those papers. She found that a week after the *Albertina* had crashed, Alport had sent a standard memo back to Britain. But attached to it in the archive, Williams found, was a secret report from Neil Ritchie, an MI6 operative under diplomatic cover and a close colleague of Park's. Williams was shocked. It was so strange to find such a secret document out in the open that she presumed it must already be public knowledge. It was not.

The document revealed, first, that Britain must know more about events in the Congo in September 1961 than it has said. And it revealed an uncomfortable duality between Britain's official position—support of the United Nations to reunite the Congo—with its more expedient private position, which was to befriend and work with anyone. Most notably, the British government was closely enmeshed with Union Minière, the mining company that provided support to the white mercenaries who hated Hammarskjöld and the UN.

The mercenary pilot Beukels had told de Kemoularia that his aerial interception of Hammarskjöld had been ordered by a mysterious Mr. X, an executive who represented European interests in Katanga. No persuasive evidence for that theory has ever surfaced. But Ritchie's memo does show that there were plenty of Union Minière officials involved at the highest levels in Katanga and who were present on the night of the crash. Any one of them might have been considered Mr. X—an eminence grise, directing matters behind the scenes.

Ritchie's task, in the days before the *Albertina* crashed, had been to track Tshombe down and deliver him to the meeting with Hammarskjöld. The task was necessary because Operation Morthor, the UN's brutal attempt to end the Katangese secession by force in September 1961, had left the Katangese government scattered. Some ministers were in Salisbury, the capital of the Rhodesian Federation, to ask Sir Roy Welensky for help. Others were simply unaccounted for.

Communications were key, Ritchie wrote. So Union Minière had provided Ritchie with a radio and an operator, who traveled with him on his mission to find and deliver Tshombe. When Ritchie had to send messages back to his superiors, he and the radio operator would first transmit them to Union Minière's top man in Elisabethville, Maurice van Weyenbergh. Van Weyenbergh would then cross the street to the British consulate to pass them along.

Henri Fortemps, an assistant director general of Union Minière, was with Tshombe in a safe house. Union Minière, which was funding, supplying, and arming the Katangese and their mercenaries in their fight with the UN, therefore knew everything the British government did in Katanga.

Ritchie spoke, also, of a meeting with Sir Ronald Prain, the British president of the Rhodesian Selection Trust, a mining company that was interlinked with Union Minière. And he does not seek to hide his disdain for the UN, or his respect for the Katangese government and its European advisers.

Life rarely falls into neat political categories. It makes sense that Ritchie worked closely with secessionist Europeans, and that British officials in Katanga took a different view of the UN's actions than their superiors in London. None of them had the luxury of seeing events in black and white. But it remains striking that powerful forces aligned with, and funding, Tshombe's mercenary army were so interwoven with sympathetic British diplomatic and intelligence efforts. And it makes it more likely that the British knew something of mercenary and Rhodesian activities that night.

Park, the best connected spy in the Congo, who shared a network with the CIA's Larry Devlin, must have filed a report like Ritchie's about the days surrounding the crash of the *Albertina*.

But the British government says no such thing exists in its archives. Neither, if one is to interpret its gnomic statements about relevant material broadly, do any records from MI5, Britain's domestic intelligence agency, which also operated in Africa. Or from GCHQ, Britain's own signals intelligence branch.

With the exception of Ritchie, Britain's entire intelligence apparatus in the Congo, the British official position holds, recorded nothing on the night of September 17, 1961.

Chapter 37

"Flail chest"

Susan Williams released her book, titled simply *Who Killed Hammarskjöld?*, during the fiftieth anniversary year of the crash, 2011. It examined, in forensic detail, each of the theories of the crash. Accident. Hijack or sabotage. Aerial attack. And each of the forces that might have influenced those attacks or helped cover them up. Business interests like Union Minière and Tanganyika Concessions. Katangese mercenary forces. Transnational white supremacists. Britain and America. The Soviet Union. The Federation of Rhodesia and Nyasaland.

New fragments of information emerged in its wake—memories long buried, or documents nobody had thought might have been important. Williams's aim was to reactivate the UN investigation. And in 2013, as part of that effort, an independent panel of judges, known as the Hammarskjöld Commission, examined the new evidence.

It comprised Sir Stephen Sedley, who had sat on Britain's highest courts and the European Court of Human Rights; Ambassador Hans Corell, a Swedish diplomat, judge and former UN undersecretary for legal affairs; South African justice Richard Goldstone, who had been chief prosecutor during UN criminal tribunals regarding Yugoslavia and Rwanda; and from Holland, Justice

Wilhelmina Thomassen, a former judge with the European Court of Human Rights in Strasbourg.

They decided that the three previous inquiries—the Rhodesian technical investigation, the Clayden inquiry that had called witnesses in Ndola in 1962, and the UN investigation the same year—were significantly flawed. The first reached a balanced verdict but had limited evidence. The second was determined to blame the pilots, and it dismissed evidence from inconvenient witnesses as untrustworthy. The UN had used much of the same material as the Rhodesian inquiry, and had followed its conclusions that black African witnesses, eight of whom had reported another plane in the sky, were not to be relied on.

Despite those three inquiries, the body of evidence still contained significant and infuriating gaps, they found. Most notably, photographs of Hammarskjöld's body, at the scene of the wreck and during the postmortem, were missing. So were the X-rays. National archives in America, Britain, Sweden, and elsewhere that might shed light on key issues were closed.

The record was also marked by what seemed like artifacts of a bitter war of disinformation between Soviet and American spies. A former senior KGB official, Oleg Kalugin, wrote in a memoir in 2009 that when "the esteemed U.N. Secretary-General Dag Hammarskjöld died in a plane crash, I and my fellow officers did everything we could to fuel rumors that the CIA was behind it."

The judges unearthed an investigative report in the August 1978 issue of *Penthouse* magazine* by the journalists Joe Trento and Dave Roman, which was mostly about Russian spies in America. In a short aside, it referred to a report the CIA had sent Kennedy in 1962 about Hammarskjöld's death. It quoted from the

---

* In the 1970s, a heyday for American journalism, well-reported and edited stories appeared even in pornographic magazines. *Penthouse* had a conspiratorial bent, but it published great reporters like Seymour Hersh. And the previous issue had included a story by James Baldwin.

report: "There is evidence collected by our technical field operatives that the explosive device aboard the aircraft was of standard KGB incendiary design."

It's possible that this was a real document. It's possible it was invented by one of the bitterly anti-Soviet American spies quoted in the piece to smear the Russians. It's possible it was something else entirely. Without the original document, the judges decided, it was impossible to say much at all. So they set the issue aside.

Their aim, with the reams of more reliable material that was available to them, was to narrow the dozens of plausible narratives for the last minutes of the *Albertina* down to the most substantial and worthy of further investigation.

They dismissed the seventeenth man theory. It was possible there was a hijacker on board, but since no evidence for such a thing existed, it was not worth exploring. It dismissed, too, the Operation Celeste documents. They contained nothing that a forger, working later, could not have known from the public record. Without the originals, which could be subjected to forensic examination of the paper and ink, the theory had to be set aside.

The judges hired three eminent pathologists to examine the very last moments of Hammarskjöld's life, in the forest next to that blazing plane. They knew from photographs and contemporary descriptions that he had been found slightly away from the wreck, sitting up against a termite mound. He looked remarkably unscathed. Photographs of his body on a stretcher at the crash site showed a playing card, said to have been the ace of spades, on his body.

He had massive chest injuries, the pathologists deduced. His ribs, spine, and sternum had been crushed. His cause of death was most likely respiratory failure, as his lungs gave out amid the shattered bones and internal bleeding. (It is known, evocatively, as "flail chest.") But given the missing X-rays and photographs, nobody could be sure without exhuming his body.

In the aftermath of the crash, two Swedish observers, Björn Egge and Knut Hammarskjöld, Dag's nephew, had spoken of seeing head injuries, including a possible bullet hole on Hammarskjöld's body that did not appear in the official reports.*

The remaining postmortem photographs showed no such hole. The images did look a little strange in places, including his forehead. Perhaps they had been retouched—a manual process in 1961, but still possible—to hide evidence of a crime by obscuring the bullet hole. But the pathologists felt the strange marks in question were likely on the body itself—and likely the result of pressure pallor as his body had apparently lain and settled on a flat surface after death.

That conclusion was supported by the positions of Hammarskjöld's limbs in rigor mortis, and by the blood tracks on the body. He had first lain flat on his front as he had died in the Ndola woods that night. But he had also been laid on his back at some stage. And when police officers had found the wreck and begun examining the scene, he had been sitting up.

That would mean that before the authorities had officially found the wreckage, someone had found the body and turned it over to see whether Hammarskjöld was alive or dead, then pulled him to sit up against the termite mound. That person or persons could also have placed the card in his collar.

It might have been hostile forces, checking in on a murder. But it could equally have been looters, or curious bystanders. It remained suspicious, though, that whoever had moved the body had apparently not reported the crash.

At the same time, a team put together by the commission painstakingly cross-referenced all the previous witness accounts of the last moments of the *Albertina* from the night of September 17, 1961. Many contradicted each other, they found. But, the

* See chapter 14.

judges realized, that did not mean that one or the other was true, or that neither was true, or that both were true. It simply meant more evidence was required.

It was notable, though, that almost none of the accounts described a gentle descent into the ground followed by the plane spontaneously igniting—which is what must have happened if the official accounts of controlled flight into terrain were true.

In fact, four new witnesses had come forward whose accounts closely matched those of the black Africans dismissed by the investigations. A charcoal burner, John Ngongo, had gone into the woods that night and seen a plane coming down in a tilted position. He could see that it had already caught fire, particularly on its wings and in its engines. After it had crashed nearby, he heard the sound of another aircraft, a jet. The fire was too intense to allow him to get too close to the wreckage.

A local woman, Emma Malenga, was keeping watch for chicken thieves when she noticed a plane circling above her. It went around twice. The third time it came around, she said, it was on fire. Two others had similar tales.

Another witness spoke of a local legend, almost a horror story, that had spread around Ndola in late 1961. It told of a woman who had been thrown clear of the crash and been caught in a tree, where she screamed until she died. This was perhaps a reference to Sergeant Harold Julien, the last survivor of the crash. He had lain grievously injured, and screaming for help, in the forest for fifteen hours before later dying in a hospital.

Julien had regained consciousness briefly, to give an account that suggested strange events, including an explosion, before the plane went down. The official line had been that he was delirious and could not be relied on.

Mark Lowenthal, the doctor who had looked after Julien, broke years of silence to speak about the incident. Julien had been strong, Lowenthal, now a professor in Israel, recalled. It was one of his great regrets, he said, that he had not insisted that the Americans fly him to the United States for immediate treatment. He might have survived. It lent new credence to Julien's description of an explosion.

The judges took Harry S Truman's equally mysterious statement—suggesting that Hammarskjöld had been killed—on September 19 seriously, too. "It is unlikely in the extreme," the report said, "that he was simply expressing a subjective or idiosyncratic opinion. It seems likely that he had received some form of briefing."

Truman's words helped narrow their focus. There were, broadly, five options to explain the crash. It might have been an accident. It might have been a hijack or sabotage—something aboard the plane. It might have been a ground attack, or it might have been an aerial attack.

The judges felt that one of those theories formed what they called a golden thread.

Chapter 38

"Buzzed"

It had been forty-six years since the mercenary pilot Beukels had met with Claude de Kemoularia and confessed to causing the crash. And in that time, others had also come forward with tales of attacking or disrupting the *Albertina* from the skies.

Errol Friedmann, a former Associated Press reporter, told the judges that he had covered the 1962 Rhodesian inquiry. On about the fourth day, he recalled, two Belgian mercenary Fouga pilots told the courtroom that they had not been flying on the night of September 17, 1961.

But later, in a hotel bar, one of the pilots—he could not recall a name—told him they had "pulled the wool over the eyes of the commission." They had, in fact, been flying on the night of the crash. The same pilot, the more talkative of the two, said they had been in contact with the *Albertina*, and that when it got near Ndola they had "buzzed" the DC-6. It took evasive action. The pilot said he buzzed it again and forced the plane to lose altitude. Friedmann asked whether he'd seen the plane crash. The man's only response was to laugh out loud. Friedmann's editor forbade him from testifying to the inquiry about the incident and sent him immediately to Johannesburg instead.

And the judges discovered that in 1974 a petty criminal named Bud Culligan had tried to bargain his way out of jail for check fraud by saying he'd worked for the CIA and had flown a plane involved in Hammarskjöld's death. The letter he wrote made it as far as the attorney general of the United States, and was passed on for Senate investigation. This raised the suspicion that someone, somewhere, felt it might merit further scrutiny.

Mercenaries like Beukels, Culligan, and the Belgian pilots, the judges decided, were more often guilty of passing others' exploits off as their own than of making up stories wholesale. They agreed, in other words, with the UPI correspondent Ahier who had felt that all of the mercenary tales contained some element of truth, though none had all of it.

And those tales echoed the evidence that Ivan Smith, Virving, Williams, and others had gathered. Even the snippets that Charles Southall, the former NSA officer, and Tore Meijer, the pilot who had been messing around with a radio, said they had heard that night matched.

The golden thread through all of them was the notion that an aerial attack or diversion could plausibly have taken place that night. It might not have directly caused the crash. Perhaps it was immaterial, in fact, and the *Albertina* had crashed during a controlled flight into terrain. But the question needed to be asked.

The existing evidence, alone, demanded it. It was baffling that it had ever been dismissed. Davison Nkonjera, a storeman at the African Ex-Servicemen's Club, about a mile from the airport, had testified to the initial UN inquiry that he had seen the entire crash.

In the skies over the airport he had first seen a plane, presumably the *Albertina*, arrive from the north and circle. Then, as he watched, he said, the runway and control tower lights at Ndola went out. Out of the darkness he heard two jets take off in the direction of the plane that had been circling. Nkonjera felt that something was wrong, and so he went toward the planes on his scooter. He said he saw a flash or a flame from one of the jets, to the right, strike the larger plane. His testimony was corroborated by a colleague.

Two charcoal burners, Lemonson Mpinganjira and Steven Chizanga, said they, too, had seen two smaller planes following a larger one as it circled. As the larger plane turned, they said, the lower of the two jets repositioned above it. Then they saw a red flash on the larger plane and heard a loud explosion followed by a series of smaller ones.

A former diplomat told the judges that there might be a new way to verify or disprove those accounts. On the tarmac at Ndola that night, he said, were two American aircraft. It was well known that they had powerful and advanced radio equipment, and it was said they were in touch with Hammarskjöld's plane. Their engines were running, which was most usually done to allow transmissions. Their mission was overseen by the US air attaché in Pretoria, South Africa, Don Gaylor. He was an intelligence officer (but had been at pains to point out that he had not been operating in that capacity that night).*

When combined with Southall's testimony that the NSA had recorded radio communications from that night, it was overwhelmingly likely that in American security vaults lay transcripts that would provide a more complete picture of Hammarskjöld's last moments. The panel asked the American government for any relevant material. The response was that there were three documents that were pertinent. Two were marked TOP SECRET and would likely never be released. They heard nothing about the third.

The panel recommended that the UN investigation be reopened. Perhaps it would have more luck persuading America, Britain, and others to disclose what they knew.

In Sweden, a new government had taken power in 2014. It

---

* A candidate for the ancient journalistic maxim: *Well, he would say that, wouldn't he.*

helped push the resolution. On December 29, 2014, the UN agreed and appointed Mohamed Chande Othman, a Tanzanian judge, to oversee the detective work.

For the first time in more than five decades, the investigation into Hammarskjöld's death had a dominant theory. One that would be examined not by devotees, but by the only body that had both the right to the truth and the ability to push beyond national boundaries: the UN itself.

Chapter 39

"Other interference"

O thman, a soft-spoken, gray-haired man with a round face and a neat mustache, is in his mid-sixties. He has the affect of a kindly uncle, and listens more than he talks. He and two colleagues, Kerryn Macaulay, an Australian aviation specialist, and Henrik Larsen, a ballistics expert from Denmark, quickly decided that the keys to the mystery lay in government vaults around the world.

When they mapped those leads, in 2015, the dotted lines led in fourteen directions—to secret, or undisclosed, documents in Angola, Belgium, Canada, the Congo, France, Germany, Portugal, Russia, South Africa, Sweden, the United Kingdom, the United States, Zambia, and Zimbabwe.

His aides argued that he should apply all the force at his disposal. That these countries needed to be pressured into disclosure. Othman had been chief justice of Tanzania before his appointment to head the new investigation. And before that he had been lead prosecutor in international trials for atrocities in Rwanda and East Timor, among other high-profile international roles. He had developed a strong stomach. But he had come to feel that quiet determination would serve him better. So he asked for help instead of demanding it. Politely. Respectfully. But repeatedly.

He found that though the passage of time had dulled

memories, it had also removed heat and stigma. Many who had wrestled quietly with their consciences for decades finally lost the fight and came forward, or provided documents. Intelligence agencies that had starkly reported, repeatedly, that they had no information suddenly discovered relevant documents. New details flooded forth.

The Swedish government declassified its own autopsy and medical records on Hammarskjöld. And the panel found a complete set of X-rays of all of the victims, including Hammarskjöld, and a detailed pathology report in the personal archives of the Rhodesian doctor who had performed the autopsy in 1961.

The X-ray of Hammarskjöld's skull showed no bullet wound in his forehead. And a team of pathologists told Othman that the injuries his chest X-ray revealed would have been so catastrophic as to render a gunshot pointless anyway. He had not been assassinated *after* the crash.

A Danish-produced documentary, *Cold Case Hammarskjöld*, had come out in 2019. It focused on the Operation Celeste letters and the mysterious South African Institute for Maritime Research that claimed to have assassinated Hammarskjöld. It found evidence that SAIMR had existed, and that it had sinister motivations.

And the researcher who had found the letters in the first place, Terreblanche, told Othman that she recalled dimly that the documents had been on old paper, and that the letterheads may have been in color—both indications that they may have been originals.

But the Celeste letters themselves could only be corroborated by forensic analysis. And the South African government did not respond to a request for help in finding the original documents. Without them, it was impossible to verify whether the communiqués were real or an elaborate forgery.

Othman, like each investigator before him, ended up looking to the skies. He was most convinced by the golden thread theory, or "aerial attack or other interference," as he put it. Though the

Belgian and French governments had said they had no information on Beukels, Othman got hold of de Kemoularia's papers—including correspondence, notes, and diaries—from his daughter.

They corroborated de Kemoularia's meetings with the Belgian mercenaries. They also revealed that he had reported what he had heard to the French police in July 1969, and to the Swedish government* in November 1974. It lent credence to de Kemoularia's work that he had attempted to have it verified and acted on. It was not recorded why the French and Swedish authorities declined to investigate further.

It was just one of many strange new details Othman pieced together over four painstaking years and countless dull meetings with dismissive representatives of uninterested governments. Gradually, he built a picture of Katanga and its surroundings during its ill-fated secession between 1960 and 1963.

It had played host to more espionage and double dealing, usually in the service of proxy games between governments, than many large and ancient nations. A web of seasoned, brutal spies and assassins, a pervasive eavesdropping apparatus, nefarious commercial interests, dirty international deals. And a wild and uncontrollable Fouga Magister jet that was on the attack every few hours.

I have combined Othman's work with the material Ivan Smith, Virving, Rösiö, and Williams revealed, and new fragments of information I and others have gathered. It provides a very different account of the crash of the *Albertina*.

---

* Namely Axel Edelstam, who had denied to Rösiö ever meeting de Kemoularia.

Chapter 40

"He would return and attack again"

As the *Albertina* lifted into the air in Leopoldville just after 4 p.m. on Sunday, September 17, 1961, Hammarskjöld's mind must have been on the nation below him.

He knew that Operation Morthor had raised the stakes. If he failed to persuade Tshombe to cease fighting, it would mean the end of his tenure as secretary-general. He knew that Britain and America were displeased. He knew that the Katangese despised and suspected him, and that the Rhodesians supported them. The capitalists called him Communist, and the Communists called him capitalist.

But he had grown comfortable under pressure. He felt he understood what was happening well enough to navigate regardless. He was wrong. A second war, more chaotic, secretive, and vicious, seethed beneath the one he thought he was fighting.

Part of the evidence for that, though he could not possibly have known it, sat in a box near him aboard the DC-6. It contained a small gray machine for sending encrypted messages. It was made by a Swiss company called Crypto AG. Model number CX-52. He typed messages into it. The machine encoded them via a series of pinwheels that could be arranged in virtually unbreakable combinations. The coded messages were transmitted and then decoded on the ground using an equivalent machine.

Cracking the code would have required a team of mathematicians and a thousand years. So British and American intelligence didn't bother. They just co-opted the manufacturer and built in a back door—the means to decrypt any message. Hammarskjöld's most secret communications had been compromised.*

The rest of his messages were being gathered by Rhodesian intelligence using what Welensky described in one message to London as "wireless intercepts" and "signals intercepts." The Rhodesians had long been recording details of UN plans, and even troop movements, and sharing them with the British (and by extension the Americans) and the Katangese. By the time the sun set over the *Albertina*, about two hours after takeoff, its movements and intentions were broadly known.

And the intercepts were just one small part of the intelligence network. Though Devlin never mentioned it, the CIA had an operative, David W. Doyle, in Katanga, and three other named operatives across both nations. They were running more, and more mysterious, missions than Hammarskjöld could possibly have guessed. In fact, many of the details still remain redacted.

One of those missions, code-named WICLAM, had something to do with pilots and planes. And the agent code-named WIROGUE, who had worn the wig and boasted unknowingly to a fellow CIA agent in the bar of the Memling Hotel in Leopoldville, had remained in the Congo.

WIROGUE, a former citizen of the Soviet republic of Georgia named either David Tzitzichivili or David de Panasket, had been a mercenary, a forger, and a bank robber in his past lives. The CIA

---

* It was later revealed in the *Washington Post* that the cooperation went even further. The CIA and West German intelligence came to co-own Crypto-AG, which was the center of a sprawling eavesdropping operation.

had given him flying lessons, plastic surgery, and training in small arms and demolitions.

He had been assigned to fly a CIA station plane code-named YQCLAM. The precise purpose of his flights is redacted. But he was certainly running an air intelligence unit. And he seems to have been working in some capacity with West Germany. He had traveled there that September. Another CIA report reveals that the West German security service, the Bundesnachrichtendienst or BND, had an operative named Hans Germani in Katanga on the night of September 17, 1961.

The German aircraft manufacturer Dornier had also supplied Katanga with Do 27 and Do 28 propeller planes. The Dorniers were excellent for bush flying because they required only a short runway to take off and land. They had been used across Africa, fitted with rocket launchers and other weapons. At least one of those planes was in Katanga before Hammarskjöld's death, according to West German records, and may well have been equipped to attack UN planes.

The CIA knew about the Dorniers, and had done its own investigations into Katangese air capabilities. The State Department released information that showed Katanga had secretly received three Fouga Magister jets in February 1961, likely sent by Belgium. It is fair to assume that one or more would have been airworthy by September. And that they were patrolling the skies that night, tracked by the United States.

In the days before the *Albertina*'s last flight, the US ambassador to Leopoldville, Edmund Gullion, who worked closely with Devlin, had sent urgent messages to headquarters. On September 15, he described a "single-engine jet fighter attack on Kamina," a UN air base in Katanga. "Tower in voice contact with fighter. Pilot appears to be Belgian. Pilot stated after attacking with rockets and machine guns he would return and attack again."

The next day, Gullion sent another message. It spoke of a commercial pilot who had been flying above Katanga when he heard and felt a jet fighter nearby. When he looked over, it was flying wing-to-wing with him, close enough that he could see into the cockpit. He recognized the pilot. It was a large, bearded man named Van Risseghem. On September 16, Gullion had elaborated, and reported "two Magisters believed operable."

Hammarskjöld was himself aware of Van Risseghem. He had sent a message to the Belgian foreign minister, Henri Spaak, on that day, September 16, requesting help to stop Van Risseghem's attacks on the UN and on civilians.

Belgian secret services told Othman that when they tried to piece together the pilot's movements, they found that a pilot named Jan Van Risseghem had flown in Katanga. But he had returned to Belgium between September 8 and 16 that year, as recorded by immigration authorities. Given that it took days to get to Africa in 1961, he could not have been at Ndola on the seventeenth.

Van Risseghem himself had denied any involvement in the crash of the *Albertina*, in an interview with Rösiö that the Swedish government provided Othman. He even provided his flying logs to prove his point. But the innocuous details for the month of September looked different from the other months. Almost in different handwriting. Different stamps and signatures were used. And different information was recorded—including takeoff and landing locations.

Another pilot in Katanga, Bracco, provided logs to a French author, Maurin Picard, that disputed some of the details in Van Risseghem's accounts. Othman suspected the logs for that month had been created at a different time, possibly by a different person. It was plausible they were falsified.

UN records also showed Van Risseghem as present for the hostilities of Operations Rumpunch and Morthor just days before the *Albertina* went down. And someone had definitely been flying the Fouga, or more likely two Fougas, in those days even if it wasn't him. The sheer quantity of attacks indicated as much.

There had been many other pilots—named as Fouquet, Pence, de Radiques, de Stoute, Dubois, Hedges, Puren, Delcors, Mans, Heuckets, Hislier, Boutet, Bertaux, Volont, Pier, Hirsch, and Osy—capable of flying such missions. Another was named as Melot—a name exceedingly similar to that of the mysterious copilot, Mertelot, whom Beukels had named to de Kemoularia.

And though the pilots went to great lengths to tell anyone who would listen that they could only operate from their main air bases, some were accomplished and reckless enough to put a Fouga down on a dirt strip, risking its jet engines as they sucked up billowing dust.

As midnight approached, one of the pilots most likely climbed into the cockpit of a Fouga, a Dornier, or a de Havilland at one of dozens of possible makeshift air strips near Ndola, levered down a glass canopy that framed a 180-degree view of the black above, and powered up his engines.

Fifteen minutes before the *Albertina* landed, it transmitted a mundane message to the control tower at Ndola about its arrival time. That message never appeared in the tower logs. But the British consul in Elisabethville overheard it. He did not record how the British came to be listening to, or communicating with, the *Albertina*. But he worked closely with MI6's man in Katanga that night, Neil Ritchie, who had secured radio equipment from Union Minière.

Another operative, this one for Britain's domestic intelligence agency, MI5, which helped oversee the remnants of the empire, was nearby. As was a more mysterious figure—an MI5-linked operative named Gordon Hunt. He had an ambiguous job that seems to have included meeting British representatives, commercial interests, the Belgian government, mercenaries, Union Minière, and the Rhodesians. Daphne Park and a more junior operative, meanwhile, were in Leopoldville.

Their precise activities that night have not been detailed. But the Canadian government picked up a hint in September 1961 at Britain's foreign ministry. The head of the Africa Department, Basil Boothby, told a colleague that the British had been pressured into dubious actions in Katanga by Tanganyika Concessions, a British conglomerate that owned as much as 40 percent of Union Minière. Its chairman, Sir Charles Waterhouse, was a former Conservative MP who liked to joke that Union Minière had ways to deal with political inconveniences.

Shortly before midnight, Hallonqvist, the *Albertina*'s captain, asked Ndola for clearance to descend. He locked the landing gear into position and set the flaps at a conventional thirty-degree angle. "Your lights in sight," he told the tower after midnight, "overhead Ndola, descending, confirm."

His radio must have crackled with a response from the Federation's operatives. They had been placed at Ndola and given instructions to shoot if required, out of a fear that hostilities in Katanga would spill over Rhodesian borders. They asked for details of its passengers, intentions, and destination. But the *Albertina* did not respond.

As the DC-6 prepared to land, lights flashing against the dark-blue sky, five new eyewitnesses reported another plane screaming closer to it. I believe that a hostile aircraft approached the *Albertina* as a warning, as an act of intimidation or violence, or in the service of some other plan too arcane and ridiculous to be guessed at now. And that the *Albertina*'s pilots, convinced quite legitimately they were under attack, took the evasive actions we know they were trained to take—to dive, veer sharply, and head for an airfield.

Perhaps, under pressure and facing confusing topography around Ndola airfield, they miscalculated and the plane crashed, killing all aboard with the brief exception of Julien, just seconds from safety. It is the only theory that encompasses all of the evidence, including the denials.

There may still be ways to know for sure. The details of this moment—the heart of the mystery—were almost certainly noted or recorded by the invisible network of radio signals connecting the *Albertina* to the ground.

The US Air Force had Dakota transport aircraft on the tarmac at the airport in Ndola, equipped with high-powered radios capable of transmitting or relaying messages as far as Washington. They had been in nearly continuous contact, according to one account, with Leopoldville, Elisabethville, New York, and Washington and from time to time with United Nations aircraft in the air. Those Dakotas, according to an account Devlin gave later that was partly corroborated by British Intelligence, had been in touch with the *Albertina* that night.

In Cyprus, according to Southall's account, the NSA intercepted a transmission suggesting that a pilot, possibly French-speaking, had targeted the DC-6. And in Iraklion, Greece, about five hundred miles away from Southall's station, a US Air Force security services officer named Paul Abram was listening to radio signals in a similar facility. His job was to monitor five or six different radio channels with a specific eye toward information about the war in the Congo: troop movements and arms sales, among other things.

He had been listening all night to what sounded like a group of American ground forces. At around midnight he heard someone say: "Here comes the plane...the plane is well lit." Then, on another frequency, he heard a non-American voice—he could only recall that it was not French- or Spanish-accented—saying "the Americans just shot down a UN plane." Then his radio blew up with chatter.

Seven new witnesses noted that the DC-6 was on fire before it hit the ground.

In the long hours between the last communication of the *Albertina* and the discovery of the wreckage, as fifteen people gave in to their injuries and Julien screamed alone in the forest, Gullion sent another memo.

"Hammarskjöld's plane believed lost in vicinity Rhodesian border, near [Ndola]. There is possibility he was shot down by the single pilot who [has] harassed UN operations and who has been identified by one usually reliable source as Van Risseghem,* Belgian, who accepted training lessons with so-called Katangan air force." Gullion asked that influence be brought to bear in Brussels and Salisbury to ground this pilot.

It didn't work. Later that day, one of the American Dakota transport planes departed Elisabethville to fly to Leopoldville. Shortly after it took off, a Fouga attacked and wounded it in mid-air. The plane was damaged, but it managed to evade the Fouga and complete its journey.

At around 2 p.m., an hour or so before the wreck of the *Albertina* was officially discovered, Lord Alport landed in Salisbury, the capital of the Rhodesian federation. He was told of the crash, before anyone else it seems. He returned to Ndola, where he made sure he took possession of Hammarskjöld's briefcase and his Crypto AG machine.

A Rhodesian official known only as Mr. Steadman also rushed to the scene of the crash. He followed Julien to the hospital in Ndola. And he listened very carefully when he was there. He reported back to his government that he had discovered important information. Julien had been speaking to his doctors.

Julien had told them, apparently lucidly, that "Mr. Hammarskjöld

---

* The original memo contains a typo, or a mistake, and spells the name "Van Riesseghel."

had changed his mind while the plane was over Ndola and had decided to go to Katanga. He said that shortly after leaving Ndola there was a big explosion on board, followed by a series of smaller explosions as the plane was forced to the ground. Julien escaped by throwing himself through a safety hatch."

Shortly after that, a Rhodesian official named as Colonel Archer contacted the hospital to say that no medical staff should talk about what they had heard, especially about sparks in the sky. He cited the "security angle."

It was part of a concerted cover-up operation by the Rhodesians, led by Welensky, that would ramp up alongside the investigations. The government withheld evidence from the Rhodesian inquiry, according to other documents, and had hoped that by appointing a UN representative as part of it, they could prevent the UN from starting its own investigation. When they could not, Rhodesian officials sought to influence UN investigators away from the notion of hostile activity instead.

In a letter in late November 1961, in the middle of the Rhodesian inquiry, Welensky's transport minister Kenneth Towsey had told an official named as Major Cox that the Rhodesians should "show as much cooperation as we reasonably can without giving away any important positions." Major Cox responded that the Rhodesian investigation was "of course, the best safeguard which those who were involved in the accident have."

> The devils enter uninvited when the house stands
> empty. For other kinds of guests, you have first to
> open the door.
>
> —*Dag Hammarskjöld*

Othman does not feel he uncovered the whole story. Each new piece of intelligence indicates the presence of other documents that must logically exist and would reveal more of the final minutes of the flight. As of this writing it is uncertain whether he will continue his investigation—the UN will ultimately decide.

Prime among the missing evidence must be the Ndola tower logs from the night of September 17, 1961. It is simply not plausible that they were accidentally destroyed. And it is hard to trust the reconstructed versions put forth by the Rhodesians given the admission that they were seeking to protect those involved.

The airport manager, John Williams, who would have known what happened, said it was not a normal flying accident. The British government went to great lengths to make sure that Rösiö could not see him to ask more. And I could find no current trace of him.

The original logs may be buried in an archive somewhere, unmarked. If they are gone forever, someone still alive might know why they were destroyed, and what they contained. Or the secret died with its last keeper.

If that is the case, there could still be a way to peer into those last minutes through the interceptions that Britain and America were gathering. But in 2014 the NSA, or American officials acting on its behalf, had mounted a quiet campaign to persuade the UN and concerned governments to stop pursuing the information.

Officials connected with the agency showed a few people, including a colleague of Othman and at least one Swedish government minister, copies of two classified documents that they said were relevant to the crash. These promised to be the holy grail—transcripts that clearly defined what had happened in the air that night. But in the end, according to two people who described the documents to me, they were nothing. Intercepts of irrelevant UN communications. The reason they had been held so secretly was that it was embarrassing that the United States spied, and presumably continues to spy, on the UN.

It is likely this was an attempt to evade further scrutiny rather than a total disclosure. The agency still refuses to either verify or disprove Southall's account and Abram's new story from that night. The British government, too, refuses to acknowledge its own intercepts—though we have ample evidence that they existed.

There were, by my count, at least a dozen spies—working for America, Britain, and West Germany alone—on the ground the night that Hammarskjöld died. The fragments of their work that have emerged, in the form of the report from Neil Ritchie, and the information Gullion sent to Washington, suggests ample useful contemporary reporting on the events of that night. But officially they don't exist. And the INR report that drew together the work of all the American spies has not been released.

I decided to contact the two analysts who had put that report together, Karen Enstrom and Bowman Miller. I hoped enough time had passed that one or both might be willing to discuss the matter, even if only to tell me that their report had been innocuous.

Enstrom never replied. Miller told me, by email, that I was misinformed. That he knew nothing more about the crash of the

Albertina than had appeared in the news, and so it was pointless to talk. When I pushed, politely, his tone changed. "I wish you luck with your researches," he wrote. "End of story."

Bengt Rösiö died in early 2019. The Swedish government still has material on Katanga that it did not release to him, and has never released. I was told this is because it contains evidence that Swedish soldiers had been cannibalized there. The government had swept it under the carpet at the time, and it would be embarrassing for them to admit the truth to the families of those soldiers now.

Munongo kept no diaries or papers, his son told me. None that he knew of anyway. He had been very careful to avoid writing things down, he said.

Susan Williams does not believe it likely there will be any grand revelation. "There's an idea that in the NSA or CIA archives there will be a smoking gun, but in my experience that is not the case," she says. "It rarely happens like that." More likely, she said, is an aggregation of evidence and clues that add up to something more.

That process would be infinitely easier if the British and American governments opened their secret archives. The topic can no longer present any security threat. Most of the people involved are dead, and some of the nations involved no longer even exist. The only risk would seem to be exposing their methods. Which we already know about, from the public material.

Nor would such a revelation set a difficult precedent. Similarly sensitive documents, which revealed that eleven prisoners had been beaten to death in British colonial Kenya during the 1950s, were released in 2012. The CIA released thirteen million pages of classified material from a similar era in 2017.

Shortly after I began writing this book, on a blustery blue day in Uppsala, I visited Hammarskjöld's grave in a gated cemetery not far from the castle in which he grew up.

It is a small, rectangular stone, no more than two feet by one, worn and pitted over the years, laid flat into the grass. It sits in a family plot and says simply:

Dag Hammarskjöld
29.7.1905—18.9.1961
United Nations
Secretary-General

I was taken aback by the fact that the tombstone of his father, Hjalmar, a looming, asymmetrical monolith that must be ten feet tall, towers above it. About halfway through writing, that eternal act of dominion started to feel like a metaphor.

Hammarskjöld was not a saint. But he was, in some fundamental sense, good. He sought to persuade rather than force. To do the kind thing even when it hurt. His father preferred battle.

I suspected, too, that he would be denied the simple justice of a complete and honest account of his death. But as I reported, I came to realize that truth has its own quiet power. It cannot dominate or bully. It triumphs quietly, in the feelings of others.

If Hammarskjöld had been another fearful leader, focused on expedience, Ivan Smith, Virving, Rösiö, Williams, and Othman would perhaps have given up a little earlier, or thought twice about taking that last trip or making that last call. Their work means that the noise, for me anyway, has resolved itself into signal.

Nobody visits Hjalmar's grave. Sometimes, someone visits his son's. When they do, they stand and think.

Acknowledgments

Writing is a humbling experience. Never more so than when I consider how much kindness and inspiration I have received from so many people during the course of this book.

I must start by thanking those whose stories I have been allowed to tell. It is an unsettling thing to be written about, and an act of trust and generosity to allow some writer you've never heard of to try.

Without George Ivan Smith and Bo Virving, this mystery would have died long ago. And without the help of their children, Edda Ivan-Smith and Björn Virving, I would never have understood these men or their work. Bengt and Görel Rösiö, Susan Williams, and Mohamed Chande Othman all took the time to talk to me, patiently, over messages, calls, visits, and meetings. And Simon Thomas at the United Nations was so helpful that I still get occasional pangs of guilt.

They were part of a broader community of Hammarskjöld obsessives—including Roger Lipsey, Hans Kristian Simensen, Maurin Picard, and countless others—who were unfailingly generous with this newcomer.

Without the love, inspiration, and support of my wife, Caroline, to whom this book is dedicated, I'd still be staring at a blank page. As if that were not enough, she also explained Sweden, her home nation, to me, found and translated source material, and was my most trusted reader and adviser. Any parts you enjoyed were probably due to her.

My father, Raj, died shortly before I began writing. He felt that there were certain writers every child should read: P.G. Wodehouse, Gerald Durrell, Roald Dahl, Spike Milligan. He and my mother, Hershi, bought them for me, in heavy stacks I couldn't see over, when we could barely afford them.

Our downstairs bathroom was filled with books by authors that I came to appreciate later—Clive James, Simenon, Sir Arthur Conan Doyle, Graham Greene, James Cameron (the journalist, not the filmmaker), Gay Talese, George Orwell. These wonderful voices added up to a spirit—kind, curious, seeking the universality of human experience over the fevered groupthink of the day—that Hammarskjöld embodied and that I strive to emulate.

My mother also bailed me out, and worried about me, and laughed at my jokes and kept me sane as I wrote. My sister Suniti read my first draft and responded generously, which anyone who has read a first draft knows is a profound act of love.

John Burns, David Carr, Jo Becker, Chris Chivers, and numerous others at the *New York Times* taught me whatever I know of the act of looking at the world and writing down what you see. Richard Zacks generously took the time to read and to answer my questions about narrative nonfiction when he absolutely did not have to.

Lajos Egri's *Art of Dramatic Writing* is a wonderful guide to how longer stories function. I took apart Thomas Harris's *Silence of the Lambs* and Douglas Preston's *Monster of Florence* to see what thriller authors were up to. I could not have picked more beautiful machines to examine.

My agent, Kris Dahl, has been a kind, supportive presence for as long as I remember. She read my drafts, gently guided me, and reassured me at every turn. Gordon Wise, at Curtis Brown in London, was unfailingly enthusiastic and nice. Tamara Kawar and Caroline Eisenmann at ICM were calming presences.

My publisher, Sean Desmond, should be canonized for services to patience and wit. He's the type of reader and editor every writer dreams of: He can see and sense, but he is kind. He and Rachel Kambury, and my publishers in Britain, Jack Ramm and Tom Killingbeck, and in Sweden, Martin Kaunitz and Sara Nyström, were nothing but generous of spirit.

I wrote most of this book in the Allen Room at the grand New York Public Library on Fifth Avenue. It's an amazing place, with amazing staff. They bring, virtually to your desk, any book you can imagine. Lucy McCann at the Bodleian Library, at Oxford University, was a fabulous guide to the papers and materials over which she meticulously watches. She dealt patiently with my urgent requests for some oddity or another, as did Amanda Leinberger at the United Nations archives.

They and their colleagues at other institutions helped me realize that libraries and archives are churches for books and writing. I was reminded every day that I was joining a fellowship of people through the ages who had determined to set down, however imperfectly, a story, or a piece of wisdom, or hard-won information, that they felt needed remembering. I think it is how civilization endures.

Henrik Hammargren and the staff of the Dag Hammarskjöld Foundation—Mats Svegfors, Carl Bildt, Annika Söder, Göran Björkdahl, Bengt Wicksen, Annika Rembe, and the Villard family—helped me understand Hammarskjöld, Sweden, and countless facets of the mystery.

Paddy Hayes explained Daphne Park and her world to me. Jean Sackur shared her memories of both Park and the Congo in the 1960s. Patrick Munongo helped me understand his father, Godefroid, and the way the Katangese saw secession. James

Dunnett, whose father, Denzil, was the British consul in Elisabethville, provided both recollections and materials. Others, who preferred not to be named, explained the world of secrets, and that it is subject to the same forces, human foibles, and slapstick as everything else.

Maria Dimitrova dug into the British archives for me and listened to my neuroses. Clifford Waldman, Jessica Weisberg, and Kristian Harborg reassured me that those neuroses were normal. Maggie the dog didn't care either way, which was equally important.

Morgan, Abraham, Jordan, Enzo, and Phillipe at 11th Street Cafe provided caffeine, food, and low-pressure socialization. My colleagues at Columbia University were patient and kind. Curtis Summit taught me to stop saying sorry. So instead of apologizing to anyone I have forgotten here, I will just say: Thank you.

Source Notes

The descriptions and details in this book are drawn from interviews with those present at the events in question, from contemporary documents, archival materials, and press clippings and news footage made available to me through the astounding databases and research tools of the New York Public Library. The Mary Ferrell Foundation was an invaluable source of declassified US intelligence materials.

There were a few key texts that recurred throughout, as sources, guides, verifiers of details, or references, and to which I'd like to draw special attention (in alphabetical order): Larry Devlin's *Chief of Station, Congo*, Paddy Hayes's *Queen of Spies*, Roger Lipsey's *Hammarskjöld*, Christopher Othen's *Katanga 1960–63*, David Van Reybrouck's *Congo*, Brian Urquhart's *Hammarskjöld*, and Susan Williams's *Who Killed Hammarskjöld*.

I've detailed any particularly key sources—those that formed the spine of a particular chapter—below; a select bibliography follows that. And if you have any information you'd like to share, you can reach me at HammarskjoldBook@gmail.com.

Introduction

The account of Truman's daily routine was drawn from a September 3, 1961, Associated Press report, "At Home with Harry," by Saul Pett, which profiled the ex-president in retirement. The version I used appeared in the *Hartford Courant*.

Reports by UPI, as printed in the *New York Times*, and by the *Independence Examiner* detailed the presentation of the check and his comments about Hammarskjöld.

Laila's story is drawn from a talk given by Hammarskjöld's friend Sture Linnér on Sveriges Radio, "Sommar i P1," on July 11, 2007.

A variety of contemporary press reports detailed the Congolese guard of honor and the protests outside the UN. The accounts from inside the UN are drawn from the Hammarskjöld biographies by both Brian Urquhart and Roger Lipsey, as well as from interviews.

Prologue

The descriptions and details of the Congo and its history are drawn from V.S.
Naipaul's *Congo Diary*, David Van Reybrouck's *Congo*, Larry Devlin's *Chief
of Station: Congo*, Ian Scott's *Tumbled House*, and Adam Hochschild's *King
Leopold's Ghost*, as well as contemporary photographs, press clippings and
film footage, and interviews with those present in Leopoldville at the
time.

The details of the riot, and the events that preceded it, are drawn from a Belgian parliamentary report into the events; from Van Reybrouck's *Congo*;
from Janssens's memoir, *J'étais le général Janssens*, and an obituary that
appeared in the Belgian newspaper *Le Soir* on his death in 1989; and from
contemporary press clippings and news report films.

The Congolese history draws on Van Reybrouck's *Congo*, Hockschild's *King
Leopold's Ghosts*, and historical documents connected with the establishment and operations of the Congo Free State.

The descriptions of the young Congolese bills are drawn from the photographs of Jean Depara and from Van Reybrouck's *Congo*.

Chapter 1

The history of the UN is from the UN itself.

The biographies by Lipsey, Urquhart, and Kelen form the spine of the biographical material on Hammarskjöld and his work on the Congo crisis,
along with materials from the Dag Hammarskjöld Foundation, archival
materials from both the UN and the George Ivan Smith papers at the
Bodleian Library at Oxford University, and interviews.

Hammarskjöld's own writings—speeches, correspondence, and his diaries—
gave great insight into his state of mind, as did Sture Linnér's body of
work on his friend.

The material on the Congolese election and its aftermath is drawn from contemporary reports, interviews, Van Reybrouck's comprehensive history,
and Zeilig's *Lumumba*.

The details of the mutiny at Camp Thysville come from a Belgian parliamentary report and from contemporary journalism.

Chapter 2

The material on Thiriart and white supremacy in the 1960s comes from Othen's
Katanga, Bourseiller's *Extrême Droite*, Lee's *Beast Reawakens*, Coogan's
Dreamer of the Day, Laroche's *Salan Devan L'Opinion*, O'Donoghue's *Irish
Army in the Congo*, Laurent's *L'Orchestre Noir*, and from Thiriart's own
words, available online.

The material on Katanga comes from Othen's *Katanga*, Puren's *Mercenary Commander*, O'Brien's *Katanga and Back* and his *My Life and Times*, Gerard-Libois's

Katanga Secession, an unpublished memoir by the British consul Denzil Dunnett, and from Gordon Hunt's memo "Hotline to Katanga," as well as the descriptions of those present and material from the UN archives, the Ivan Smith papers in Oxford, and the British National Archives.

The material on Tshombe comes from contemporary press reports and from interviews with those connected with him.

Chapter 3

The descriptions of the fifteenth UN General Assembly are drawn from contemporary accounts and news reports, as well as Kelen's Hammarskjöld biography and the recollections of those present.

Biographical details on Hammarskjöld are drawn from sources noted for Chapter 1, with a particular focus on Lipsey's biography, which was a central guide to locating relevant letters and documents. Hammarskjöld's ascent to secretary-general was covered in myriad press reports, most notably the wonderful interview conducted by Abe Rosenthal for the *New York Times*.

I have also drawn from Hammarskjöld's own writings, as collected by the Hammarskjöld Foundation, Ivan Smith's papers, the essay written by W.H. Auden to introduce the translation of Hammarskjöld's diaries into English (published as *Markings*), and the recollections of those who had known him.

Chapter 4

Leopoldville in 1960 was described to me by several people present in different parts of the city, including Bengt Rösiö and Jean Sackur. I drew also from Scott's *Tumbled House*, which documents the daily chaos; and Naipaul's *Congo Diary*, which describes the aftermath of this crisis; as well as contemporary news and governmental and UN reports.

The bulk of the chapter refers to Devlin's memoir, *Chief of Station, Congo*, declassified US intelligence materials, Senate testimony, news reports, and corroborating interviews, as well as other accounts Devlin gave through the course of his later life in retirement.

Hammarskjöld's responses are drawn from his speeches.

Chapter 5

The references to the SIS report, and the attached notes to Prime Minister Harold Macmillan, are drawn from the copy of the report available in the UK National Archives. Some of Macmillan's own responses are detailed in his memoir, *Pointing the Way*.

Paddy Hayes's *Queen of Spies* was the central text in describing and interpreting Park, guiding me to a plethora of materials in the shape of speeches and talks she had given, as well as obituaries and memorial materials for her funeral, including recollections from those who had known her most closely (which were kindly provided by Sir Gerald Warner, the former deputy chief of SIS). I also drew on a longer interview Park had provided the BBC correspondent Gordon Corera for his book *The Art of Betrayal*. The quotes attributed to her are from talks and discussions later in her life, most notably an appearance in connection with the Royal Society of Literature.

The British strategy on the Congo was outlined in declassified materials from the Foreign and Commonwealth Office and other branches of the government, and the attitude of SIS chiefs was detailed in Williams's *Who Killed Hammarskjöld*, and in a strange pseudo-memoir by George Kennedy Young, another former deputy chief of SIS, obtained and published by *Lobster Magazine*.

Chapter 6

The events surrounding Lumumba's arrest, imprisonment, and murder are drawn from declassified US and UK government materials, usually in the shape of correspondence within the governments, from Hayes's *Queen of Spies*, Devlin's *Chief of Station: Congo*, and from Ludo de Witte's peerless account, *The Assassination of Lumumba*.

The CIA's activity in the Congo and elsewhere was examined by the 1975 United States Senate Select Committee to Study Governmental Operations with Respect to Intelligence Activities, more commonly known as the Church Committee for its chairman, Idaho senator Frank Church. I have drawn heavily on testimony there by Devlin (under a pseudonym) and others.

The UN's perspective was provided in Brian Urquhart's biography of Hammarskjöld, in interviews participants in the conflict later gave to historians, and in contemporary memos that have since been made public. Some of the more gruesome details come from Othen's *Katanga 1960–63*.

All of the above was confirmed and contextualized by interviews with those present, some of whom declined to be named as sources, and from contemporary press accounts.

Chapter 7

The scene reconstruction is drawn from contemporary sources: descriptions of the Memling Hotel and its atmosphere from those present in Leopoldville and from pictures. The substance of the exchange comes from declassified CIA materials describing the incident and the backgrounds of the two men in detail.

Chapter 8

The material on Hammarskjöld, and his monkey, is drawn from the biographies by Lipsey, Urquhart, and Kelen, as well as materials from the Dag Hammarskjöld Foundation.

The material on Katanga is drawn from the recollections of those present, from archival documents, Othen's *Katanga 1960–63*, Jerry Puren's *Mercenary Commander*, O'Brien's *My Life and Times* and *To Katanga and Back*, and Hunt's *Hotline to Katanga*.

The material on France and on the Organisation Armée Secrète of Algeria is drawn from Devlin's memoir and from press accounts, and characterizations of the way French soldiers were seen in Katanga comes from declassified UN materials and from O'Brien's memoirs.

Trinquier's theories are drawn from an English translation of *Modern Warfare*. Faulques's day-to-day actions were described by Puren and Pottinger.

The UN's decisions in this period were described in archival materials, most notably the communications and ordnances mentioned, and contemporary press coverage.

Chapter 9

O'Brien's misgivings about Hammarskjöld come from the endnotes to his play, *Murderous Angels*.

The reconstruction of Operation Mortor comes from archival materials, mostly the UN and George Ivan Smith's papers at the Bodleian Library, and from the copious press coverage, in both print and newsreel, covering the conflict. The dispatches of David Halberstam of the *New York Times* were particularly vivid and useful. The description of Faulques was drawn from Puren's memoir.

Details about the operations's fallout come from declassified UK, US, and UN materials; also, vital context was provided by the Zimbabwean government.

Chapter 10

The UN and Rhodesian reports into the crash of the *Albertina* described the bullet lodged in the engine, some of the circumstances surrounding it, and its subsequent flight to Leopoldville. I drew from those available details and information on mercenary activities that night, along with contemporaneous images and video, to build this interpretation of events.

The detail on Noork's birthday comes from the recollections of Kjell Peterzén, as published on a website dedicated to the company he worked for, Transair. (It was made known to me by Williams, who references it in *Who Killed Hammarskjöld*.)

Chapter 11

The description of the events at Leopoldville airport is drawn from a video taken that day. It has been expanded with the views of the participants from their own memoirs (in Hammarskjöld's case his diaries, *Markings*), with extra details from later investigations, including the UN's.

The details aboard the plane come from the recollections of Linnér, who briefly boarded the *Albertina* and described Hammarskjöld there. The descriptions of his feelings are drawn from the accounts by Urquhart, Lipsey, and William.

Chapter 12

The eyewitnesses gave detailed accounts of their memories of the night of September 17, 1961, to both Rhodesian and UN investigators. This chapter is comprised mostly of material from transcripts of those interviews.

The descriptions of what Daka must have seen come from videos and images taken of the crash site the next day.

Chapter 13

The precise events of the period after the crash, essentially the early hours of September 18, 1961, were drawn from the Rhodesian and UN reports, *Who Killed Hammarskjöld*, archival UN cables, declassified UK and US government communications, and material uncovered by Rösiö.

The O'Brien incident was detailed in his memoirs. The description of the crash site is drawn from *Who Killed Hammarskjöld*, from images and filmed footage taken there, and from later investigations. Julien's words and behavior in the hospital were recalled in witness statements by a Rhodesian police officer and by the doctors and nurses who had treated him there.

Chapter 14

The details of the Rhodesian investigation are drawn from the report it eventually generated and the reams of ancillary materials—appendices, images, and witness statements—that went along with it.

Where I have described a map or image, I have drawn on a copy of it. The recollections of Egge and Knut Hammarskjöld are drawn from later UN reports, from material uncovered by Rösiö, and from *Who Killed Hammarskjöld*.

Details of Julien's last moments are from sources provided in the previous chapter.

Chapter 15

Ivan Smith's daughter, Edda Ivan Smith, was kind enough to provide details of her father's life in an interview. It supplemented and illuminated his extensive archive at the Bodleian Library at Oxford University, which covers virtually his entire life. His thoughts on Hammarskjöld are mostly drawn from correspondence with friends.

External views of Ivan Smith appeared in writings by O'Brien and in contemporary press clippings. The details of the global response to Hammarskjöld come mostly from news reports, which Ivan Smith also collected and archived.

Chapter 16

Ivan Smith detailed his kidnapping, and his thoughts on it, in correspondence. This account also draws from a UN Oral History Project interview given by Sir Brian Urquhart in 1984, and Thomas Dodd's version of events, which appeared in *Time* magazine in December 1961.

Chapter 17

Ivan Smith detailed his investigation of copious documents in his archive. Portions were first uncovered in an essay by Manuel Fröhlich, "The Unknown Assignation: Dag Hammarskjöld in the Papers of George Ivan Smith," published by the Dag Hammarskjöld Foundation in 2008.

The background details on the progress of the formal inquiries are drawn from Williams's *Who Killed Hammarskjöld*. The details of the Clayden inquiry are drawn from its report and associated appendices, as well as from Bo Virving's own account of events, kindly provided via documents, images, and interviews by his son, Björn Virving.

Chapter 18

The chapter is comprised largely of material from the Rhodesian report itself, "Report of the Commission on the Accident Involving Aircraft SE-BDY."

Chapter 19

Virving's report was provided to me by his son, Björn, and was supplemented by Björn's recollections of his father's experiences.

Chapter 20

The swirl of rumors and new details that emerged in the wake of the Rhodesian investigation was detailed in the UN report of 1962, which forms the spine of this chapter, and in Blandori's unpublished appendix to it. Supplemental material was supplied from correspondence, papers and clippings in Ivan Smith's archive, the later UN investigations overseen by Mohamed Chande Othman, and Arthur Gavshon's *Mysterious Death of Dag Hammarskjöld*.

Chapter 21

Material for this chapter is drawn primarily from correspondence between Welensky and Ivan Smith, available in their archives, supplemented with basic public biographical information from a variety of sources, as well as insight and direction from Williams's *Who Killed Hammarskjöld*.

Chapter 22

Much of the chapter is drawn from the published version of *Murderous Angels* and its comprehensive endnotes, supplemented by contemporary press accounts and reviews of the play.

The list of nicknames, and some of the notions of how O'Brien was seen, come from an essay Christopher Hitchens wrote about him for the now-defunct magazine *Grand Street* in 1987.

I drew also on sections of Trinquier's *Modern Warfare*, as well as an article O'Brien had written for the *Guardian* covering his misgivings about the crash, which described the incident with Welensky.

The crash group detail was mentioned by Williams, and details of it are drawn here from contemporary UN communications.

Chapter 23

The chapter is drawn from materials in Ivan Smith's archive, including transcripts of his television appearances, supplemented with interviews, most notably with his daughter, Edda Ivan Smith.

Chapter 24

Ivan Smith's experiences with De Kemoularia, and his efforts to piece the mystery together, are detailed in tapes of their meetings and in a long transcription of those tapes available in his archive.

Chapter 25

The history of the Katangan secession and the siege of Jadotville is drawn primarily from Gerard-Libois's *Katanga Secession*, O'Donoghue's *Irish Army in the Congo*, and contemporary press clippings describing the events here. The information on the prevalence of hijackings is drawn from

Brendan Koerner's *The Skies Belong to Us: Love and Terror in the Golden Age of Hijacking*.

The continued story laid out by Grant is from sources described for Chapter 24.

Chapter 26

Material is drawn largely from sources provided for Chapter 24.

Chapter 27

The chapter is built around Ivan Smith's 71-page memo to De Kemoularia, supplemented with correspondence and other papers from that moment in Ivan Smith's life.

Chapter 28

The account of Munongo's last day was kindly supplied in an extensive interview with his son, Patrick Munongo. It is supplemented by O'Brien's writing on Katanga and UN documents that detailed Kanyinda's accusation, as well as contemporary press accounts.

Chapter 29

The chapter is drawn from extensive interviews with Bengt Rösiö, who also supplied the other materials on his investigation cited here, notably his book on the crash and a translation of his report, which appeared in the *Journal of African Studies*. He also wrote witty letters to me, addenda to his body of work, which expanded on his theories.

Chapter 30

The chapter is derived from sources provided for chapter 29.

Chapter 31

The existence of the INR report was first unearthed by Susan Williams. This chapter is drawn from interviews with those with experience of the agency (who did not want to be named as sources), press clippings about the agencies, and copies of Southall's exchange with Miller and Enstrom kindly supplied by Williams, along with the FOIA document mentioned.

Chapter 32

The material on Rösiö is derived from sources listed for chapter 29. The information on Southall, and the details of his account, come from Williams's

Who Killed Hammarskjöld, a short University of Beirut biography of South-all, and testimony he gave later to investigators that appeared in reports from the UN and others.

Chapter 33

Correspondence and interviews with Rösiö described his experiences. Edda Ivan Smith supplied the details of her father's last days, which are supplemented by press clippings, including letters he wrote to the *Guardian* newspaper.

Chapter 34

The details of Tutu's press conference come from archival video of the event. The details of the Celeste letters come from copies of the eight mentioned. The context comes from contemporary press clippings, many of which were first unearthed by Susan Williams.

Chapter 35

Susan Williams kindly offered an interview, and she described her experiences with this story, which I supplemented with the published account available in her book. The context in South Africa is drawn from contemporary press clippings.

Chapter 36

Post-Leopoldville biographical information about Daphne Park comes from *Queen of Spies* and from her obituaries. Susan Williams outlined the moment she found the Ritchie report, and I drew on a copy of the report itself.

Chapter 37

Material for the chapter is drawn from *Who Killed Hammarskjöld* and from a copy of the Hammarskjöld Commission's report, supplemented by Susan Williams herself.

Chapter 38

Material for the chapter is derived from the sources listed for Chapter 37.

Chapter 39

The chapter is drawn from interviews and exchanges with Mohamed Chande Othman himself and Simon Thomas of the UN, as well as Othman's initial report.

Chapter 40

The chapter is drawn from, essentially, all of the sources in the previous chapters and built around the new work done by Othman, supplemented by a large quantity of new material supplied by the Zimbabwean government.

Select Bibliography

Aldrich, Richard James, *GCHQ: The Uncensored Story of Britain's Most Secret Intelligence Agency*

Bourseiller, Christophe, *Extrême Droite*

Conrad, Joseph, *Heart of Darkness*

Coogan, Kevin, *Dreamer of the Day: Francis Parker Yockey & the Postwar Fascist International*

Cordier, Andrew W., and Wilder Foote, editors, *Public Papers of the Secretary-Generals of the United Nations*

Corera, Gordon, *The Art of Betrayal: The Secret History of MI6*

De Witte, Ludo, *The Assassination of Lumumba*

Devlin, Larry, *Chief of Station, Congo: Fighting the Cold War in a Hot Zone*

Doyle, David W., *Inside Espionage: A Memoir of True Men and Traitors*

Gavshon, Arthur L., *The Mysterious Death of Dag Hammarskjöld*

Gerard-Libois, Jules, *Katanga Secession*

Hammarskjöld, Dag, *Markings*

Hayes, Paddy, *Queen of Spies: Daphne Park, Britain's Cold War Spy Master*

Hochschild, Adam, *King Leopold's Ghost: A Story of Greed, Terror, and Heroism in Colonial Africa*

Janssens, Emile, *J'étais le général Janssens*

Kalugin, Oleg, *Spymaster: My Thirty-Two Years in Intelligence and Espionage Against the West*

Kelen, Emery, *Dag Hammarskjöld: A Biography*

Laroche, Fabrice, *Salan Devan L'Opinion*

Laurent, Frederic, *L'Orchestre Noir*

Lee, Martin A., *The Beast Reawakens: Fascism's Resurgence from Hitler's Spymasters to Today's Neo-Nazi Groups and Right-Wing Extremists*

Lipsey, Roger, *Hammarskjöld: A Life*

Macmillan, Harold, *Pointing the Way, 1959–1961*

Marks, Leo, *Between Silk and Cyanide: A Codemaker's War, 1941–1945*

Naipaul, V.S., *A Bend in the River*

_____, *A Congo Diary*

O'Brien, Conor Cruise, *Memoir: My Life and Times*

_____, *Murderous Angels: A Political Tragedy and Comedy in Black and White*

_____, *To Katanga and Back: A UN Case History*

O'Donoghue, David, *The Irish Army in the Congo, 1960–1964: The Far Battalions*

Othen, Christopher, *Katanga 1960–63: Mercenaries, Spies and the African Nation that Waged War on the World*

Puren, Jerry, as told to Brian Pottinger, *Mercenary Commander*

Rösiö, Bengt, *Ndola*

Scott, Ian, *Tumbled House: The Congo at Independence*

Svegfors, Mats, *Dag Hammarskjöld*

Trinquier, Roger, *Modern Warfare. A French View of Counter-Insurgency*

Urquhart, Brian, *Hammarskjöld*

Van Reybrouck, David, *Congo: The Epic History of a People*

Virving, Björn, *Termitstacken: Om olychkan dar Dag Hammarskjöld omkom i Belgiska Kongo*

Williams, Susan, *Spies in the Congo: The Race for the Ore That Built the Atomic Bomb*

_____, *Who Killed Hammarskjöld?: The UN, the Cold War and White Supremacy in Africa*

Zeilig, Leo, *Lumumba: Africa's Lost Leader*

Index

He just wanted a decent book to read ...

Not too much to ask, is it? It was in 1935 when Allen Lane, Managing Director of Bodley Head Publishers, stood on a platform at Exeter railway station looking for something good to read on his journey back to London. His choice was limited to popular magazines and poor-quality paperbacks – the same choice faced every day by the vast majority of readers, few of whom could afford hardbacks. Lane's disappointment and subsequent anger at the range of books generally available led him to found a company – and change the world.

'We believed in the existence in this country of a vast reading public for intelligent books at a low price, and staked everything on it'
Sir Allen Lane, 1902–1970, founder of Penguin Books

The quality paperback had arrived – and not just in bookshops. Lane was adamant that his Penguins should appear in chain stores and tobacconists, and should cost no more than a packet of cigarettes.

Reading habits (and cigarette prices) have changed since 1935, but Penguin still believes in publishing the best books for everybody to enjoy. We still believe that good design costs no more than bad design, and we still believe that quality books published passionately and responsibly make the world a better place.

So wherever you see the little bird – whether it's on a piece of prize-winning literary fiction or a celebrity autobiography, political tour de force or historical masterpiece, a serial-killer thriller, reference book, world classic or a piece of pure escapism – you can bet that it represents the very best that the genre has to offer.

Whatever you like to read – trust Penguin.